AF352699

THE MIRROR OF TRUE PENITENCE

TRANSLATED BY MICHAEL SHERBERG

Jacopo Passavanti

The Mirror of True Penitence

UNIVERSITY OF TORONTO PRESS
Toronto Buffalo London

ISBN 978-1-4875-6313-4 (cloth)   ISBN 978-1-4875-6315-8 (EPUB)
                                     ISBN 978-1-4875-6314-1 (UPDF)

Library and Archives Canada Cataloguing in Publication

Title: The mirror of true penitence / Jacopo Passavanti ; translated by Michael Sherberg.
Other titles: Specchio della vera penitenzia. English
Names: Passavanti, Jacopo, approximately 1297–1357, author |
    Sherberg, Michael, translator
Series: Toronto Italian studies.
Description: Series statement: Toronto Italian studies | Translation of: Lo specchio della
    vera penitenzia. | Includes bibliographical references and index.
Identifiers: Canadiana (print) 20250295148 | Canadiana (ebook) 20250295164 |
    ISBN 9781487563134 (cloth) | ISBN 9781487563141 (PDF) |
    ISBN 9781487563158 (EPUB)
Subjects: LCSH: Repentance – Catholic Church – Early works to 1800. | LCSH: Christian
    life – Catholic authors – Early works to 1800. | LCSH: Repentance in literature.
Classification: LCC BT800 .P3713 2026 | DDC 234/.5 – dc23

Cover design: Val Cooke
Cover image: The Print Collector / Alamy Stock Photo; iStock.com/
Oleg Sibiriakov

The manufacturer's authorised representative in the EU for product safety is Mare
Nostrum Group B.V., Mauritskade 21D, 1091 GC Amsterdam, The Netherlands.
Email: gpsr@mare-nostrum.co.uk.

We wish to acknowledge the land on which the University of Toronto Press
operates. This land is the traditional territory of the Wendat, the Anishnaabeg, the
Haudenosaunee, the Métis, and the Mississaugas of the Credit First Nation.

University of Toronto Press acknowledges the financial support of the Government of
Canada, the Canada Council for the Arts, and the Ontario Arts Council, an agency of
the Government of Ontario, for its publishing activities.

Contents

Acknowledgments

I am first of all very grateful to my editor at Toronto, Suzanne Rancourt, for supporting this project with her usual enthusiasm and generosity. I thank as well the two anonymous reviewers whose readings she solicited, and who offered meticulous advice about revisions and corrections. Finally, at Toronto Barbie Halaby copyedited the manuscript with a sharp eye to detail, and Barb Porter carefully supervised production. Any faults that remain are entirely my own.

Finishing up this project coincided with my retirement, and that has put me in a reflective mood. What follows is a list, doubtless incomplete, of mentors and colleagues whose kindness and friendship have sustained me over the course of my career. Some are gone but their memory is a blessing. The list is alphabetical because, with only a few exceptions, no other order makes any sense: Fabian Alfie, Albert Ascoli, Tili Boon-Cuillé, Eric Brown, Daniel Bornstein, Theodore Cachey, Mirella Cheeseman, Paolo Cherchi, Fredi Chiappelli, Alison Cornish, Marga Cottino-Jones, Luisa Del Giudice, Robert Henke, Martin Eisner, Roberto Fedi, John Garganigo, Pascal Ifri, Ignacio Infante, Victoria Kirkham, Christopher Kleinhenz, Richard Lansing, Joseph Loewenstein, Dennis Looney, Suzanne Magnanini, Christian Moevs, Kristina Olson, Michael Papio, Stanley Paulson, Randolph Pope, Joy Potter, Regina Psaki, David Quint, Meredith Ray, Lucia Re, Robert Rodini, Sherry Roush, Ignacio Sánchez Prado, Francesca Savoia, Margery Schneider, Julie Singer, Elzbieta Sklodowska, Janet Smarr, Jon Snyder, Justin Steinberg, Cynthia Stollhans, Harriet Stone, Wayne Storey, Lynne Tatlock, Ed Tuttle, Jane Tylus, Carolyn Valone, Bill Wallace, Mark Weil, Rebecca West, Lynn Westwater, Gerhild Williams, Iva Youkilis, and Sergio Zatti.

And, of course, my beloved Simeon, *sine qua non* for 30 years, and our three amazing sons, who have filled our lives with so much joy.

My career would not have happened but for Elissa Weaver, to whom I dedicate these pages with help from the immortal Ariosto: "Quel ch'io vi debbo, posso di parole / pagare in parte, e d'opera d'inchiostro; / né che poco io vi dia da imputar sono; / che quanto io posso dar, tutto vi dono."

THE MIRROR OF TRUE PENITENCE

Introduction: The Man and the *Mirror*

A son of Florence, the Dominican intellectual Jacopo Passavanti wrote *The Mirror of True Penitence*[1] at a critical moment in his city's history, less than a decade after the cataclysmic Black Death of 1348 and at a time when the Italian vernacular was gaining traction in an expanding literary marketplace. Passavanti witnessed, and in some ways recorded, the transition from a late medieval worldview to one associated with rising humanism, at a time of consolidation of a number of economic forces that would drive the Renaissance. The *Mirror* comes to us as a document of Dominican theory of penitence, as well as a marker of many of these transitions, one that helps us better understand the complexities of a moment that is critical not just in the history of Florence but more broadly in the history of Western culture. In its original Italian vestments it reveals much about its cultural circumstances, and in translation it speaks to a wider audience about the relationship between late medieval piety and the expanding energies of the urban lay world of the mid-fourteenth century.

Passavanti began to draft *The Mirror of True Penitence* in 1354, encouraged, he tells us in his introduction, by those who had heard his Lenten sermons that year, both laypeople and clerics.[2] As originally conceived,

---

1 The bibliography of this work is predominantly in Italian. General studies include Marcello Aurigemma, *Saggio sul Passavanti* (Florence: Le Monnier, 1957) and Giovanni Getto, "Umanità e stile di Jacopo Passavanti," in *Letteratura religiosa del Trecento* (Florence: Sansoni, 1967), 3–105. Both are somewhat antiquated at times but still valuable. More recently, see Ginetta Auzzas, "Dalla predica al trattato: Lo *Specchio della vera penitenzia* di Iacopo Passavanti," *Lettere italiane* 54 (2002): 325–42.

2 As M. Michèle Mulchahey points out, however, the Roman Province prohibited the direct circulation of sermons to readers outside of the Dominican order. She continues: "Passavanti circumvented the prohibition by publishing the substance of his preaching in an altered form" (*"First the Bow Is Bent in Study": Dominican Education before 1350* [Toronto: Pontifical Institute of Mediaeval Studies: 1998], 447).

the plan ambitiously involved not just the Italian text that has served as the basis for this translation but a Latin version as well, intended to be more theologically dense for better-prepared clerical readers. No sure copy of the Latin version survives, though Giancarlo Rossi has offered a compelling argument that a manuscript conserved at the Biblioteca Medicea Laurenziana in Florence is it.[3] Passavanti's Italian text remains incomplete, at least according to his own plan. What we do have nevertheless acquaints us with his thinking about the problem of sin and penitence, his mode of reasoning, his writing style, and his language. It reveals to us a thoughtful preacher whose project, over the course of his writing, evolved from a text-based summa on penitence to a cautiously empirical investigation of human psychology.

The treatise bears the imprint of Passavanti's career as a Dominican preacher, and so it is perhaps best to start with his life. His biography straddles the tumultuous decades of the Florentine fourteenth century, from the exile of the "white" Guelphs, including Dante Alighieri, to the Black Death and its aftermath. The documentary record of this life was summarized more than a century ago by Carmine Di Pierro.[4] Passavanti was born around 1302, in Florence, to the nobleman Banco Passavanti and his wife, Francesca de' Tornaquinci, and likely entered the Dominican order at the prescribed age of fifteen. Early on he demonstrated the intellectual gifts that would earn him a posting, by his late twenties, to Paris to further his education. Returning to Tuscany in 1333, he settled initially in Pisa, first as an instructor in theology and later as a preacher, and then took postings in Pistoia and elsewhere. By 1348 he was firmly established in Florence as the prior of Santa Maria Novella. He remained in this city for the rest of his life, tending a flock of industrious souls. The extant documents also suggest that between 1350 and 1352 he served as vicar general of the Florentine diocese. He died in 1357.

As prior of the great Florentine church, Passavanti oversaw its growth. Projects included the expansion of the monastery library as well as of the physical property of the complex.[5] As early as 1348 he received a gift from the estate of Turino Baldesi for a fresco cycle of

---

3 Giancarlo Rossi, "La 'redazione latina' dello 'Specchio della vera penitenza,'" *Studi di filologia italiana* 49 (1991): 29–58.

4 Carmine Di Pierro, "Contributo alla biografia di frà Jacopo Passavanti fiorentino," *Giornale storico della letteratura italiana* 47 (1906): 1–24, which synthesizes Passavanti's life using the *Necrologium* of Santa Maria Novella as well as other early sources.

5 The library today is named for Passavanti, marking his critical relationship to it and to the monastery.

Old Testament stories.[6] Baldesi also designated a gift for the construction of the main door of the church. By 1356, Passavanti's success in managing generous gifts was such that the Florentine banker Niccolò Acciaiuoli, the grand seneschal of Naples, entrusted him with projects related to the construction of the Certosa of Galluzzo, the capstone of Acciaiuoli's life.

The biography of Passavanti that emerges thus resembles a triptych, with the preacher as theologian in the centre panel, the Dominican administrator on the left, and on the right the development director, matching projects with wealthy donors. While medieval in form, this tripartite content suggests how in his life Passavanti mediated the religious concerns of his order, directed at the salvation of souls, and the economic opportunities presented by Florentine wealth. As Passavanti's contacts with Acciaiuoli and Baldesi make clear, already in the mid-fourteenth century wealthy donors were endowing projects that would mark their generosity. This practice of making pious gestures coincided with an ongoing secularization, both driven, at least in part, by the strong Florentine mercantile and banking economy.[7] As wealth spread, investors sought ways to devote at least some of their money to good works. At the same time, this cultural evolution challenged laypeople to reconcile the pleasures of this world with concerns about the next. The investment in religious projects helped alleviate any compunctions about how they might be spending their time or their money.

Along with the material enticements offered by the mercantile economy, in terms of goods and services available for purchase, there were the intellectual pleasures offered to an increasingly literate population

---

6 This would have been a major gift; Richard A. Goldthwaite estimates that "in the fourteenth century a large fresco commission for a chapel – for example, in Santa Croce at Florence – cost as much as 500 florins (*Wealth and the Demand for Art in Italy 1300–1600* [Baltimore: Johns Hopkins University Press, 1993], 61). Paolo Uccello eventually executed this project in the mid-fifteenth century, painting frescoes in the Chiostro Verde. See John M. Najemy, *A History of Florence 1200–1575* (Oxford: Blackwell, 2008), 325, who points out that by the mid-Trecento Santa Maria Novella had become an important locus for commissions by wealthy Florentine families who competed for recognition.

7 On the history of the Florentine economy, see Gene Brucker, *Renaissance Florence* (New York: John Wiley, 1969), 51–88; and Najemy, *History of Florence*, 96–123. Brucker makes the important point (53) that already in the late Middle Ages private money helped pay for the construction of the Palazzo della Signoria as well as the major Florentine churches, so this patronage tradition was not new to the city. For a thorough economic analysis of the relationship between wealth and patronage, see Goldthwaite, *Wealth*.

in the form of lay literature.[8] The fourteenth century saw a vast growth in manuscript production, with some counts numbering around 800,000 individual manuscripts.[9] The demand for, and circulation of, written texts suggests not just a growing lay literacy in some sectors, Florence among them, but also a growing intellectual curiosity, all of which appears to have resonated as threatening to the Dominicans. In 1335, Di Pierro reports, Florentine Dominicans themselves were prohibited from reading books of poetry, a sign that lay culture had penetrated the monastery. The ban appears to have had little effect, for twenty years later we find Passavanti scolding Dominicans for reading Ovid, Juvenal, Terence, romances, and love poetry, even as the *Mirror* itself bears a record of his having dipped a toe or two into this very stream.[10] The list of problematic texts doubtless reflects the type of material in general circulation, a mix of Latin classics and late medieval vernacular material that was popular in the early fourteenth century.

Indeed, the fourteenth century bears evidence of a tug-of-war over access to literary texts. Dante Alighieri had anticipated Passavanti's concerns about the threat posed by courtly love literature, directing his worries at lay readers, as evidenced in the famous episode of Paolo and Francesca in the fifth canto of the *Inferno*, for whom indulgence in erotic reading led to deadly erotic play. Passavanti's contemporary Giovanni Boccaccio also understood the power of literature as an erotic mediator, though he celebrated this function rather than condemn it. These conflicting positions on the social and ethical value of literature, both recorded in Passavanti's lifetime, reflect changing worldviews, with Dante believing that human curiosity about things erotic should be managed as a moral problem and Boccaccio accepting it as an inevitable part of life. Passavanti aligns himself with Dante and pursues a similar strategy to combat the concern, offering up a number of narratives,

8 As Vittore Branca documented years ago in *Boccaccio medievale*, the *Decameron* spread rapidly in the fourteenth century, a sign not only of an expanding readership base but also of a growing interest in vernacular literature. Even Dante's early poetry, not to mention *La divina commedia*, was repeatedly copied, including by Dante himself; see Justin Steinberg, *Accounting for Dante: Urban Readers and Writers in Late Medieval Italy* (Notre Dame, IN: University of Notre Dame Press, 2007).

9 Ross King, *The Bookseller of Florence: The Story of the Manuscripts that Illuminated the Renaissance* (New York: Atlantic Monthly Press, 2021), 151.

10 The Dominican campaign against lay reading continued into the fifteenth century. In his *Regola del governo di cura familiare*, written between 1400 and 1405, the Florentine Giovanni Dominici advocated the burning of "pagan" books. See Arthur Field, *The Intellectual Struggle for Florence: Humanists and the Beginnings of the Medici Regime, 1420–1440* (Oxford: Oxford University Press, 2017), 104.

borrowed from the *exemplum* tradition, that feature sexual temptation and transgression and its consequences.

The Dominican ban on secular books was both general and specific, in the latter sense that it targeted, along with the Latin authors named, Dante himself.[11] Evidently the *Commedia*'s deep piety and Dante's own interest in the salvation of souls did not rescue him from opprobrium, as the direct access offered by the *Commedia* to a variety of religious questions threatened the monopoly on theology that ecclesiastics reserved for themselves. Dante's decision to have Thomas Aquinas voice a critique of Dominican decadence in *Paradiso* 11 may also have figured into the injunction. The prohibition nevertheless remains striking, not least because it implicitly recognizes the poem's status as an instant classic that was attracting hungry readers. Here too, in any event, Passavanti appears to have ignored the advice, as the *Mirror* references all three parts of the *Commedia*, as well as *Il Convivio*, Dante's vernacular commentary on several of his poems, and *De vulgari eloquentia*, his linguistic treatise extolling the "illustrious vernacular," written in Latin. Passavanti may have wanted to know the enemy, but the order's repressive attitude suggests an understanding of how exposure to lay culture might put the hegemony of Christian morality at risk.

Indeed, the Dominican ban on reading signals alarm over the power of literature to draw people into the orbit of sin and, perhaps worse, to think for themselves. In this context, Passavanti's decision to organize his sermons into a written text looks like a way of combating this growing trend by offering an alternative to the vernacular texts of which he disapproved while simultaneously recognizing that people pursued them. As well, by penning a lengthy text directed beyond the physical walls of his church, he appears to have sought affirmation not just as a preacher but as a member of a group with growing cultural status: writers. In this context, Passavanti's decision to couple a vernacular version of the *Mirror* with the Latin version is telling.[12] As mentioned above, he planned to write the treatise in both Italian and Latin, thus affirming what Giovanni Getto describes as a traditionally medieval division of the world into laypeople and clerics, but also perhaps recognizing, as Getto suggests, the superior ductility of the vernacular, at

---

11 Di Pierro, "Contributo," 6–7.

12 It is also consistent with a recognition, on the part of Dominicans, of the growing reach of the vernacular; see Rita Librandi, "L'italiano nella comunicazione della Chiesa e nella diffusione della cultura religiosa," in *Storia della lingua italiana*, vol. 1, *I luoghi della codificazione*, ed. Luca Serianni and Pietro Trifone (Turin: Einaudi, 1993), 343–7.

least as far as the *exempla* are concerned.[13] If traditionally, therefore, the Dominicans had relied on sermons and visual representations – recall that Turino Baldesi had endowed a new fresco cycle of Old Testament narratives – for their messaging,[14] Passavanti aimed to leverage the growing cultural capital of the written word, in Italian, to advance this purpose. To the extent that his decision assumed a growing population of lay readers, it also signals the embrace of written texts as vehicles for Dominican voices.

The Mirror of True Penitence thus comes to join an expanding corpus of vernacular prose literature, as the world of the Italian Trecento increasingly accommodated the demands of readers of Italian. Vernacular texts included a number of works that had been brought from Latin or French into Italian, as Alison Cornish has extensively documented,[15] as well as a growing canon of original works in Italian, including those of Passavanti's predecessor Domenico Cavalca; Dante's *Vita nuova* and *Convivio* (both works, to be sure, combining prose and poetry); and Boccaccio's early romance, the *Filocolo*, and of course the *Decameron*. These authors were adapting their Italian for a variety of discourses, even as they addressed a novel audience.[16] Their texts bear evidence of how they thought about their readers and sought to accommodate their needs. They struggled with lexical roadblocks, sometimes coining neologisms to fill a gap or, in the alternative, devising complex circumlocutions. They pushed back against an early reliance on parataxis, exhibited in the anonymous thirteenth-century *Novellino* and other early prose texts, with an increasingly complex syntax, inspired at times by Ciceronian Latin, producing beautifully balanced periods that elevated their prose. And they were formally experimental, applying their skills to a variety of genres, including Passavanti's decision not to publish his sermons qua sermons, but rather to redeploy them as part of a more broadly conceived treatise on penitence.

Passavanti's familiarity with Dante and the Italian tradition was only part of the friar's vast textual culture, in both Latin and the vernacular.

---

13 Getto, "Umanità e stile," 23.

14 Goldthwaite, *Wealth*, 77.

15 See, among her many studies devoted to this topic, Alison Cornish, "Vernacular Translation in Medieval Italy: *Volgarizzamento*," in *A Companion to Medieval Translation*, ed. Jeanette Beer (Leeds: Arc Humanities Press, 2019), 107–23.

16 Cavalca's role in the development of the vernacular is perhaps less well known than that of the others; for background see Librandi, "L'italiano," and Mario Sassi, "The Language of a Preacher: Cavalca, Passavanti, and the First Steps toward a National Vernacular," *Rivista di storia e letteratura religiosa* 58 (2022): 27–49.

As mentioned above, among his other activities he sought to expand the library at Santa Maria Novella, likely focusing on religious texts in Latin. While there is no extant contemporary inventory of the library,[17] the *Mirror* helps fill out the picture of Passavanti's own education and voracious readerly curiosity. The text itself includes literally hundreds of quotations. Not surprisingly, the Old and New Testaments figure heavily into the mix, though Passavanti demonstrates a marked predilection for some books over others. These include, in addition to the Gospels, Psalms, Proverbs, Ecclesiasticus, some of the prophets (Isaiah, Jeremiah, Ezekiel), and many of the Pauline letters. Church fathers feature as well, with scores of quotations from many works by Augustine, as well as Bernard, Gregory, and Thomas Aquinas. Finally, there are some authors from Latin antiquity: Cicero, the benighted Ovid, Valerius Maximus, and Virgil.

How Passavanti accessed his citations is unclear. Given his fierce intelligence, and the fact that medieval writers relied heavily on memory, he may very well have organized them in his own brain, or he may have catalogued them on paper, topically, as part of an armamentarium of quotable material. The scores of citations serve to consolidate his arguments, either because they directly address the question at hand or because they reflect a worldview that is consistent with Passavanti's own. Often he does not name the text or author he is citing, leaving his reader to guess whether the quote comes from, say, Augustine or Ecclesiasticus. The basis of authority lies not in the author, however; rather, it lies in the fact that Passavanti cites in Latin, even as he does not expect his "unlettered" reader to understand it. This approach may be a way of validating the accuracy of his translations, as in the *Mirror* Passavanti criticizes some translators for their sloppy work.[18] As well, it serves to signal the authority of the quotes because they speak the accredited language of the Church. By including the Latin alongside its translation, Passavanti effectively demystifies the Latin quotations, by translating them, while simultaneously remystifying them by reminding his readers of their origins in a language associated with the sacred. Even as he writes the *Mirror* in contemporary Tuscan for the benefit of his lay and undereducated clerical readers, he implicitly embraces a linguistic hierarchy that

---

17 The earliest extant inventory dates to 1489 and lists 932 titles. See https://www.parrocchiasantamarianovella.it/s-maria-novella-prima-parte/. The manuscript containing the inventory is now housed at the Biblioteca Nazionale Centrale in Florence, Conventi Soppressi B.I.971.

18 See p. 215.

favours Latin, which transcends history, over Italian, the language of immanence.

Passavanti entitles the work *Lo specchio della vera penitenzia* (*The Mirror of True Penitence*), perhaps in homage to earlier works that feature the word *specchio*, such as *Specchio di croce* (Mirror of the Cross) and *Specchio dei peccati* (Mirror of Sins) by his fellow Dominican Cavalca. He may have thought as well about the tradition of the *specula principum*, or mirror of princes, that arose in the twelfth century. Either way, Passavanti's use of the word suggests that he comes to an understanding of the word's association with a genre of didactic literature, and that by using it he can alert his readers to the nature of its content. His use of the mirror image appears to have less to do with the reflective quality of mirrors themselves and more with a notion of modelling; in the Prologue he names St. Jerome as one "whose life and doctrine are an example and mirror of true penitence." So too then the book itself, which models true penitence not through actions but rather through words. The adjective in the title anticipates the argument, which Passavanti will advance, that there is such a thing as false penitence, which leads to no good end.

The treatise's content bears the marks of Passavanti's pedagogical approach to the subject at hand. Early on, he announces six topics: the definition of penitence; those things for which we should repent; those things that keep us from repenting; the parts of penitence and what is required to perfect it, especially contrition; confession; and, finally, satisfaction. Having made this outline, Passavanti proceeds through a series of arguments, each one carefully rubricated. Their elaboration follows a general model. First, Passavanti makes his claim with a reasoned defence. The appeal here is largely logical and occasionally scholastic in its format, in the sense that he sometimes poses a question and then proposes an answer. To bolster the logical argument, Passavanti offers his Latin citations. Not surprisingly given medieval practice, the quotations appear outside of their original context, and there is no attempt to recontextualize them. Their original setting may or may not be relevant to the argument at hand; here the pithy is clearly the enemy of philology. Occasionally, Passavanti strings together more than one Latin quotation without sourcing them, thus giving the impression that they all come from the same text even though they do not. Finally, as a complement to the expository passages, Passavanti sometimes includes an *exemplum*, which illustrates either a point he has already made or a new one. This practice too would reflect his sermonizing; as Jacques Le Goff has defined it, an *exemplum* is "a brief narrative offered as true and destined to be inserted in a discourse (generally, a sermon) to convince an audience of a salutary lesson."[19]

In introducing his discussion of confession, Passavanti avers that the "principal purpose" of his treatise is to teach people how to make good and effective confessions. Over many pages he details what is anything but a streamlined process. He answers questions about the frequency of confession, its structure, the sins that must be confessed, to whom the confessant must confess, the circumstances that allow or mandate that the confessant turn to a confessor other than the parish priest, and so forth. The *Mirror* thus offers another advantage to the reader as a resource to keep all these instructions straight. One certainly has the impression of bureaucratic oversight of what should be a straightforward process, whose success would depend uniquely on the sincerity of the regret offered. But it is precisely Passavanti's insistence that intention is not a sufficient precondition for grace, and that confession, in the prescribed format, along with satisfaction is, which centres the role of the confessor, making him a key manager of the confessant's relationship with God.

The culture of confession reflected here certainly anticipates the culture of surveillance that Michel Foucault, in *The History of Sexuality* and other works, saw as emerging in the seventeenth century. However, such an interpretation should not overlook the concerns, both spiritual and psychological, that inform the *Mirror*. Every page of this text is marked with a profound interest in the fate of the human soul and the risk of falling short. Even if one were to discount Passavanti's preoccupation with what becomes of the soul after death, there is here an interest in ethical behaviour and self-examination as ends in themselves. Confession, after all, is the second step of a process that begins with contrition, which involves recognizing that one has done wrong. This acknowledgment is precisely the complicating factor that raises the question of whether confession is also necessary, because already in contrition there is regret.

Passavanti sets this process against the backdrop of an increasingly complex world, one that generates not new types of sin but rather new opportunities for sin. In a telling paragraph, he lists the types of contracts that may involve some form of graft, ranging from business transactions to bank loans to real estate and family law. His awareness of the range of legal issues suggests that in his tripartite career as priest,

---

19 Qtd. in Carlo Delcorno, *Exemplum e letteratura tra medioevo e Rinascimento* (Bologna: Il Mulino, 1989), 8.

administrator, and development director he dealt with a variety of legal issues, both directly and indirectly. Many of the questions to which he refers, ever so briefly, pertain to the urban environment of fourteenth-century Florence: contracts and other business dealings, real estate transactions, banking. Passavanti recognizes that daily life could entail unforeseen ethical and moral entanglements that can be easier to ignore than to confront.[20] The role assigned to the confessor thus involves not simply that of facilitating the process of confession but also ensuring that the work conducted in this life is oriented towards the good.

For all that he tries to stick to his plan, Passavanti also struggles to stay on task. Sometimes he will cut himself short, announcing that he does not want to run on too long, presumably not to overtax his reader by plumbing the minutiae of theological argument (he says he is saving those arguments for the Latin version of the work). At the same time, he belabours the importance of certain practices, particularly regarding confession, because of what is at stake for his lay readers. Questions regarding what to confess, and when, and to whom populate the treatise, with Passavanti's dissection of them suggesting a strong desire on the part of confessional authorities to micromanage the lives of lay Christians.

The *Mirror*'s many *exempla* have attracted more than their fair share of attention, a sign perhaps that narrative remains compelling not just to the human imagination writ large but to the critical eye as well. The preacher had ready access to these narratives though another type of resource that emerged in the late Middle Ages, the compendium of exemplary narratives. Several such works circulated, including Stephen of Bourbon's *De septem donis Spiritus Sancti*, the first such manual organized, as the title suggests, around the seven gifts of the Holy Spirit. A later text, the *Liber exemplorum ad usum praedicantium*, was the first to sift its narrative material alphabetically by topic. The Dominican Arnoldus of Liège, who died around 1308, also compiled a collection known as the *Alphabetum narrationum*, with helpful cross-references within the text.[21] This popular work founds its way into English as the *Alphabet of*

---

20 As Gene Brucker pointed out, "knowledge of the law was particularly valued in Florence, where social and economic relations were governed by a complex and sophisticated legal code" (*Renaissance Florence*, 102). More recently, Justin Steinberg has documented the legal complexities of late medieval life in *Law and Mimesis in Boccaccio's* Decameron: *Realism on Trial* (Cambridge: Cambridge University Press, 2023).

21 See Delcorno, *Exemplum*, 14–15.

Tales in the fifteenth century.[22] Angelo Monteverdi's thorough research, conducted early in the twentieth century, confirms that Passavanti's source for his *exempla* was in fact the *Alphabetum narrationum*.[23]

Passavanti's use of *exempla* is consistent with the preacher's practice; after all, the manuals that collected these short, instructive narratives were designed to facilitate sermon-writing.[24] Their inclusion here suggests how Passavanti transferred his sermonic material into the *Mirror*, as well as how preaching might have informed some of the other narrative material that emerged during this period. One of Passavanti's *exempla* features a narrative that famously found its way into Boccaccio's *Decameron*, as the eighth story of the Fifth Day.[25] While we cannot know how the account made its way to Boccaccio – he too could have had access to a preacher's handbook of *exempla*, and he would have been aware of Dante's use of this narrative in *Inferno* 13 – it is fascinating to imagine how this great author, hearing such narratives in sermons, might have thought to repurpose them into the brilliant stories that compose his masterpiece. In this regard, he certainly pays his debt to Passavanti's church, Santa Maria Novella, having his group of ten young storytellers first decide to leave Florence in the spring of 1348 while gathered together in that very building.

Passavanti's combination of argument, citation, and *exemplum* reaches peak density in the third chapter of the Fifth Distinction, the section of

---

22 The English translation attributes the text to Etienne of Besançon, and indeed there appears to be some dispute over its authorship.

23 Angelo Monteverdi, "Gli esempi dello 'Specchio di vera penitenza,'" *Giornale storico della letteratura italiana*, Parte Prima, 61 (1913): 266–344; Parte Seconda, 63 (1914): 240–90. Monteverdi located versions of the *exempla* in a number of sources and observed that Passavanti's versions consistently tracked in form and narrative detail with the version that appears in the *Alphabetum*. More recent studies on Passavanti's *exempla* include, in addition to Aurigemma and Getto, Pina Robuschi, "Gli *esempi* del Passavanti," *Rinascimento* 9 (1958): 114–19; Ginetta Auzzas, "Tradizione caratterizzante e interpolazione di 'exempla' nello 'Specchio della vera penitenzia,'" *Filologia italiana* 1 (2004): 61–71; and Myriam Carminati, "La pénitence, 'médecine de l'âme': Nuit et terreur dans les *exempla* de Jacopo Passavanti," *Revue des langues romanes* 110 (2006): 407–24. Finally, Francesco Valli addresses several of the *exempla* in his essay "Iacopo Passavanti," in *Letteratura italiana: I minori* (Milan: Marzorati, 1961), 1:306–21. For a general overview of the medieval *exemplum* see Delcorno, *Exemplum*.

24 It makes sense, therefore, as Rossi reports, that the *Theosophya*, which he hypothesizes is Passavanti's missing Latin companion to the *Mirror*, contains no *exempla*: Dominican preachers would have other available resources and in theory would not themselves require the moral teaching that the *exempla* offer.

25 It is the *exemplum* of the purgatorial pursuit, witnessed by the charcoal vendor, in the second chapter of the Third Distinction.

the treatise devoted to confession. Here the author expostulates on the utility and effect of confession. He lists five effects: It frees the soul from death (i.e., from condemnation to hell, as well as from bodily death); it opens the way to paradise; it gives hope for salvation and the remission of sins; it frees the sinner from punishment or diminishes it; and it hides the sin from God. As usual, the expository approach can be challenging. Passavanti first addresses how confession frees the soul from death. He relies on a statement by St. Ambrose, then follows up, not surprisingly given the scholastic nature of the argument, with a quote from Thomas Aquinas. Next he introduces a counterargument that casts doubt on his initial claim, wondering whether contrition is a sufficient condition for grace or whether confession is required as well. The answer: Contrition itself is not sufficient, but a vow or intention to confess is a precondition for grace. The problem, which becomes clear as the argument progresses, is that if contrition alone is a necessary precondition for grace, then confession becomes unnecessary. To rescue confession from the dustbin, he again summons Aquinas, who makes the point that through confession the grace grows.

This first argument thus comes down to a theological reassertion of the need for confession as part of the process of penitence. Perhaps aware of the density of his reasoning, Passavanti then introduces a subpoint, the striking claim that confession frees the confessant not just from damnation but from mortality as well. Shelving his scholasticism for the moment, Passavanti introduces an *exemplum* involving a poor clerk who murders a goldsmith to steal his wares. The killer draws his sister into the crime after the fact, and when they are arrested, she urges him to confess in order to save both their souls. He refuses, so she confesses on her own, and when they are both put to the flame, the fire quickly consumes him but leaves her unharmed.

As an illustration of the positive effects of confession, the tale makes sense here. As well, it reflects Passavanti's attitude towards the *exempla*. He betrays no doubts about the "truth" of the tale: in other words, that a human being, having made a full and sincere confession, can survive being burned alive. While he may never have witnessed such a miracle himself,[26] he trusts that the *exemplum*, as a record of the miraculous, is a historical record – in this case of an event that took place in the

---

26 Though Passavanti may not have witnessed this particular miracle, people in the late Middle Ages firmly believed in the possibility of miracles, as a number of extant miracle collections attest. The Church itself had established procedures for verifying miracles; see Michael E. Goodich, *Violence and Miracle in the Fourteenth Century: Private Grief and Public Salvation* (Chicago: University of Chicago Press, 1994). As if acknowledging its ubiquity, Boccaccio takes aim at this aspect of the faith in the first tale of the *Decameron*.

French city of Arras – and not a fiction. For him to think otherwise and nevertheless to present the tale as historically true would be an act of charlatanism not unlike that described by Boccaccio in the story of Friar Cipolla (*Decameron* 6.10), in which a flimflamming preacher exploits the gullibility of his audience. Moreover, Passavanti is fully aware that such deceitful preachers exist, offering an unvarnished condemnation of them in his discussion of vainglory.[27] In like manner, he would expect his reader to accept the tale as verisimilar and to limit analysis of it to a determination of whether the narrative accounts for a natural phenomenon, a miracle, or the work of the devil.[28]

Inasmuch as he offers the supernatural events recounted in *exempla* as part of the historical record, Passavanti does not include the *exempla* simply for their illustrative value; he includes them because they enjoy the same authoritative status as his abundant Latin quotations. If, as some readers have suggested, Passavanti uses *exempla* in an effort to frighten his readers into compliance, this would be consistent with the general practice of *exempla*, as Carlo Delcorno has observed.[29] It is not, however, Passavanti's only purpose. The *exempla* bear witness to God's power on earth, for it is God, we are invited to assume, who intervenes to block the natural effect of fire on the clerk's sister, as it is God who enables the other supernatural events described in these tales. Passavanti seeks to remind his readers that, even as they may never have witnessed miracles themselves, the potential for such events, as modelled on the miracles recorded in the Gospels, is everywhere and always. Readers should therefore never lose faith, for God's power can work to both generous and deleterious effect at all times.

In this chapter alone, Passavanti employs the pattern of argument followed by *exemplum* five times. After the discussion of how confession opens the path to paradise, he includes a story of how a dead woman returned to life during her funeral in order to confess one last sin so that she would go to heaven. When explaining how confession frees us from due punishment or diminishes it, he introduces an account, again from Arras and attributed to the thirteenth-century hagiographer Caesarius of Heisterbach, of a group of heretics condemned to the flame. One of them, induced to confess, does so on the pyre, whereupon the fire dies down and his burns heal. After the discussion of how confession hides the record of sin from God, Passavanti adds a narrative from the legend of St. Constance, archbishop of Canterbury, about a young monk

---

27 See p. 211 of the text.
28 Delcorno, *Exemplum*, 105.
29 See Carminati, "La pénitence," on the fear element of Passavanti's *exempla*; and Delcorno, *Exemplum*, 104–5.

who, thanks to demonic possession, acquired the ability to identify mortal sinners, which he regularly deployed. Finally, once he explains how confession without contrition (and without a commitment not to sin again) is useless, he offers a narrative, set in Bramante, concerning another demoniac who had the same ability to identify sinners and who exposed a man who had made an insincere confession.

In citing these *exempla*, Passavanti relies not just on his talent as a raconteur; he also takes care to validate their historicity. In four of the five stories he names the locale, either Arras or Bramante or, presumably, Canterbury; elsewhere he specifies the year in which the event occurred. And while he attributes the story of the woman who came back to life to "leggende," he takes this word not as denoting a fiction but rather in its historical meaning as a short work associated with saints and so called because they were typically read among groups of people.[30] Passavanti appears to like these narratives not just because they colourfully make his point but also because they impose different cognitive demands on the reader than does his scholastic argumentation. In other words, and here he is relying on his own experience as well as on that of other preachers who use *exempla* in their sermons, he recognizes that moral lessons offered through narrative may help his readers understand his claims. Given the density of some of his paragraphs, which he leavens via the *exempla*, one has to wonder how well an audience listening to one of his sermons in Santa Maria Novella might have followed along. Here then we can see another advantage to the transfer of the sermons, designed for oral delivery, to the written text: It affords the reader the time and the opportunity to digest Passavanti's complex thinking on the problems of sin and penitence, encouraged perhaps by the anticipation of brief narrative whose message will be easier to grasp.

The text thus proceeds in an orderly fashion according to Passavanti's initial plan, following its argumentative scheme until, suddenly, it appears to wander. As part of his study of sin, Passavanti pens treatises on pride and its opposite, humility. He begins with pride because it is largely understood to be the root of all sin, he explains. There follows another treatise, this time on vainglory, identified as a corollary of pride but with important differences, detailed over many pages. Next comes what some earlier editions labelled the "Treatise on Dreams," almost a document apart from the rest of the work but in fact included here as

---

30 See Tommaseo-Bellini, *Dizionario della lingua italiana*, www.tommaseobellini.it, s.v. "leggenda." I have translated this word as "account."

part of his investigation of vainglory; Passavanti sees the widespread belief that dreams are legible as exemplifying this sin. Given that Passavanti had promised to write about all seven of the deadly sins, as well as their corresponding virtues, and there was still the announced section on satisfaction to write, the treatise begins to look almost impossibly unwieldy; and besides that there was the Latin version to attend to. And then everything stops.

We can speculate as to why the friar never finished his work; the common assumption attributes it to his death. But Passavanti may have lost interest or, understandably, felt overwhelmed by the text's metastatic growth (at one point he admits that "the material is multiplying in my hands"). We also do not know how much sermonic material Passavanti had at hand; in other words, we do not know how many of the deadly sins he had managed to discuss in his Lenten sermons of 1354. There is another possibility as well, as the text itself marks a subtle shift in Passavanti's thinking that no longer comported with a project devoted to penitence.

The first evidence of this shift comes late in the discussion of vainglory, when Passavanti, setting aside his practice of citing, takes a much more discursive approach based on straightforward argument and simple logic. This practice continues in the subsequent discussion of dreams, where it is clear that he has done his homework. He affirms the importance of the topic by reminding his reader of the pivotal role played by dreams in biblical narratives. He acknowledges the two master dream interpreters in the Bible, Joseph and Daniel, and recognizes that others have claimed the same talent. The problem, he explains, is that people who believe they can interpret dreams correctly, no matter how sincere their conviction, may in fact have unwittingly fallen prey to the devil. In other words, regardless of whether one can interpret dreams correctly or not, there is the graver problem, insoluble from the point of view of the interpreter, of whether such efforts actually constitute a sin because of diabolic entrapment. Making matters worse, a sinner unaware of his or her own sin cannot repent for it, and failure to repent dooms one to hell. Under these circumstances, the confessor's role becomes paramount, as only he can ferret out the truth about sinful behaviour.

Passavanti proceeds to summarize his own research into dream theory, which points to dreams as either causes or effects. The discussion of dreams as effects is fairly straightforward. Dreams, the friar explains, can result from environmental, psychological, or physiological factors, including one's sleeping position. He discounts claims that herbs and stones can influence dreams, though he does admit that dreams can contain divine revelations. Here some cracks appear, however: Passavanti openly wonders why such revelations come only through dreams and not in conscious visions, and he also worries about how the dreamer can tell the difference between a true vision and a fantasy, particularly given the possibility that dreams result from diabolical intervention. Moreover, while he accepts that dreams may accurately foretell the future, he denies that we can be sure of the accuracy of those who claim to understand what they signify. "Experience," he writes,

> which teaches certain things, shows that the so-called interpreters are wrong; because that judgment could be about dreams other than those we have offered as an example. The only thing they have going for them is that for somebody who had one or another of those dreams or had them interpreted by others, what they were said to mean had in fact happened. But the dreaming could be for some special reason, because one person dreams in a way that another does not, and one person has truer dreams than somebody else. There is no doubt a great difference in how people dream, according to their constitutions and thoughts, feelings, and the variety of their jobs, studies, and activities, which are the reason for dreams.

Moreover, he argues, "whoever reads or hears this treatise should recall whether he ever dreamed any of the aforesaid dreams, and whether what these blowhards stubbornly affirm ever happened. If not, as I believe, he should hold them to be liars." His doubts about dreams extend as well to visions, which constitute another problem for him inasmuch as one cannot tell the difference between true vision and fantasy. To the extent that Passavanti does not offer a litmus test to prove the veracity of either dreams or visions, he establishes a baseline of scepticism regarding the interpretation of observed phenomena.

The evolution away from a scholastic practice and towards a growing reliance on logic rooted in the observed world, with the corollary that Passavanti increasingly trusts his own ability to solve problems, suggests that the preacher himself may have felt the influence in a growing civic spirit that privileged the agency of the human intellect. Along the way of ordering his thoughts, Passavanti appears to rely more and more on himself, trusting in his own ability to make sense of what he observes. In this way, his work reflects the emerging ethos of midcentury Florence, with its reliance on human ingenuity, and which Boccaccio captures so well in the *Decameron* and other works. It is almost as if Passavanti has reinterpreted the image with which he opens the text, in which he encourages his reader to grab hold of the plank of penitence when shipwrecked in a choppy sea.[31] Passavanti still believes in the role of chance in human affairs, but by the end of the *Mirror* the act of reaching out for the plank of penitence is not merely a gesture of faith in God; it participates in the human intelligence that looks to solve problems.

In the context of dream theory, then, Passavanti's decision to transform his sermons into a written text also assumes new importance, as part of a broader interrogation of reading and its dangers. Passavanti frames the *Mirror* as a treatise designed to help save us from ourselves. As he makes clear early on, borrowing a narrative from Peter Damian, he knows that people can make fatal mistakes by misinterpreting signs. The story he cites involves the popular belief that when Mount Etna acts up, the volcano, assumed to be a portal to hell, is preparing to receive a high-profile sinner. The protagonist of the narrative, a Salernitan prince, correctly interprets the sign – the suddenly active Mount Etna is in fact readying to receive a sinner – but erroneously assumes that the volcano is preparing for someone other than himself. Thus, when he suddenly dies while bedding one of his lovers, off he goes to hell. The tale does not deny that naturally occurring events can be harbingers of the future. However, it calls into question the reliability of our interpretation of signs, which applies to the interpretation of dreams as well. Generalized as a problem of reading, it suggests that independent readers may take their own lessons from what they read, particularly as their own inclinations may influence them. Along with his Dominican brothers, Passavanti may undertake to leverage his authority to direct his readers to proper reading choices and a correct understanding of what they read, but his efforts to exercise control betray a growing worry that control may be slipping away. It is an ironic footnote to Passavanti's project that even as he worries about the souls of his lay audience, he capitalizes on the very interest that puts them at risk: vernacular reading.[32]

---

31 On Passavanti's use of this metaphor, see Timothy Kircher, *The Poet's Wisdom: The Humanists, the Church, and the Formation of Philosophy in the Early Renaissance* (Leiden: Brill, 2006), 184–201.

32 Passavanti himself acknowledges this danger: "It seems the time has come, indeed it did come (were it not so!), as St. Paul predicted when, as he writes to Timothy, the impeccable doctrine of Holy Scripture and of the true faith will not endure, but people follow their appetites in looking for teachers and preachers who will scratch the itch on their ears, i.e., who will tell them what they want to hear for their pleasure and not their benefit, and they will turn away from the truth and lend an ear to fables."

The *Mirror* thus reflects not only a theory of penitence; it reflects as well a changing world and a writer who appears, perhaps unknowingly, to be changing along with it. It is a text that lays its foundation on concerns about the post-mortem status of the soul, but it does so while making concessions to a social and cultural dynamic that prizes human intelligence as a gift that enables new, independent ways of thinking. It fascinates not simply because of its charming prose, careful analysis, and lively narratives, but also because it struggles so tellingly with its historical moment, confronting a transition that is as worrisome as it is inevitable. Readers have justly compared Passavanti to both Cavalca and Boccaccio, for in some ways his work straddles those of these two seminal authors, marking a path from one to the other. Since today there are many English translations of the *Decameron*, but this is the first full English translation of the *Mirror*, we know how the story ends.

Aspects of Passavanti's Language and Style, and a Note on the Translation

Passavanti is a highly colloquial writer, and his lifelong experience as someone who wove words for their spoken, as opposed to written, impact is everywhere evident in this text. In his review of its critical history, Marcello Aurigemma noted how the *Mirror* quickly earned praise for its style – a praise that no doubt would have both pleased and disappointed Passavanti, since it effectively fetishized the work as a model of good Italian at the expense of its moral content.[33]

Indeed, it is not clear that Passavanti thinks about the difference between writing as an exercise in recording speech and writing as an exercise distinct from speaking. In structuring his arguments, he relies frequently on the scholastic model borrowed from written works like Aquinas's (Latin) *Summa theologica*, itself a reflection of classroom pedagogy, and he thinks carefully about the organization of both the individual sections of the text and the work as a whole. Nevertheless, his vernacular writing is replete with the tics of speech. Indeed, he occasionally uses the verb *parlare*, to speak, when referencing his writerly

---

33 Marcello Aurigemma, "La fortuna critica dello *Specchio di vera penitenza* di Jacopo Passavanti," in *Studi in onore di Angelo Monteverdi*, 2 vols., ed. Giuseppina Gerardi Marcuzzo (Modena: STEM, 1959), 1:48–75. Such praise informs Getto's reading of Passavanti, who by his account practises "un geometrico lavoro di intarsio" ("Umanità e stile," 20). At the same time, however, Getto acknowledges that the text's occasional musicality reflects "con più calda memoria la predicazione quaresimale da cui attinge, compilando il suo trattato" (40).

activity, a sign of how thoroughly embedded his mind was in the speaker's way of thinking. Individual sentences begin with conjunctions like "and" and "whereupon"; compound subjects are matched with verbs in the singular; and there is frequently a wordiness that one would associate with extemporaneous utterance. The use of synonymic pairs for emphasis, while not unique to orality, nevertheless creates frequent redundancies. The verbs *essere*, to be, and *avere*, to have, dominate. The register is decidedly quotidian, even as Passavanti's language provided valuable fodder for the composers of the *Vocabolario degli Accademici della Crusca* in the early seventeenth century; where Passavanti might have chosen a more elegant word to capture a thought, he leans towards circumlocution in simpler language. There is as well a marked effort to untangle complex arguments about sin for an audience of lay readers who do not share his background in theology.

The present translation addresses Passavanti's style out of respect for the demands of English and the expectations of the English-language reader, even at a certain risk to the stylistic integrity of the original. As much as possible I have cut the unnecessary conjunctions that begin sentences; some remain as representative traces of Passavanti's practice. Subjects and verbs now agree in number. Passavanti's lengthy periods, carefully balanced and often quite elegant, read as run-on sentences in English, so I have had to break them down. I have sought to eliminate the wordiness wherever possible.

The question of the verbs *essere* and *avere*, on the other hand, is more problematic. Here we enter into the critical terrain of the range of Passavanti's vocabulary, which is actually fairly narrow, a reflection in part of the limited vocabulary of the medieval vernacular and in part of the desire to keep things simple for his readers. Moreover, it is unclear how much of the relatively small corpus of Italian vernacular literature Passavanti may have read, beyond the works of someone like Cavalca. While the *Mirror* offers the picture of Passavanti as a voracious reader, he very likely did most of his reading in Latin. His language therefore reflects the language of his everyday experience, and in particular of conversation with others who did not have a broad or sophisticated Italian vocabulary. So when I replace "to have" with "to acquire," what the text gains in precision it loses in both homogeneity and authenticity. While such modifications to Passavanti's linguistic practice remain invisible, I have frequently had to balance respect for Passavanti's linguistic universe with an impulse to concision that an English-language reader would appreciate. I can only ask Passavanti's forgiveness if I have trespassed the limits of his own register in an effort to align his text more closely with contemporary English style.

Finally, there is the question of the gendering of Passavanti's prose. Not surprisingly, he hews towards the masculine, frequently referring to *un uomo*, a man, and *uomini*, men, as generic terms for people. Only rarely does he refer to women, and elsewhere, when he writes about men, he appears to be referring to human beings in general. The practice strikes me in part as reflexive, because Italian does use masculine forms in generic ways. However, it also reflects the way in which, in his own mind, Passavanti lives in a world of men – not just the world of Dominican men but the world of men in general, who are the predominant social drivers of Florentine public life. So the gendering of his text remains an important marker of Passavanti's social world and his way of thinking, and to erase it completely would be to erase this evidence. Therefore, I have attempted to temper, but not wholly eliminate, the rampant masculine forms that clutter the text, substituting "person" and "people" wherever possible. Occasionally I have used the first-person plural ("we," "us") or the second person as a means to achieve a more neutral balance.

Ginetta Auzzas's critical edition of *Lo specchio della vera penitenzia* forms the basis of this translation. Auzzas conducted a thorough collation of the previous editions of the treatise, identifying and removing spurious material. Interested readers should consult her apparatus, which provides much useful information.

Auzzas also undertook to identify the source of the many quotations that populate Passavanti's prose. I have credited her work in my own notes with [GA], though I have not gone so far as to specify the location of the quote within the text from which Passavanti borrowed it. Auzzas does do this work, though in many cases locating the quote in context requires recourse to the same edition she used. Auzzas also notes the source for the many biblical citations, and I have reconfirmed each one against the biblical texts.

Bibliography

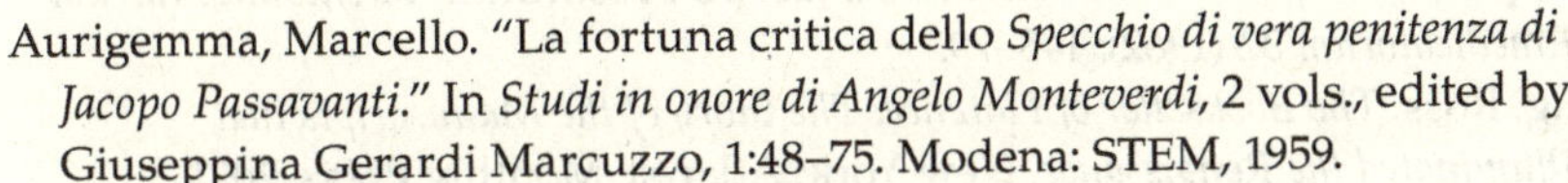

Aurigemma, Marcello. "La fortuna critica dello *Specchio di vera penitenza di Jacopo Passavanti*." In *Studi in onore di Angelo Monteverdi*, 2 vols., edited by Giuseppina Gerardi Marcuzzo, 1:48–75. Modena: STEM, 1959.

– *Saggio sul Passavanti*. Florence: Le Monnier, 1957.

Auzzas, Ginetta. "Dalla predica al trattato: Lo *Specchio della vera penitenzia* di Iacopo Passavanti." *Lettere italiane* 54 (2002): 325–42.

– "Per il testo dello 'Specchio della vera penitenza': Due nuove fonti manoscritte." *Lettere italiane* 26 (1974): 261–87.

– "Tradizione caratterizzante e interpolazione di 'exempla' nello 'Specchio della vera penitenzia.'" *Filologia italiana* 1 (2004): 61–71.

Battaglia Ricci, Lucia. "*Exemplum* e novella." In *Scrittura religiosa: Forme letterarie del Trecento al Cinquecento*, edited by Carlo Delcorno and Maria Luisa Doglio, 37–57. Bologna: Il Mulino, 2003.

Branca, Vittore. *Boccaccio medievale*. Milan: BUR, 2010.

Brucker, Gene. *Renaissance Florence*. New York: John Wiley, 1969.

Carminati, Myriam. "La pénitence, 'médecine de l'âme': Nuit et terreur dans les *exempla* de Jacopo Passavanti." *Revue des langues romanes* 110 (2006): 407–24.

Cornish, Alison. "Vernacular Translation in Medieval Italy: *Volgarizzamento*." In *A Companion to Medieval Translation*, edited by Jeanette Beer, 107–23. Leeds: Arc Humanities Press, 2019.

Delcorno, Carlo. *Exemplum e letteratura tra Medioevo e Rinascimento*. Bologna: Il Mulino, 1989.

– "Letteratura in forma di sermone: Introduzione." In *Letteratura in forma di sermone: I rapporti tra predicazione e letteratura nei secoli XIII–XVI; Atti del Seminario di studi (Bologna 15–17 novembre 2001)*, edited Ginetta Auzzas, Giovanni Baffetti, and Carlo Delcorno, 1–8. Florence: Leo S. Olschki, 2003.

– "Nuovi testimoni della letteratura domenicana del Trecento (Giordano da Pisa, Cavalca, Passavanti)." *Lettere italiane* 36 (1984): 577–90.

Del Popolo, Concetto. "Una tessera Iacoponica in Passavanti." *Lettere italiane* 53 (2001): 397–400.

Di Pierro, Carmine. "Contributo alla biografia di frà Jacopo Passavanti fiorentino." *Giornale storico della letteratura italiana* 47 (1906): 1–24.

Field, Arthur. *The Intellectual Struggle for Florence: Humanists and the Beginnings of the Medici Regime, 1420–1440.* Oxford: Oxford University Press, 2017.

Getto, Giovanni. "Umanità e stile di Iacopo Passavanti." In *Letteratura religiosa del Trecento*, 1–105. Florence: Sansoni, 1967.

Goldthwaite, Richard. *Wealth and the Demand for Art in Italy 1300–1600.* Baltimore: Johns Hopkins University Press, 1993.

Goodich, Michael E. *Violence and Miracle in the Fourteenth Century: Private Grief and Public Salvation.* Chicago: University of Chicago Press, 1994.

Kaeppeli, T. "Opere latine attribuite a Jacopo Passavanti." *Archivum Fratrum Praedicatorum* 32 (1962): 145–79.

King, Ross. *The Bookseller of Florence: The Story of the Manuscripts that Illuminated the Renaissance.* New York: Atlantic Monthly Press, 2021.

Kircher, Timothy. *The Poet's Wisdom: The Humanists, the Church, and the Formation of Philosophy in the Early Renaissance.* Leiden: Brill, 2006.

Librandi, Rita. "L'italiano nella communicazione della Chiesa e nella diffusione della cultura religiosa." In *Storia della lingua italiana*, 3 vols., edited by Luca Serianni and Pietro Trifone, 1:335–81. Turin: Einaudi, 1993.

Meiss, Millard. *Painting in Florence and Siena after the Black Death: The Arts, Religion, and Society in the Mid-Fourteenth Century.* Princeton, NJ: Princeton University Press, 1978.

Monteverdi, Angelo. "Gli esempi dello 'Specchio di vera penitenza.'" *Giornale storico della letteratura italiana*, Parte Prima, 61 (1913): 266–344; Parte Seconda, 63 (1914): 240–90.

Mulchahey, M. Michèle. *"First the Bow Is Bent in Study": Dominican Education before 1350.* Toronto: Pontifical Institute of Mediaeval Studies, 1998.

Najemy, John M. *A History of Florence 1200–1575.* Oxford: Blackwell, 2008.

Passavanti, Iacopo. *Lo specchio della vera penitenzia.* Edited by Ginetta Auzzas. Florence: Accademia della Crusca, 2014.

Robuschi, Pina. "Gli *esempi* del Passavanti." *Rinascimento* 9 (1958): 114–19.

Rossi, Giancarlo. "La 'redazione latina' dello 'Specchio della vera penitenza.'" *Studi di filologia italiana* 49 (1991): 29–58.

Sassi, Mario. "The Language of a Preacher: Cavalca, Passavanti, and the First Steps toward a National Vernacular." *Rivista di storia e letteratura religiosa* 58 (2022): 27–49.

Steinberg, Justin. *Accounting for Dante: Urban Readers and Writers in Late Medieval Italy.* Notre Dame, IN: University of Notre Dame Press, 2007.

– *Law and Mimesis in Boccaccio's* Decameron: *Realism on Trial.* Cambridge: Cambridge University Press, 2023.

Valli, Francesco. "Iacopo Passavanti." In *Letteratura italiana: I minori*, 1:307–21. 4 vols. Milan: Marzorati, 1961.

Key to Abbreviations

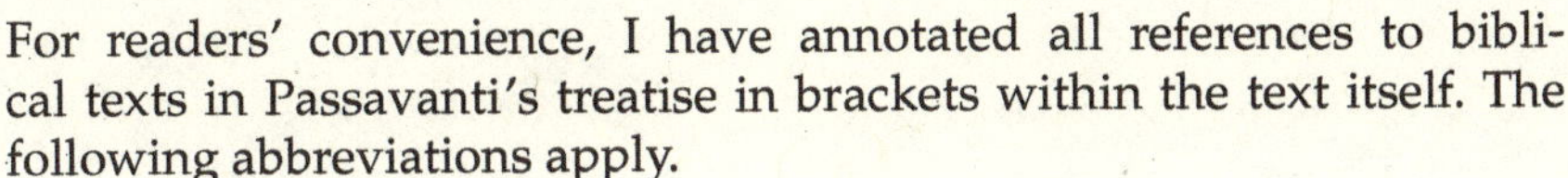

For readers' convenience, I have annotated all references to biblical texts in Passavanti's treatise in brackets within the text itself. The following abbreviations apply.

Ac	Acts of the Apostles	1 Jn	1 John
Am	Amos	Jr	Jeremiah
1 Ch	1 Chronicles	2 Kg	2 Kings
1 Cr	1 Corinthians	Lk	Gospel of Luke
2 Cr	2 Corinthians	Lv	Leviticus
Dn	Daniel	1 Mc	1 Maccabees
Dt	Deuteronomy	2 Mc	2 Maccabees
Ec	Ecclesiasticus	Mh	Micah
El	Ecclesiastes	Ml	Malachai
Ep	Ephesians	Mt	Gospel of Matthew
Es	Esther	Nb	Numbers
Ex	Exodus	Nh	Nahum
Ez	Ezekiel	Ph	Philippians
Gl	Galatians	Pr	Proverbs
Gn	Genesis	Ps	Psalms
Hb	Hebrews	1 Pt	1 Peter
Hg	Haggai	2 Pt	2 Peter
Hk	Habakkuk	Rm	Romans
Hs	Hosea	Rv	Revelation of John
Is	Isaiah	1 Sm	1 Samuel
Jb	Job	2 Sm	2 Samuel
Jd	Judith	1 Tm	1 Timothy
Jg	Judges	2 Tm	2 Timothy
Jh	Jonah	Tt	Titus
Jl	Joel	Ws	Wisdom of Solomon
Jm	James	Zc	Zachariah
Jn	Gospel of John		

THE MIRROR OF TRUE PENITENCE

The Mirror of True Penitence

HERE BEGINS THE PROLOGUE to the Book entitled MIRROR OF TRUE PENITENCE, COMPILED BY THE FRIAR JACOPO PASSAVANTI OF THE ORDER OF FRIARS PREACHERS

According to the venerable doctor St. Jerome, "Poenitentia est secunda tabula post naufragium": penitence is the second plank after the danger of the shipwreck. The holy doctor speaks of penitence by comparing it to people shipwrecked at sea, where it often happens that, when a boat breaks apart by chance or because of a tempest, those who are most alert hold fast to one of the planks of the broken boat, and, staying afloat, do not sink but reach the shore or port having escaped the danger of the tempestuous sea. The same thing happens to those who live in this world, which is called a sea because of its continuous movement and instability, for both the tempestuous adversities and serious dangers that are there, in which most people perish. Between the weight of human flesh and that of original or present sin, which all the children of Adam bear on their shoulders, and given the force of the fortuitous waves of temptation and worldly and bodily tribulations, they cannot swim. Only Jesus Christ our saviour, God and man unburdened by sin, skimmed the sea of this world. He showed this when his disciples were in the boat on the Sea of Galilee and at great risk given the strength of the opposing wind, and he came to them walking lightly over the waves of the turbulent sea. St. Peter could not do this; indeed, he would have sunk to the bottom were it not for the virtuous hand of Jesus Christ that helped him. This suggests that everyone will drown in this dangerous sea without the aid of divine grace, which has supplied us with a light and sturdy little boat for the salvation of human beings. Jesus Christ built it with his own hands from the wood of his most holy cross and the sharp nails of his passion, painting and decorating it with his precious blood. This little boat is baptismal innocence, which all who are baptized through Jesus Christ may enter. If captained and steered well, it will carry those who stay aboard, as true and straight Christians, safe and sound to the port of eternal life. The blessed Virgin Mary crossed the sea of this life in this sturdy and intact little boat, as did St. John the Baptist and many other saints, who were sanctified in the belly of the mother or preserved and safeguarded by a special divine grace, so that they would not fall into mortal sin in their lives. All the innocents cross there too: the ones who, before reaching such an age when, by distinguishing good from evil, they might consent to the evil of sin, to which our corrupt nature is inclined more than to the good, were taken by natural death or forced from the present corporeal life after receiving the grace of baptism. They cross not by their own merit, because they could not steer the light and beautiful boat, but thanks instead to that patron who built it, and who with his presence and grace steers it. Thus, with no obstacle in their path, they arrive at the secure and tranquil port of the heavenly city. We see this clearly in the Holy Gospel, when Jesus Christ, coming to his disciples who were in the little boat in the middle of the sea and who faced a great tempest because of the contrary wind, which they were helpless to resist, climbed aboard and ordered the winds and the sea, which were attacking and overwhelming the small boat, and he stopped the tempest, so that with good humour and tranquillity they arrived safe in port, not by their own deeds but by the virtue and presence of Jesus our saviour.

The heavenly father, God, in some ways leaves the governance and care of the movement and direction of the little boat to the power and faculty of free will. He leaves it to man, making him the helmsman when he reaches the age of such discretion that, with oar in hand and careful work, he can persevere in the safeguarding and guidance of such a noble vessel in which God had lodged and placed him. But man, out of either negligence or ignorance, or a desire for worthless pleasure, or sensual and corrupt concupiscence, or presumptuous hope, or imprudence, or stubbornness, or by lack of foresight, lets it venture far into the high sea, abandoning the arguments of wise and thoughtful management. Whereupon, either thrust by contrary winds or striking the rocks in its path, or because it hits upon ruinous waves, or because of the tossing and swirling waves or their destructive force, or because of the excess of the swollen sea or the harm done by its sprays, or the cleft of the deep sea or the darkness of the shadowy night, or out of fear of fierce beasts, or because of the sweet song of the lovely sirens or the attack of cruel pirates or the deceit of false friends, having no defence it breaks apart and shatters. These things help explain the reasons for the vices and sins that cause us to lose and break the sturdiness of pure innocence, and they become more serious as they increase in number, shattering and breaking all the more, leaving man bereft of every grace and virtue. Nor is there any remedy for this coming apart, no way to rebuild the broken little boat of holy innocence. Indeed, one is left deep in the abyss, abandoned and naked in the middle of the tempestuous sea, without hope of any good help at all.

Merciful God, who does not want us to perish and die, has provided only one refuge for when, by our own doing, the sturdy and light little boat, which He had provided that we might save ourselves, is shattered and broken. This is penitence, which anyone who wants to be saved after broken innocence must hold on to carefully and tenaciously. This is what the holy blessed doctor St. Jerome meant when, speaking by analogy, he said that there was a second plank after the danger of the shipwreck, i.e., a remedy and secure refuge after the first innocence was broken.[1] He notes that those who are shipwrecked need to be very careful to grab on to any plank or wood of the broken boat before the waves carry them away, notwithstanding the fear, dismay, uncertainty, anxiety, exhaustion, terror, forgetfulness, mental confusion, and other serious troubles that those whom fortune opposes must endure. Likewise, someone who loses his innocence by mortal sin must turn to penitence at once and without delay, notwithstanding any impediment or reluctance that the sin committed might induce. As he must quickly take the remedy of penitence, so too must he tenaciously hold tight to it. Holy Scripture says so when it says: *Lignum vitae est hiis qui apprehenderint eam: et qui tenuerit eam, beatus* [Pr 3:18]: It, that is, penitence, is the wood of life for him who takes it; and he who holds on to it will be blessed. This plank of penitence takes its strength from the same source as the little boat of innocence, i.e., from Jesus Christ, and from his passion. This perhaps is what was meant by that plank hung atop the cross, where it was written: "Jesus the Nazarene King of the Jews," in three languages, Hebrew, Greek, and Latin, suggesting that in the plank over the cross, that is, in penitence, which overcomes innocence and is linked to the cross (in other words, by the power and efficacy of Christ's passion), are contained well-being and salvation, which Jesus shows not only to one people or in one language but to all peoples in all languages. As Jesus Christ said to the apostles after the passion and his resurrection: *Euntes docete omnes gentes, baptizantes eos in nomine Patris et Filii et Spiritus Sancti* [Mt 28:19]: Go and teach all peoples, and baptize them in the name of the Father and the Son and the Holy Spirit. St. Luke writes in his Gospel that Jesus Christ, appearing to his disciples after the resurrection, told them, among other things, to preach penitence and

---

1 In the *Treatise on Psalms* (Epistle 106) [GA].

remission of sins in his name among all peoples [Lk 24:47]. Mary Magdalene wisely took hold of this second plank of penitence, where there is salvation for most humans, after her broken innocence. St. Peter took it, St. Paul took it, as in general do all those who are saved, absolved of sin by the redeemer's grace. We sinners should endeavour to be on this list, so that we do not perish by leaving the intact and sturdy little boat of innocence, having fallen into the open sea of the world, uncertain and anguished, and sunk in mortal sin.

In order that we may quickly reach out and grab on to this necessary and virtuous plank of penitence, and hold tight until it brings us to the shore of the celestial realm to which we are called, with fervent desire for our own salvation and with all neglect and ignorance removed, I, friar Jacopo Passavanti, of the lesser Order of the Friars Preachers, decided to compose and organize a certain special treatise about penitence. I was moved to it by zeal for the salvation of souls, to which the profession of my order especially directs its friars. I was provoked by the affectionate urging of many spiritual and devout persons, who begged me to organize, in vernacular prose, just as I had preached to them in our Florentine vernacular, those things about true penitence that I had preached to the people, for their utility and consolation, over many years, and especially during Lent of the present year, 1354, in order that those who want to read them might likewise find utility and consolation. So as not to deny what charity fruitfully and dutifully requires, I apply my talent to write, both in the vernacular, as was requested primarily for the benefit of those who are not learned, and in Latin for clerics, for whom it may be useful both for themselves and for those whom they have to teach, by either preaching or advising or hearing confessions, trusting always in the worth of the father of preachers, St. Dominic,[2] sovereign preacher of penitence, and also by making devout recourse to the highest doctor, St. Jerome, whose life and doctrine are an example and mirror of true penitence. Nevertheless, I humbly ask those who read this book to offer a special prayer to God for me, so that, as I have preached to the people about penitence for a long time, and now, not without great effort, write about it, the grace may be granted to me to live and persevere up to the end in true penitence, so that at the hour of my death divine mercy might receive me unto salvation. *Amen.* And because in this book we show clearly what we are asked to do, and what others should be careful about, so that they might make true penitence, it is necessarily and rightly called *The Mirror of True Penitence.*

---

2 The Spaniard Dominic (1170–1221) was the founder of the Dominican order.

Here Begins The Book of Penitence, Named
The Mirror of True Penitence

Anyone who wants to write and speak usefully and insightfully about penitence needs a well-ordered doctrine, and to speak openly and clearly, so that readers can easily understand what is said in writing and effectively enact what is most clearly understood. Therefore, proceeding in order, we shall principally consider six things about penitence. First, we will say what penitence is and where it gets its name; second, what are the things that lead us to penitence; third, we will say what things keep us from penitence; fourth, we will show what the parts of penitence are, how many things are required to make perfect penitence, and how the first part of penitence is contrition, which we will also treat here; fifth, we will discuss the second part of penitence, i.e., confession; sixth, we will talk about the third part of penitence, satisfaction.[3] By setting forth our treatise in the proper order, the doctrine of true penitence will be complete.

First Distinction.

Wherein we show what penitence is.

First Chapter

First of all, following our order, we should say what penitence is. St. Ambrose says of it: *Poenitentia est mala praeterita plangere, et plangenda iterum non committere. De Poenitentia d. 3:*[4] Penitence is crying about past wrongs, i.e., sins committed, and from then on never again committing those acts which we had reason to cry over. St. Gregory says the same thing: *Poenitere est ante acta peccata flere: et flenda iterum non committere.*[5] It is the same statement. St. Thomas says[6] that the above-cited words show what penitence is by its effects, which are two. The first has to

---

3 The contemporary language of the sacrament of Penance (or Reconciliation) calls the third part reconciliation or celebration, in addition to satisfaction. I have adopted this latter word as it resonates with Passavanti's *soddisfazione*. Current language also adopts "conversion" as a synonym for Passavanti's *contrizione*, here translated as "contrition." Finally, some models add a fourth element to the process, absolution.

4 The reference to Ambrose appears to be through Gratian, who cites him in the Treatise on Penitence in the *Decretum*, which he cites below [GA].

5 *Regulae pastoralis* 3 [GA].

6 *Scriptum super sententiis* 4 [GA].

do with past sin, and therefore he says we should cry for past sins; the other effect has to do with future sin, and therefore he says we should never again do those things that give us reason to cry. We understand this second statement to mean that just as someone who has true penitence must suffer and cry for his past sins, so too should he intend to abstain from them in the future. And if it so happens that someone falls again into sin, the first penitence was nevertheless valid.

We must repent over again for sins into which we have fallen again, notwithstanding what some seem to say, as the Master of Sentences[7] says of St. Augustine, and St. Isidore, and St. Gregory, and some others whom the *Decretum* also mentions in the Treatise on Penitence. These statements must be understood as referring not to different times but to one and the same time, that we must cry for past sins and not commit them anymore: In other words, just as someone suffers and cries for the sin committed, he must also not commit, nor intend to commit, either that same sin that he is repenting having done or any other grave sin for which he must needs repent. But should he happen to sin again, either by that same sin or another, the first penitence was useful, and the second will be useful, and however many he shall make all the way to death. This is because divine mercy, which takes human fragility into account, has provided for the sacrament of penitence to be made and received not just once, like baptism, but as many times as we sin throughout life. This is what Jesus Christ meant when he asked St. Peter: *Quoties peccabit in me frater meus et dimittam ei? Usque septies? Non dico tibi usque septies, sed usque septuagies septies* [Mt 18:21]. St. Peter asked Him how many times one should forgive the sin, and if seven times were enough; and merciful and courteous Jesus Christ said: Not just seven times, but seventy-seven, or even seven times seventy; in other words, forgive him as many times as he sins, or can sin, when he returns to penitence. That said, the sin into which man falls again after penitence is much more serious than the first one, for many reasons which the saints attribute to us, but especially because it shows ingratitude towards the grace received from God. It is not that, once the sin has been forgiven, it returns, but rather that, because of the ingratitude, it is more serious with regard to its effect than it was the first time. This is what Jesus Christ meant when He said in the Gospel: *Cum immundus spiritus exierit ab homine, etc. ed adducit alios septem spiritus nequiores se, etc. et fiunt novissima hominis illius pejora prioribus* [Mt 12:43–5]. He said

---

7 Peter Lombard (1096–1160), in the fourth of the *Libri Quatuor Sententiarum* [GA]. He
   earned the title *Magister Sententiarum* thanks to this work, which became a standard
   theological text widely taught at medieval universities.

that when the evil spirit, which first had left man because of penitence, returns when a person falls into sin again, it is seven times worse, and the condition of the fallen man is worse than before. He spoke likewise to that sick man whom He had healed: *Vade, ed amplius noli peccare, ne deterius tibi aliquid contingat* [Jn 8:11]: Go, and do not want to sin anymore, so that something worse does not happen to you. Wherein we should note that He said *noli*, do not want, and He did not say *non pecces*, do not sin, suggesting that, as we said above, for repentance the intention is enough and the will not to sin, even if one sins again later.

Later on we will talk about how grave it is to fall again into sin, and how many evils it does to the ungrateful soul.

Second Chapter

On the word penitence.

This word "penitence" comes *a poenitendo*, that is, "from to repent"; because through penitence a man repents the evil he has done. Or it is called penitence, almost as *poenae tentio*, i.e., holding on to punishment, by which the wrongs that someone has done are punished, so that to repent is almost to hold on to punishment. Thus, penitence almost means "punishtence."[8] As St. Augustine says: *Poenitentia est quaedam dolentis vindicta, puniens in se quot dolet commisisse:*[9] Penitence is a vendetta by which a man punishes himself for what he regrets having done.

Second Distinction.

Wherein we show how many things there are that lead us to penitence, and not to delay it.

The second thing we have to say about penitence, according to our order, is what things lead us to penitence, and not to delay it. There are seven things: first, love of justice; second, fear of divine judgment; third, the uncertainty of death; fourth, God's patience and kindness; fifth, the difficulty of repenting after the long practice of sin; sixth, the

---

8 Passavanti here introduces a neologism to create a pun, analogizing the Italian word *penitenzia* to his new word, "punitentia," rooted in the verb *punire*, to punish. I have sought to conserve this wordplay with the word "punishtence."

9 In *De vera et falsa poenitentia* [GA].

injury that we do to God and to His angels by not repenting; seventh, the example and the doctrine of Christ and of the saints who made it and taught it.

First Chapter

Wherein we show how love of justice leads us to penitence.

The first thing that leads us to penitence is love of justice. Justice is a virtue that keeps the scale level and renders unto each of us what is our due, which every good and upright soul should love in himself and in others. Just as, according to the dictates of justice, someone who does good and lives virtuously deserves reward and merit, so too does one who does bad and lives a life of vice deserve torment and punishment. Therefore, because we are all evildoers and sin by disobeying God's law (for to sin, as St. Ambrose says,[10] is nothing other than to trespass God's law and disobey His commandments), it follows that we justly deserve torment and punishment. The punishment for sin, according to divine justice, must be eternal and endless, but divine pity, which looks kindly upon human frailty, mitigates the severity and rigour of justice with the sweetness of its mercy; and it trades eternal punishment for temporal punishment in those who repent of having done wrong and of having offended divine goodness by sinning. Wherefore it has provided the sacrament of penitence, which has infinite virtue from the infinite merit of the passion of Christ, and the sin is punished temporally. It is through penitence that we reconcile ourselves to God, who with infinite virtue removes eternal guilt and punishment from us. This is the justice that punishes sin, and we must love and grab on to it, even though there are few who love it. Whence the prophet Jeremiah laments, saying: *Non est qui poenitentiam agat super peccato suo* [Jr 8:6]: There is no one who repents of his sin.

Now what pity is this, what pain, what confusion, what shame, that does not find those who, for love of justice, might keep from sinning or repent of having sinned? What we do not do for love, let us at least do out of fear of God's harsh justice!

We read, and the Venerable Bede writes,[11] that in the year of our Lord 806 a man passed from this life in England, and before he was buried, his soul returned to his body. Frightened and alarmed because of the

---

10 In *De Paradiso* [GA].

11 In the *Historia ecclesiastica gentis Anglorum* [GA]. A more direct source, however, appears to have been the *Alphabetum narrationum* (*Alphabet of Tales*), a collection

punishments and grave torments that he had seen the souls endure in the other life, even as his relatives and friends were caressing him and rejoicing, he was not happy at all. Suddenly, terrified, he fled into the desert and, building a little cell next to a river, lived there until his death, where he afflicted himself with penitence. Fully dressed, he would enter the stream up to his neck when it was coldest, and coming out he would stand there with his clothes on, so wet against the wind and the cold and the cloudless sky that his flesh froze. Then he would heat up a huge pot of water, which he got into when the water was boiling and with those frozen clothes still on. From there he would go back into the river, and then into the pot. He would do this all day long, and he kept on doing so up until the end. And when he was asked why he tormented himself so cruelly, he answered that if others had seen what he saw, they would do the same and more, and that he wanted to do justice to himself in life lest he should have to endure elsewhere what he had seen others endure without end, because his punishment was light by comparison to what he had seen, and it would soon have to end. We will speak more specifically about this in the next chapter.

Second Chapter

Wherein we show how fear of divine judgment leads us to penitence.

The second thing that leads us to penitence is fear of divine judgment, which those who do not undertake to purge their sins in the present life will have to endure, harsh and hard, after death. What purges sins is penitence, by which a man judges himself and rights himself by punishing the wrongs that he has done. This way he escapes and does not have to fear another judgment, for as Scripture says, God does not punish the same thing twice. Indeed, the apostle Paul says: *Si nosmet ipsos iudicaremus, non utique iudicaremur* [1 Cr 11:31]: If we were to judge ourselves, we surely would not be judged later. Whereupon St. Gregory says:[12] The omnipotent God and merciful judge, by willingly receiving our penitence, hides our faults from His judgment. St. Augustine teaches us and says: Go into your mind, almost as to a seat of judgment, and imagine yourself as an evildoer standing before yourself; judge yourself, do not desire to put yourself behind yourself, so that God does

---

of sermons attributed to the thirteenth-century Dominican preacher Etienne de Besançon.

12 In the *Homiliae XL in Evangelia* (GA).

not put you before Himself. Which means, let a man judge himself with the judgment of penitence, so that God does not judge him with severe and harsh justice. Whence the wise Ecclesiasticus says: *Si poenitentiam non egerimus, incidemus in manus Domini* [Ec 2:22]: If we do not repent, we will fall into the hands of God. Speaking of this, St. Paul says what a fearful and horrible thing it is to fall into the hands of the living God, i.e., into the hands of His justice [Hb 10:31]. And Jesus Christ said in the Gospel: *Nisi poenitentiam habueritis, simul omnes peribitis* [Lk 13:3]: If you do not repent you will all perish together. St. Augustine says: He who truly repents does not let the evil that he has done go unpunished, and so, because he does not forgive himself, God forgives him, whose judgment no one who disdains it can escape.

O sinners, do not treat yourselves with such cruel mercy that in order to spare yourselves a little discomfort here, you allow yourselves to be condemned by the just judgment of God to the eternal flame of hell!

We read in the *Book of the Seven Gifts*[13] that a noble young man, who had been raised very carefully, entered the Order of the Friars Preachers, whereupon his father, along with his relatives and friends, wishing to remove him from it, undertook to deceive the young man's soul with promises and temptations. Among other things they said that he would not be able to endure the harshness of the order, because he was very tender and had been raised softly. To which he replied: This is why I entered the order, because seeing that I was tender and delicate and could not endure any harsh or difficult thing, I thought, how could I suffer the most serious, endless punishments of hell? Therefore, I decided – and I intend to hold fast – to endure the harshness of religion here for a while, rather than have to bear those intolerable and eternal punishments. His father and relatives, not knowing what to say, left him in peace.

---

13 As Auzzas explains, this is likely an erroneous attribution, a confusion of the *Tractatus de diversis materiis predicabilibus ordinatiis et distinctis in septem partes seu septem dona Spiritus Sanctus*, a work by Stephen of Bourbon, with the *Liber de dono timoris*, a treatise by Humbert of Romans that also refers to the seven gifts of the Holy Spirit. Passavanti likely learned about this text through the *Alphabetum narrationum*. See Iacopo Passavanti, *Lo specchio della vera penitenzia*, ed. Ginetta Auzzas (Florence: Accademia della Crusca, 2014), 171–2.

Third Chapter

Wherein we show how the uncertainty of death induces
us quickly to repentance.

The third thing that induces us to repent without delay is the uncertainty of death, for no one can be sure when it might come. Nothing is more certain than death, nor is anything more uncertain than the hour of death, and there is too great a danger that it might arrive and find us unrepentant. God has ordained that death be uncertain, according to St. Gregory,[14] so that by not knowing when it might come, we are always ready, as if it might come at any moment. As St. Augustine says,[15] God, who promises pardon for your sins if you will repent, does not promise you tomorrow in exchange for repentance. Therefore, those who vainly hope for a long life are to be strongly scolded, because this is not under their control, and they delay penitence until death. They are often deceived, because by living badly they do not deserve to end up well, and they are not worthy of receiving that grace to truly repent at death. There are many impediments that do not allow one truly to repent. Sometimes death is sudden, or the illness so brief, and one spends a great deal of time taking medicines, and the pain of illness worries him and causes travail and so distracts him that he does not realize he is going to die. Even when the illness is long, so great are the desire to get well and the hope given by doctors and relatives and friends, who hide his illness from the sick man and do not let the priest or friar talk to him, that the sick man barely realizes that he is very sick, and he often dies without realizing or thinking he might die. Indeed, the people keep the sick man from confession and other sacraments, from making his will or whatever restitution he has to do, saying – at the risk of their own souls – that they do not want him to be afraid, and therefore at the moment of his greatest doubt they say to him, lying to themselves: "You don't have a dangerous illness; soon you'll be free of it; the doctors are keeping you safe from this sickness."

O mortal people! Remedy such a dangerous mistake, and do not allow yourselves to be deceived by the false promises of ignorant doctors, the evil temptations of false friends, the copious tears of traitorous relatives, the affectionate love of your poorly loved wife and your poorly regarded children, the lying comfort of your foolish household, the hopeful wish that you might soon recover: put the salvation of your

---

14 In the *Moralia in Job* [GA].
15 In his *Sermons* [GA].

soul before all else! If it is not directed at holiness, or not sufficiently so that once we fall ill, before serious things happen that create an impediment and distraction, a man must do what he must do: confess, make restitution, make his will, request all the sacraments of the Church like a faithful Christian, and choose a church burial, and then wait for God's grace and mercy! Whence it is expressly ordered in the Decretal[16] that, when they examine the sick man for the first time, the doctors are to speak to him about confession, arguing that if he does not do it, they may not proceed with any cure, nor examine him again. If the one does not do it, then the other does not do it, and everyone says they do not want to be the messenger or frighten the sick man. If this were the custom, the sick would not be afraid.

No one cares about the salvation of the soul except when a sick man is so bad off that he cannot do what he should do, and so either does nothing or does it badly and defectively, or does not do it freely, as he should, but has to do it as someone else wants. He should do it therefore when it can be done well. If not, once the body is dead, the suffering soul, finding itself in cruel torments and dolorous punishments, realizes its error and uselessly regrets not having made a useful repentance while it was living with the body and had the use of free will, by which a man can repent and make arrangements and prepare himself to receive the grace of having true penitence. Therefore, although it is said that repenting on one's deathbed is dubious and risky, and especially that most of the time the reason for such repentance is fear of punishment and not love of justice, and that a man abandons sin when he does not believe he can sin anymore – or rather, as St. Augustine says,[17] the sins leave the man, the man does not leave his sins, as it is by necessity and not by will – nevertheless, it is undeniable that penitence is possible while the soul is with the body, because God's mercy and grace can work immediately in those He chooses for eternal life. And He chooses in different ways, places, and times, to demonstrate the infinite expanse and copious abundance of His grace.

There are the examples of the thief on the cross and many others. One, written by Caesarius,[18] is of a worldly knight who, living with

---

16 Specifically in the *Liber extravagantium decretalium* or *Extravagant Decretals of Gregory IX* [GA].

17 In *De vera et falsa poenitentia* [GA].

18 The tale appears in the *Dialogus miracolorum*, a collection of nearly 800 miracle stories, by the Cistercian Caesarius of Heisterbach (ca. 1180–1240). Passavanti will cite Caesarius throughout the text, but he likely knew these stories through the *Alphabetum narrationum*, where they also appear; see Passavanti, ed. Auzzas, 478.

many sins in a most evil way, was assaulted and killed by his enemies. While they were knifing him and killing him, ashamed and repenting of his evils he said: *Domine, Miserere mei*: Lord God, have mercy on me. Now it so happened that, as many people were gathered around this knight's tomb, the devil entered one of them and gravely tormented him. When asked why he was afflicting the Christian in this way, the devil answered: "Many of us came to this knight's death, believing that we could take his soul away to hell without any impediment, because he had led his entire life according to our will. And yet we have no control over him at all. Indeed, God's angels have taken him from us, saying that we have no claim to him. And so, indignant and offended, we are taking revenge on this poor fellow." When the devil was asked how it was that the knight had escaped, he answered: "He said three damn words, by which he was delivered from our grasp, and if God let us say them, as this guy did, we would be saved too. But that power has been taken from us."

Now, between the uncertain and the possible, one should follow the good counsel of St. Augustine,[19] who, when speaking on this question, concludes: take the certain and leave the uncertain. Meaning, take the certainty of penitence while you are strong and well, when not only fear of punishment but also love of justice induces you to repent – by which eternal salvation is surely acquired – and leave the uncertainty of delaying penitence until death which, although possible, is not surely useful. The saviour in the Gospel, as a warning about the uncertainty of death, says: Be vigilant and you will always be prepared, for you know neither the day nor the hour [Mt 25:13]. And he offers the example of the rich man who, having had a copious and abundant harvest of all the earthly goods of life, said to himself: "Enjoy yourself now, my soul, rest, and have a good time, because you have long to live." And a voice came: "You fool you, tonight your soul will be asked for and taken from you. These things that you have put away, for whom will they be?"[20] Meaning: they are not yours, and you will not enjoy them.

A man should not allow himself to be led to the worthless hope of a long life, but he should listen to Solomon, who says: *Memor esto, quoniam mors non tardat*: Remember, death is not long in coming.[21]

Even if life were long, a man should not delay penitence for several reasons. The first is: by living in sin and continuing to do evil, a man

---

19 In his *Sermons* [GA].

20 Passavanti is condensing an anecdote that appears in Luke 12:16–20.

21 Ecclesiasticus 14:12. Like others, Passavanti erroneously attributes this work to Solomon.

distances himself more from God, and makes himself more unworthy of His grace, which is necessary for true penitence. It often happens to these types that, being incapable of the grace of doing penitence and not wanting it, when they want it later on, they cannot have it. Hence the common proverb: He who does not want when he can have it, cannot have it when he wants it. St. Paul says this of Esau, who did not find a place of penitence although he tearfully asked for it [Hb 12:17]. Scripture speaks in like manner of that haughty Antiochus.[22] The other reason is that by delaying penitence we lose much time, which will be asked of us, and we will never be able to get it back. The third reason is that as one continues to do evil, the practice becomes second nature, and then it is too hard to get past it. The other reason why penitence must not be delayed is to acquire more merit, and to live more securely and with a greater hope of salvation, and in order not to have to suffer so many pains in purgatory if God's mercy saves you from the eternal punishment of hell.

And so, you lovers of useless things, come to your senses, waste no more time, return to true penitence without delay, wait no longer for an uncertain future.

Fourth Chapter

Wherein we show how God's patience and gentleness induce us to penitence.

The fourth thing that leads us to repent quickly and without delay is God's patience and kindness, which sustains us, calls to us, and waits for us. And yet we discourteously disdain it and ridicule and scorn it, when we should instead surrender to Him and, humbling ourselves, serve Him and love Him. Like ungrateful servants, haughty and obstinate, we abuse God's kindness and feel safe in offending Him, because He is good. St. Paul scolds everyone who does not surrender to God's kindness but obstinately opposes and disdains Him, saying: *An ignoras, quod benignitas Dei ad poenitentiam te adducit? An divitias bonitatis ejus, et longanimitatis contempnis? etc.* [Rm 2:4–6]. The apostle says, Do you not know, you obstinate sinner, that God's gentleness leads you to penitence? O shameless one, do you disdain the abundance of His goodness and patience, with which He awaits you? Do you not see what you are doing with your resistance and your obstinate heart, which does

---

22 See 2 Maccabees 9 for the narrative of Antiochus's recalcitrance in the face of God's urgings that he change his ways [GA].

not repent? Gather God's wrath against you unto yourself, which He will show you on the day of His just judgment, when He will render to each according to their deeds. And so, if we were to consider carefully and diligently the greatness of the benefit that God holds for us, and that if He were to take from us the time He gives us for penitence and were to judge us by our actions, what a bad place we would be in! We should be ashamed of our ingratitude towards God's goodness, and of having misused the time He has given us. As St. Gregory says, if we do not want to fear divine justice, we should at least be ashamed by God's goodness, because even though He sees us disdaining it, He does not disdain us, nor does He stop calling to us to return and waiting for us. But when He has waited long enough and endured our sins with great patience, He will take harsh revenge on our disdain and reluctance. This is what St. Augustine means when he says, Do not be negligent and pretend not to realize that the pious Lord awaits you and sustains you, while you continue to sin; because for however long He waits for you to make amends, if you do not correct yourselves, He will judge you that much more harshly. And the prophet says that God is waiting for us: *Expectat vos Dominus, ut misereatur vestri* [Is 30:18]: God is waiting for you in order to have mercy on you. As St. Jerome explains: God waits for our penitence for a long time, so that, if we do repent of our sins, He will repent of the evils that He threatens to do to us, so that, if we change our minds about doing evil, He will change His mind about doing harm to us.[23] And it is made clear in the Proverbs of Solomon that He is calling to us, and regretting that He has not been answered, and suffers for having been disdained, protesting that He will have revenge, where He says: *Vocavi, et renuistis: extendi manum meam, et non fuit qui aspiceret: despexistis omne consilium meum, increpationes meas noluistis: ego quoque in interitu vestro ridebo et subsannabo, quando id quod timebatis, advenerit* [Pr 1:24–6]: I called you, God says, and you did not answer me, I held out my hand to you, and there was no one waiting for it; and you disdained all my advice, and you did not want to hear my warnings; so I will laugh about your death, and I will make fun of you and mock you when that which you feared comes to pass.

Therefore, dearest brothers, when we are called let us not be slow in going, for the road is long and the time is short. And we should go quickly if we consider that all the good people have gone, and the dangers of the road are many; and a good and gracious Lord awaits us, as do many dear friends and relatives who are concerned about us

---

23 In the commentary on Joel, *Commentaries on the Twelve Prophets* [GA].

and want to see us with them, in an honourable state, at the great banquet and joyous party of paradise. It is likely that if we wait too long the door may be closed to us, as it was to the five foolish virgins who put off preparing the lamps and the oil, and therefore arrived late and found the door locked, and it was not opened to them, as the Holy Gospel recounts [Mt 25]. Which means that you must be concerned about your own salvation and be prepared by living well, so that at the hour of death, when you are called, you do not have to prepare. This is something people often put off, and then it does not get done, or it gets done in a rush, or badly, or late, and there is no remedy for such a mistake. So watch out, and take my word for it: those who do not prepare when they can will not be able to prepare when they want to, or will rightly never want that which is for their own good.

We read in the Venerable Bede[24] that there was a knight in England, valiant in arms but in comportment full of corruption, who fell gravely ill. He was visited by the king, who was a holy man, and who urged him to prepare his soul by confessing like a good Christian. He replied that this was not necessary, and that he did not want to show that he was afraid, nor be deemed a coward. As his illness worsened, the king returned to him and comforted him and, as he had done the first time, urged him to penitence and to confess his sins. He replied: "It's too late now, sir, because I am already judged and condemned, because despite the need I did not believe you the other day, when you visited me and counselled me about my salvation, when – alas! – there was still time to find mercy. Now – if only I had never been born! – all hope is taken from me, because shortly before you came here two very handsome young men came by, and one stood at the head of the bed, the other at the foot, and they said: 'This one is about to die, let's see if we have any claim on him.' And the one took from his breast a little book written in gold letters, where, although I could not read it at first, I did read a few little good deeds that I had done in my youth before I sinned mortally, and I did not recall them. Just as I was rejoicing over them, two very large, very black, very cruel demons arrived, and they opened a large book before me, where all my sins were written, and all the bad deeds I had ever done, and they said to those two young men, who were God's angels: 'What are you doing here? You have no claim on him, your book has been worthless for years now.' Looking at one another, the angels said: 'They are speaking the truth.' So they departed, leaving me to the demons, who are sawing me apart with two sharp knives, the one at

---

24 Bede's *Historia ecclesiastica gentis Anglorum*, though again likely via the *Alphabetum narrationum* [GA].

my head, the other at my feet. Look now, the one at my head is cutting out my eyes, and I have already lost my sight, and the other has already sawed me up to my heart, and I cannot live any longer." Having said these words, he died.

Fifth Chapter

Wherein we see that the difficulty of repenting after long practice leads us to penitence.

The fifth thing that leads us quickly to make penitence is the difficulty of repenting after a long practice of sin, because, as St. Augustine says, the custom that one does not resist becomes force of habit,[25] and the common saying is true, that habit becomes nature. There are many who, accustomed to doing bad and living a life full of vice, do not seem to be able to abstain from sin, because their reason is so clouded and subject to the sensory appetite, and their free will so knotted up, that it cannot bring them to good unless a special grace helps them. What happens to them is what happens to sick people whose long illnesses age them in such a way that it is almost impossible or very difficult to cure them. Therefore, we should seek to cure the sickness of sin quickly and without delay, before it grows or festers, using the medicine of penitence. As St. Gregory says, the sin that is not washed away quickly with penitence draws us quickly to other sins with its weight.[26] And so, by adding one sin to another, the sickness grows, and a person runs into many difficulties. First off: the more he sins, the farther he distances himself from God, and he will need that much more time to return to Him, and whoever waits until old age or death loses the time he has to return to God. And although there are some who, repenting at death, are saved, we do not want to run this risk; because, as St. Jerome says, the privilege of the few does not create a rule for all.[27] Indeed, the saints say that God often withdraws His grace at the end from many who had rejected it when they were alive and well.

St. Gregory[28] tells us of a person who, having fallen into the sickness from which he died, and seeing a great multitude of demons coming to take away his soul, and the one who seemed to be the leader ordering that his soul be torn from his body, began to cry out: "Wait until

---

25 In Book 8 of the *Confessions* [GA].
26 In the *Moralia in Job* [GA].
27 In the commentary on Job, *Commentaries on the Twelve Prophets* [GA].
28 In the *Dialogues*.

tomorrow! Wait until tomorrow!" When those words were not obeyed, he died, moaning with painful cries, and his soul was carried off by the devils to the punishments of hell.

The other problem is that when a man puts off penitence, he sins more, and by sinning more he creates a greater burden, under which he must necessarily perish if he does not follow the counsel of St. Paul, who says: *Deponentes omne pondus, et circumstans nos peccatum* [Hb 12:1]: Let us put down the weight and the sin that surrounds us.

We read in the *Life of the Holy Fathers*[29] that St. Anselm once heard a voice that said to him: "Come, and I will show you the deeds of men." Going there, he saw someone who was cutting firewood and, having made a great bundle of it, was figuring out how to carry it; and not being able to because of its great weight, he put it back down. Cutting more firewood, he added to the bundle, and again he tried to carry it; and not being able to, he cut some more firewood, and added it to the bundle, when he should have reduced its size if he wanted to carry it. And as the weight grew evermore, he shouldered the bundle and fell beneath it. And the voice said: "These are the ones who, by adding sin to sin as they live, perish beneath it." He also saw two men on horseback who were carrying two large boards crosswise, and they wanted to pass through the door of a temple, and they could not. And the voice said that they signified those who carry the justice of good works with pride. He also saw someone by the shore of a lake who was drawing forth some water with a vessel, and he was putting it in a cistern that was full of holes and broken, so that it held nothing. And the voice said: "This one signifies those who, while having done some good works, have done so many bad ones that they cause the good ones to perish."

Therefore, don't think about how to increase the heavy weight of sin, but how to reduce it. The prophet David felt this weight and was regretful and said: *Quoniam iniquitates meae supergresse sunt caput meum, et sicut onus grave gravatae sunt super me* [Ps 37:5]: My errors are upon me, and like a heavy weight they weigh on me. But the foolish man saves the greatest weight for old age and infirmity, which he cannot carry when it is small and he is young and healthy.

The other difficulty is that the more someone sins, the more he gets twisted up and the more he resists, and therefore he will bend[30] or straighten up later with greater difficulty, just as an old twisted piece

---

29 The *Vitae Patrum* (*Life of the Holy Fathers*) is a compilation of hagiographical works dating to the fourth century. It includes three lives attributed to Jerome. Passavanti likely knew it through the *Alphabetum narrationum*; see Passavanti, ed. Auzzas, 479.
30 I.e., to God's will.

of wood sooner breaks and burns than straightens out or bends. Let us therefore heed St. Peter's advice: *Poenitemini igitur et convertimini ut deleantur peccata vestra* [Ac 3:19]: Repent and convert, so that your sins will be forgiven. And you want to do that quickly, as the prophet Joel instructs us when he says: *Nunc convertimini ad Dominum Deum vestrum, quoniam benignus et misericors est* [Jl 2:13]: Now convert to your Lord God without delay, because He is kind and merciful. And St. Augustine, explaining the psalm, says: for it to be fruitful, let your penitence not be slow or late, correct yourself today, for you are a sinner; because the one who will be your judge is today your advocate.[31] As St. John the Evangelist says: *Advocatum habemus apud patrem Jesum Christum justum* [1 Jn 2:1]: We have before the Father, as our advocate, the just Jesus Christ, in whom we must have faith, for he will win the argument for us.

Therefore, sweet brothers, make use of him now as a favourable advocate, so that he will excuse our faults, point out our natural fragility, accuse our adversaries, affirm the value of his passion, by which all our offences are pardoned. And let us not delay so much that we must have a judge for our sins, and a harsh and most just punisher of our faults.

Sixth Chapter

Wherein we are shown what leads us to penitence, and that by not doing so we do harm to God.

The sixth thing that leads us to make penitence quickly is that by not repenting or by delaying it, we do harm to God. This is because, first of all, we are being unfaithful and disloyal to God, inasmuch as the time that He has given us to spend in His service, we spend instead in the service of his adversary, and we give the devil the flower of our youth, saving what's left for God in our old age.[32] And if the servant who, because there was nothing to be gained from following it, hid his lord's will was judged unfaithful and disloyal, how much more will someone who loses his will be judged an unfaithful and disloyal servant, and even more so someone who spends it to offend and dishonour his lord? The will given to the servant, which God wants him to use for gain and to make his own, stands for the grace, knowledge, time, and good will that God gives man to use well and virtuously, always to earn honour

---

31 In the *Enarrationes in Psalmos* [GA].

32 What's left: *la morchia*, literally the remains of pressed olives.

and glory from the Lord, who gives, and for his own benefit. The hardened sinner does the contrary, as the holy Job says: *Dedit ei Dominus locum penitentiae, et ipse abutitur eo in superbiam* [Jb 24:23]: God gives man space for penitence, and he on the contrary lives in it in pride. Which means that God gives man the time to repent and return to Him, and he uses it arrogantly by sinning and disobeying God.

Is it not great arrogance and presumption for a man to arrange and organize what belongs to God, i.e., the time to come, promising himself a long life and a good death, when he has made himself unworthy of it? How can someone reasonably hope that God will graciously give him the time to come, when he has used what He has given him in a manner full of vice, doing Him harm? It is not with hope but with blind presumption that a man uselessly organizes what there is of the time to come. God often makes His judgment visible by just vendetta, taking from these people the time that they arrogantly used against God, presumptuously hoping to have a long life.

We read in Helinand[33] that in Mâcon there was a count who was a worldly man and a great sinner, arrogant towards God and pitiless and cruel towards his fellow man. Amassing wealth from his lordship and being healthy and strong, he did not think about dying, nor did he think about the material things that he could lose, nor about being judged by God. One day at Easter, he was in his palace surrounded by many knights and servants and many honourable citizens who were celebrating Easter with him, when suddenly a stranger on a large horse came through the palace door, speaking not a word to anyone and approaching the count and his company. When everyone could see and hear him, he said to the count: "Arise, count, and follow me." Fearful and trembling, the count stood up and followed this unknown knight, to whom no one dared say a word. At the palace door the knight ordered the count to mount a horse that was prepared for him. Taking it by the reins and pulling it behind him, running at full speed, he led him up in the air, where he could see the whole city. The count was moaning in pain, crying out: "Help me, citizens, help your wretched unlucky count." Shouting in this way, he disappeared from sight, and he went to reside forever in hell with the demons.

---

33 Auzzas references the *Flores* of Helinand de Froidment, a Cistercian monk and student of Peter Abelard who lived ca. 1160–1229. He is known also for his *Chronicon* and *Les Vers de la Mort*. Passavanti may have known the tale through the *Alphabetum narrationum* (see Passavanti, ed. Auzzas, 480).

To persevere in sin and delay penitence is also an offence and insult to the angel who is given to man to watch over him. St. Bernard says:[34] in every place, no matter how secret, revere your guardian angel, and dare not do in his presence what you would not do in mine. If the angel, indeed, the angels of God, are happy, as Jesus Christ says in the Gospel about the penitent sinner [Lk 15:7], so too are we to believe that they are displeased with those who offend God by persevering in sin and don't repent of it.

And we could recount certain examples written elsewhere, but in order not to write too much, I'll let them go.

Therefore, for the reasons stated above, and for many others which we could give but which for brevity's sake we are leaving out, we must repent. And we must do so quickly and without delay, and our repentance must be complete, i.e., we must suffer for all our sins, and each one individually if we can remember them all. We must try to remember them, so that, as our will was disordered because we unduly delighted in sin, it may be reordered by duly suffering for each sin. We will speak of this at greater length when we speak about contrition.[35]

Penitence must continue up until death. A person must continually and always be so disposed, not just though external acts, like fasting, wearing hair shirts, shedding tears, practising disciplines, and similar things that the penitent do, either because they are imposed by their confessor or because they voluntarily do so (which practices they can do on occasion, then abandon, and return to more or less at a convenient place and time), but also through internal acts, like suffering and repenting for the sins committed, and every time it occurs to him that he has hurt God by sinning. On this topic St. Thomas agrees with the other doctors,[36] whom I won't name here for brevity's sake. There is an example from St. Peter, about whom we read that every time he remembered having denied Christ, which happened especially when he heard the rooster crow, he cried immeasurably, and because of the many tears that he shed he wore a towel over his chest that he used to dry himself off, and his cheeks were all burned because of the many tears.

O Christian, you who are saved and purged by the blood of Christ, may you not regret having often recalled and suffered for the sins you have committed, so that you can make peace with God and His angels, whom you have offended by sinning. For it is too great a danger to have them as enemies!

---

34 In the *Sermones super Psalmum "Qui habitat"* [GA].
35 See pp. 75ff.
36 See Aquinas, *Summa theologica*, Book 3 [GA].

Seventh Chapter

Wherein we are shown how the life and doctrine of Christ and of the saints lead us to penitence.

The seventh thing that leads us to make penitence is that our saviour Jesus Christ himself taught us about it, by both words and deed. By deed, because right after the baptism he went into the desert, and he fasted for forty days and forty nights, and he was tempted by the devil [Mt 4], to serve as an example to us, not because of any need he had, but to help us, so that through his penitence and his temptation we could better bear our penitence and virtuously defeat our temptations. Likewise, according to St. Gregory, he defeated our death with his own passion and death. The words of the doctrine of his preaching began with penitence, saying: *Poenitentiam agite, appropinquabit enim Regnum Coelorum* [Mt 3:2]: Repent, for the kingdom of God approaches, as if to say: to those who make penitence, the kingdom of God will come near. Otherwise it means: since the kingdom of heaven is approaching, repent, for without it we do not acquire the kingdom of God. So too did his precursor, St. John the Baptist, who came before Jesus Christ to prepare the way, teach us and lead us to penitence both by his example and with his doctrine. By example, because at a tender and youthful age, when there was no sin, nor could there be any, he went into the desert to teach us and protect himself, and there, in place of clothes and food, he lived harshly in great penitence, according to the Holy Gospel [Mt 3]. His preaching began with penitence, with the words: *Penitentiam agite, appropinquabit enim regnum coelorum*. And he also said: *Facite fructus dignos penitentie*: Make fruits worthy of penitence. Likewise, all the saints of the Old and the New Testament teach us about penitence by their deeds and words, as something necessary for human salvation and eternal life. The holy Job, teaching his three friends, says: *Audite, queso, sermones meos, et agite penitentiam* [Jb 21:2]: I beg you, hear my words, and repent. And as he taught to others, so he did for himself, saying: *Ago penitentiam in favilla et cinere* [Jb 42:6]: I repent in the spark of the fire and in ash. Meaning, his penitence was lit by the fire of love, and it was spread by the ashes of humility. And the holy Jeremiah the prophet, sanctified in his mother's womb, said in the name of God: *Si penitentiam egerit gens ista, agam et ego penitentiam super malo* [Jr 18:8]: If these people repent, I will repent of the evil that I thought about doing to them. And the holy prophet said about himself: *Postquam convertisti me, egi penitentiam* [Jr 31:19]: Since you, God, converted me, I repent. In like manner the prophet Ezekiel said:

Convertimini et agite penitentiam [Ez 18:30]: Convert, and repent. And we read that in that great city of Nineveh they repented on the preaching of the prophet Jonah [Jh 3]. It is clear that the saints of the New Testament, who received the doctrine of Jesus Christ and the example of His life, taught by words and deeds how to make penitence. St. Peter said in his Epistle: *Nolens aliquos perire, sed ad penitentiam reverti* [2 Pt 3:9]: God does not want others to perish, but that we might return to penitence. And in the Acts of the Apostles it is written: *Testificans Judaeis atque Gentibus in Deum penitentiam et fidem* [Ac 20:21]: He insisted to the Jews and the pagans about penitence in God and the faith. And he showed it by deed: we read that, after having denied Christ and hearing the rooster crow, as Jesus Christ had preached and predicted to him, he came out of the court of the pontifex, where, when asked by the servant and the ministers if he was one of the disciples of Jesus, he denied it and said he did not know who Jesus was, he cried bitterly for his sin. It is said that he always wore a towel on his chest to dry the tears that he shed whenever he heard the rooster crow, remembering that he had denied Christ, as was written above. His food, according to the account in the book of St. Clement, was just bread with olives, and sometimes with grasses; his clothing a single tunic with a cloak, and he wanted nothing more and made do with little. And St. Paul said: *Que enim secundum Deum tristitia est penitentiam in salutem stabilem operator* [2 Cr 7:10]: That wretchedness that is according to God uses stable penitence in salvation. And elsewhere: *Iacientes fundamentum penitentie* [Hb 6:1]: Lay a foundation of penitence, if you want to build a house of eternal salvation. Not only did the apostle teach the people with words, but even more so with deeds, saying: *Castigo corpus meum et in servitutem Redigo* [1 Cr 9:27]: I punish my body, and I limit it to servitude of the spirit. Elsewhere, speaking of his penitence, he said that he suffered hunger and thirst, cold and nakedness. The other saints, who followed the apostles, do and say this: St. Martin, St. Nicholas, St. Germain, St. Augustine, St. Ambrose, St. Jerome, St. Dominic, St. Francis, St. Benedict, St. Anthony, and St. Bernard, and all the other saints, hearing and following that word of St. Luke. Indeed, Jesus Christ in the Gospel said: *Si penitentiam non egeritis, omnes simul peribitis* [Lk 13:5]: If you do not repent, you will all perish together.

Therefore, my most sweet brothers, in order that we not perish (like those of whom St. John speaks in the Apocalypse: *Non egerunt penitentam* [Rv 9:21]: They did not make penance), so that we can be saved and have eternal life, let us follow the advice of that holy lady Judith, who said: *Peniteamus, et indulgentiam cum lacrimis postulemus* [Jd 8:14]: Let us repent, and tearfully ask for God's pardon.

Third Distinction.

Wherein we show what things impede us and hold us back from penitence.

The third thing to say about penitence, following our order, is what things impede us or keep us from repenting. When the devil sees someone, no matter how great a sinner he may be, escape his grasp and save himself through penitence, he undertakes to create obstacles and prevent him from repenting, to keep him under his control while he is alive and at death lead him to damnation. It is therefore useful and necessary to show the impediments to penitence, so that they can be removed, and also to state the remedies, so that, by forbidding the former and taking the latter, we can have results worthy of penitence. According to the sages, there are four impediments that keep us from repenting, namely: shame, fear, hope, and desperation.

First Chapter

Wherein we see how shame holds you back from penitence.

Shame is the first impediment to doing the work of penitence, which consists of confessing sins, crying and striking the chest, praying, fasting, abasing oneself, avoiding partners in sin, forgiving injuries, making peace, and similar things that make penitence happen, which worldly men criticize and scorn. Many, being ashamed, thus keep from repenting, which they should not do.

First of all, if we consider natural reason, which dictates and teaches us that there is no shame, nor should there be, in washing up when one is dirty and ugly, but rather that it is shameful to get dirty, then it is also not shameful to get up when one has fallen down, but rather it is the falling down that should be a shame. Likewise, it is not shameful to win, but to be defeated. Since repenting means cleaning up, getting up, and winning, and to sin is to get dirty, fall down, and be defeated, we clearly should be ashamed of sinning and not of repenting. But, as St. Bernard says, men's blindness is such that they are ashamed of washing themselves and not of getting dirty.

The second reason is that we should not care that worldly men, who are foolish and blind, will make fun of us and scorn us. Seneca says that we should endure the accusations and scorn of the foolish with a strong and upright spirit, and that by doing good a man should disdain being disdained.[37] It would be inappropriate for someone to care about whether a blind man blamed him for taking pleasure in seeing the light, and if a cripple scorned him for walking upright, and if someone who was shipwrecked at sea and had lost his equipment made fun of someone who had saved both his own life and his belongings from fortune and the dangers of the sea. The man who through penitence returns to the light of grace and the upright state of justice, freed of the danger of the stormy sea of the world and of sin, should not care about, nor be ashamed of, the scorn of worldly men, who for the most part deserve to be scorned. And although we should be ashamed of our sin and confess it with shame, nevertheless, for the love of truth and justice, we should not care about the shame that comes from without. St. Gregory says of Mary Magdalene that her inner shame about her sin was so great that she did not believe she should be ashamed of anything from without.[38] And Solomon says: *Est confusio aducens gloriam: et est confusio aducens ignominiam* [Ec 4:25]. As St. Augustine explains, there is one type of shame that the soul feels when looking to correct its sins, and this shame is the reason for glory for the soul; and it is a different shame that keeps someone from doing good because of what people say: and this leads to confusion and vituperation.[39] I want to have the first type of confusion, so that through it I can be freed from eternal confusion. And we should not want to please evil men, nor be praised by them, nor care about their derision or mockery, because Seneca says that to displease evil men and be blamed by them is great praise.[40] And St. Gregory says that the disdain of perverse men towards our life is a way of approving of it.[41] And so, we can believe that we are pleasing God when we displease those who displease Him.

Indeed, Seneca says: a man is not happy, that is, blessed or fortunate, if the crowd does not devalue him.[42] Nor should the good man try to please the many, but just a few good men, because to please or want to please can lead to corruption. Whence the apostle: *Si adhuc hominibus placerem, Christi servus non essem* [Gl 1:10]; and the psalmist: *Deus dissipavit ossa eorum, qui hominibus placent: confusi sunt, quoniam Deus sprevit*

---

37 See *De clementia* [GA].

38 See the *Homilies on Ezekiel* [GA].

39 In the Epistles [GA].

40 Auzzas (Passavanti, 482) traces this attribution to Seneca to Vincent of Beauvais's *De morali principis institutione*.

41 *Homilies on Ezekiel* [GA].

42 Auzzas (Passavanti, 482) traces this attribution to Seneca to the *De eruditione principum* of the Dominican William Perault (ca. 1190–1271).

eos [Ps 52:6]: If I were to please men, I would not be a servant of Christ, says the apostle; and the psalmist: God has broken and destroyed the bones of those who please men, where the gloss says that those who desire to please are confused, because God has devalued them. You should not, therefore, leave behind the good that you have to do because of people's pleasure or displeasure. Jesus Christ our saviour, who was repeatedly devalued and scorned by the Pharisees, offers an example of this. He did not care about them, nor did he abandon the good of his doctrine and his miracles, so that when his disciples told him how the Pharisees were scandalized and murmured about certain words that Jesus Christ had spoken, he answered: *Sinite eos, ceci sunt et duces caecorum* [Mt 15:14]: Let them speak, don't worry about them: they are blind leading the blind; and if the blind lead the blind, they both fall into the pit. Similarly, when they scolded him, criticizing him for not observing the Sabbath when performing miracles – as is shown when he gave sight to the man who was born blind [Jn 9], and when he healed the cripple who had been by the pool for thirty-eight years [Jn 5] – he did not abandon the good work of miracles, nor did he reply to their words or show them how they were saying bad things out of either ignorance or invidious malice. We read of the apostles that they enjoyed the shame and persecutions that they endured in Jesus's name.

The third reason why one should not be ashamed of repenting is that through penitence you are excused for that which someone else should be ashamed of, namely sin. This is what St. Augustine says when commenting about those words: *Beati quorum remisse sunt iniquitates, et quorum tecta sunt peccata* [Rm 4:7]:[43] If you accuse yourself, God excuses you, and if you show yourself, God hides you. In the book of Wisdom, it is said of God: *Dissimulans peccata hominum propter penitentiam* [Ws 11:24]: God shows that He does not see the sins of men because of repentance.

The fourth reason why someone should not be ashamed of repenting is the shame and confusion that unrepentant sinners will feel when they come before God's judgment. The prophet Jeremiah says of this: They will be very confused, because they did not understand the eternal infamy which will never lessen for them [Jr 20:11].

We read in the *Life of the Holy Fathers*[44] that a young man, wanting to take a religious vocation, expressed his intention to his mother, and she sought to dissuade him, saying: "How can you leave me alone and

---

43 Augustine's comment appears in *Enarrationes in Psalmos* [GA].
44 The *Vitae Patrum*, though again likely mediated through the *Alphabetum narrationum* (see Passavanti, ed. Auzzas, 482).

abandon me, I who am a widow and have no other children, and expect to have no more?" He answered with great fervour: "Mother of mine, I must love God more than you, I want to save my soul." Whereupon, not bowing to his mother's pleas or tears, he took his vows. For some time he was spiritual and devoted, but then he began to weaken, and little by little his spirit and fervour left him, and he became dissolute and evil. Then he became very sick, and suddenly one day, he left his body and was brought before God's judgment. As he waited to be judged with great fear and trembling, he turned his eye and saw his mother, who had died some time before, and who spoke to him, saying: "What does this mean, my son? Have you come here now to be judged? What was it you said to me: 'I want to save my soul'? Is this the fervour and devotion you showed? Where is your religion?" Before he could answer he came to, confused and full of shame, and thinking again about the shame he had felt because of what his mother had said and about his great confusion, he regained his prior fervour and devotion, saying: "If I could not endure my mother's reproof and felt shame because of her words, now how can I bear that of God, the saints, and his angels?"

You should therefore be afraid of the strong reproof that God makes to the soul through the prophet Nahum: *Revelabo pudenda tua in faciem tuam et ostendam gentibus nuditatem tuam* [Nh 3:5]: God said to the sinning soul, I shall reveal your shame to your face; in other words, I shall upbraid you for those things that you will be ashamed of, and I shall show your nakedness to the people. This will be the judgment day, when as St. Paul says: *Inluminabit abscondita tenebrarum et manifestabit consilia cordium* [1 Cr 4:5]: God will shine light upon hidden things, done in shadows and in the dark, and will show the intention of the heart. In order therefore not to feel that shame and perpetual confusion, we should want to endure this small and temporary shame before people, and not abandon the work of penitence out of shame, considering what Jesus Christ says in the Gospel: *Qui me erubuerit et meos sermones, hunc Filius hominis erubescet, cum venerit in maiestate sua et Patris, et sanctorum angelorum* [Lk 9:26]: Whoever is ashamed of me and of my words, or whoever shames me and my words, the Son of the virgin will make him feel ashamed when he appears before his majesty, and that of the Father and the holy angels, that is, on the day of judgment. So it is better to endure the shame of men than that of God, keeping in mind what Scripture says in the book of Wisdom about those who were derisive, that when the scorners of the just are in hell and see in the glory of paradise the saints whom they devalued and scorned in the present life, crying out in pain and anguish they will say: *Hii sunt, quos aliquando habuimus in derisum, et in similitudinem improperii: nos insensati! Vitam illorum reputabamus insaniam et finem illorum sine honore: ecce quomodo computati sunt inter filios Dei, et inter sanctos sors illorum est* [Ws 5:3–5]: Those are the ones who, once upon a time, we held to be corrupt and devalued, whom we made fun of and scorned; because we, fools without wisdom, judged their life to be madness, and that they should end up without honour; look how they number now among the children of God, and it is their good fortune to be among the saints. Wherein we understand how grave is the sin of these deriders, scorners of the good, who, like the devil, keep many from doing good. And since St. Gregory says[45] that the greater and better sacrifice to God is the zeal of souls, so too is the greater and worst evil against God to impede the salvation of souls. And the damned deriders try to do that, of whom the Scripture says: *Delusores ipse deludet* [Pr 3:34]: God will disdain the disdainers. And Solomon says in Proverbs: *Parata sunt derisoribus iudicia* [Pr 19:29]: The judges are ready for the laughable scoffers.

Second Chapter

Wherein we show how fear keeps us from penitence.

The second impediment to penitence is fear, the fear of affliction or of corporal or worldly punishment, because men who are used to easy living and soft things and the pleasures of the flesh, and to pursuing their own ends, are afraid of giving up their common and beloved delights, in whole or in part. Those who learn to repent must nevertheless do so, for it is still necessary to suffer some punishment and discomfort in the flesh and in the mind to make up for taking pleasure in a bad way, by following their own will, both in the desires of the flesh and in the malice of the mind. The remedy for this vain fear is to consider that no sin can go unpunished. It is punished in either this life or the other, in this life by penitence, in the other by divine justice. Since the punishment of penitence is brief and slight and specific, and that of the other life – that is, of hell – is eternal and endless and heavy, indeed very heavy, more general and universal than every other punishment, those who avoid this brief punishment do not act wisely, for they end up with the endless eternal one. The weight of hell's punishment is shown not only by the Holy Scripture of the Holy Gospel and of the prophets, who speak

---

45 In the Sermons on Ezekiel [GA].

of it in many places, saying that it is very heavy and without remedy and endless, but also by certain examples of things seen and heard.

We read in the *Life of the Holy Fathers*[46] that once, when St. Macarius was in the desert, he found the head of a dead man, and touching it with his walking stick, he begged it to tell him whose head it was. The skull replied that it had belonged to a pagan priest who had gone to damnation. When St. Macarius asked him about his punishment, he answered that as far as the eye could see there was burning fire, which never went out, nor did it decrease, above his head and those of the other damned pagans and beneath their feet, and that the evil Christians were even deeper in the burning fire and with greater punishments for them.

This is further proved by what happened in Paris, where a taste of the punishments of hell was given.[47]

We read that there was a teacher in Paris named Serlo, who taught logic and philosophy and had many students. It so happened that one of his students, clever and subtle in argument but arrogant and full of corruption, died. One night, a few days later, when the teacher had gotten up, this dead student appeared before him. The teacher, recognizing him, fearfully asked what had become of him. He answered that he was damned. The master asked if the punishments of hell were as heavy as was said, and he answered that they were infinitely greater, and that one could not put them into words, but that he would give him a taste of them. "Do you see," he said, "this cloak full of sophisms that I appear to be wearing? This weighs me down more than if I had the tallest tower in Paris, or the largest mountain in the world, on my shoulders, and could never put it down. And this punishment is given to me by divine justice, because of the vainglory that I showed in appearing to know more than others, and especially in knowing how to make subtle sophisms, that is, arguments to defeat others in debate. Therefore, this cloak of my punishment is full of them, so that they are always before my eyes, to my confusion." Lifting the cloak, which was open in front, up high, he said: "Do you see the lining of this cloak? It is all coals and punishing flames of burning fire, which bursts upon me and burns me without respite. I am so punished for the dishonest sin of the flesh, of which I was guilty during my life, and I pursued all the way to my death without penitence or deciding to stop. And since I persevered endlessly in sin, and I would have preferred to live longer in order to sin more, divine justice has deservedly damned me and

---

46 The tale appears in the *Vitae Patrum* as well as in the *Alphabetum narrationum* [GA].

47 The tale appears in the *Legenda aurea* of Jacobus da Voragine, a hagiographic compilation dating to the second half of the thirteenth century [GA].

punishes me with endless torment. Woe is me! Now I get what I did not understand while I was alive, caught up in the pleasure of sin and focused on the subtle sophisms of logic: why divine justice gives man the endless punishment of hell for his mortal sin. To make my coming here useful to you, in exchange for the many lessons you gave me, give me your hand, handsome teacher." As the teacher offered it to him, the student shook one of his fingers, which was burning, over the teacher's palm, whereupon a little drop of sweat fell and made a very painful hole clean through, as if with a fiery and sharp arrow. "Now you have a taste of the punishments of hell," said the student, and screaming with painful lamentations he disappeared. The teacher was left with great affliction and torment because of his pierced and burned hand, nor did he ever find any medicine that could cure the ulcer. His hand remained pierced until he died, and many learned a useful lesson from it. Thus afflicted, between his fearful vision and the pain, and fearing that he might go to those horrible punishments of which he had had a taste, the teacher decided to abandon the school and the world. With this in mind, he wrote two verses which he recited before his students in school the next morning, recounting his vision and showing his pierced and burned hand: "*Linquo coax ranis, cra corvis vanaque vanis, / ad loicam pergo que mortis non timet ergo*": I leave the frogs to croak and the crows to caw, the worthless things of the world to the worthless men, and I am going away to a logic that does not fear the conclusion of death, that is, to holy religion. And so, abandoning everything, he took his vows, living in a holy manner until death.

If someone were to say to you, "I will not repent during my life, but I will repent at the end, and go to repent in purgatory," this statement would be foolish, because, as said above, not every person who believes he will have a good end has one. Indeed, many are deceived by this, because commonly, indeed most of the time, a man dies as he lived, as St. Gregory says: by God's just judgment the dying sinner forgets himself, as he had forgotten God while he was alive.[48]

But let's assume that someone was sure of repenting at the end. How foolish would it be to want to go to the punishments of purgatory, which according to St. Augustine[49] exceed every punishment that we can suffer in this life, instead of putting up with a little penitence here? If we accept it voluntarily, for the most part penitence makes up for the sin,

---

48 Auzzas (Passavanti, 483) has found only an indirect source for this attribution to Gregory, *Tractatus de dono timoris* (Treatise on the gift of fear) by Humbertus de Romanis.

49 Pseudo-Augustine, author of *De vera et falsa poenitentia* [GA].

no matter how small. The punishment of purgatory does not do this, and we must endure it out of necessity, no matter how great, because merit does not count. The saints say that the punishment of purgatory is very great, because however we get to purgatory – either through that place near the centre of the earth, where hell is, where the souls are purged in the same fire as that of hell, or through some other earthly place, as it is found that souls suffer purgatorial punishments in various places according to God's hidden judgment – no matter how one gets there, the punishments are very grave. If we understand purgatory to be underground, where there is the fire of hell, then there can be no doubt but that the punishment this fire gives to souls, as an instrument of divine justice, is very heavy. If we understand purgatory to be other earthly places to which divine justice has assigned certain souls, either because they sinned there when they were alive, or in order to seek help there from relatives or friends, or to teach the living, or for some other hidden judgment of God, it is certain that the punishments are very grave, according to divine justice, depending more or less on the quality and the quantity of the sins that are to be purged.

There are many examples, though I shall recount only one in order not to write for too long.

Helinand[50] writes that in the county of Nivers there was a poor man who was good and feared God. He made his living by selling charcoal. One night, having set fire to the coal pit and keeping watch over the burning pit in a little hut of his, at midnight he heard great screams. He went outside to see what the noise was about, and he saw a woman whose hair was all undone running naked towards the pit. Coming after her there was a knight riding on a black horse, with a bare knife in his hand, and from the knight's mouth and eyes and nose and those of the horse there issued a flame of burning fire. When the woman reached the burning pit she went no farther, nor did she dare jump into the pit. As she ran towards it she was overtaken by the knight who was pursuing her, and as she cried out he grabbed her by her flying hair and cruelly wounded her in the middle of her chest with the knife that he held in his hand. She fell to the ground with a great flow of blood, and he took her by her bloody hair and threw her into the pit with the burning coals. After leaving her there for a while he took her out, all fiery and burned, and putting her up on the neck of the horse he rode off in the same direction whence he had come. The second and the third nights the charcoal vendor saw the same thing. Whereupon,

---

50 In the *Flores*, though likely through the *Alphabetum narrationum* [GA].

as he was an acquaintance of the Count of Nivers through his work as a coal vendor, and because of his goodness which the count, a soulful man, appreciated, he came to the count and told him what he had seen for three nights. The count came with the coal miner to the pit, and they kept watch together in the little hut, and at the usual hour the screaming woman came with the knight behind her, and they did everything that the coal miner had seen them do. Although the count was very afraid because of the horrible scene he had witnessed, he summoned his courage, and when the pitiless knight was leaving with the burned woman lying across the black horse, he yelled to him, urging him to stay and explain what he had seen. The knight turned the horse and, crying hard, said: "Count, since you want to know of our suffering, which God has wanted to show to you, know that I was Godfrey, your knight, and I grew up in your court. This woman, towards whom I am so cruel and harsh, is Lady Beatrice, who was the wife of your dear knight Berlinghieri. The two of us, taking pleasure in dishonourable love, contracted to sin, and, in order to be able to sin more freely, she went as far as to kill her husband. We persevered in sin until the infirmity of death, but when we fell ill, first she and then I turned to penitence, and confessing our sin we received God's mercy, which changed the eternal punishment of hell into the temporary punishment of purgatory. So we are not damned, but what we do, as you have seen, is our purgatory: and our torments at some point will end." The count asked him to explain their punishments more specifically, and he answered with tears and sighs: "Because this woman killed her husband out of love for me, her punishment is that every night, as divine justice has ordained, she endure painful death by knifing at my hand, and because she had that burning love of carnal concupiscence for me, every night I throw her into the fire to burn, as you saw. And as we once looked at one another with great desire, now we see one another with great hatred, and we pursue one another with great disdain. And as we were each the reason for the other to burn with dishonourable love, so too is each of us the reason for the other's cruel torment, because with every punishment that I make her feel I suffer too. The knife I use to wound her is made of a fire that never goes out, and as I throw her in the fire and remove her from it, and carry her about, I am always burning with the same flame that burns her. The horse is a demon that torments us. We are punished in many other ways as well. Pray to God for us, give alms and say masses, so that our suffering will be reduced." Having said this, he disappeared, like a bolt of lightning.

Let it not displease us, my most beloved ones, to suffer a little punishment here so as to avoid those horrible punishments and painful torments of the other life, to which, whether we like it or not, we must necessarily go.

Third Chapter

Wherein we show how vain hope impedes penitence.

The third impediment to penitence is hope, by which some persevere in sin, saying: "God's mercy is great; He loves us; He has saved us with His precious blood; He does not want to lose us." In this way people do not repent and continue to sin. Scripture says of them: *Maledictus omnis, qui peccat in spe*: Every man who sins in hope is damned by God.[51] And St. Bernard says: It is a faithless faith, worthy of damnation, when we sin in hope: and these men are rightly called damned, because they are blasphemers and scorners of God's goodness and mercy, and when they should find reason not to sin, on the contrary they sin more.[52] St. Paul says of them: *An ignoras quod benignitas Dei ad poenitentiam te adducit? etc.* [Rm 2:4], as was explained above.[53]

St. Paul shows the seriousness of this sin when he says: *Inritam quis faciens legem Moysi, etc., et Spiritui gratiae contumeliam fecerit?* [Hb 10: 28–9], where the gloss says that those who sin with the hope of receiving mercy disrespect and harm the spirit of grace and the blood of Christ. Because of that mercy a man should keep himself from sin, considering, as St. Paul says, *Secundum suam misericordiam salvos nos fecit* [Tt 3:5]: God saved us according to His mercy. Those who have a noble heart, who avoid sin out of love and not fear, do just that. But for those who do the opposite, it happens, as Scripture says, that they are punished for their sins. Thus, someone who does harm to God's mercy by persevering in sin is abandoned by God's mercy, especially at the moment of greatest need, i.e., the hour of death. We can prove this with many examples from St. Gregory, which are contained in both the legends of the saints and in the *Life of the Holy Fathers*, which we shall not put down here, because many others have written them, and in order not to write too long a treatise.

Scripture speaks against this vain and presumptuous hope and says: do not say that God's mercy is so great that He does not recall my sins,

---

51 The sentence does not in fact appear in the Bible but may originate with St. Bernard (Passavanti, ed. Auzzas, 172).

52 In his sermons [GA].

53 See p. 42.

because you must know that wrath and vendetta proceed from Him as quickly as does mercy. Although God is merciful, He does not want someone to offend Him while trusting in Him. Therefore St. Gregory says: Given that God is just, we do not want to leave our sins without penitence; and given that He is merciful, a man should not despair.[54] And so, those who want to make amends for their bad life can hope for God's mercy, but not those who want to persevere in this evil with this hope. Foolish faith comes down to this worthless hope of many to live for a long time and die a good death, so they delay their penitence, not heeding what Scripture says through the wise Ecclesiasticus: *Ne tardes converti ad Dominum et ne differas de die in diem; subito enim veniet ira illius, et in tempore iracundie disperdet te* [Ec 5:8]: Do not put off converting to God, and do not delay from day to day, so that His wrath does not send you off to hell. In other words, on the day of your death, when you are judged, may He not damn you. St. Gregory says: he who has been held up for a long time is quickly carried away.[55] Which means that when someone does not give thought to this, when God has put up with him for a long time, waiting for penitence, he is carried off at once by death and by God's judgment.

We read in Peter Damian[56] that in Salerno there was once a prince, held by common agreement to be great and noble, who lived for a long time in much worldly prosperity of lordship, wealth, and carnal pleasure. He used to say that one who does well in this world does well in the next, understanding the proverb materially, as he lived, and not according to its correct intention. It so happened that, as he thought he was enjoying the greatest worldly prosperity he had ever had, one morning, while staring for a time at Mount Etna, that is, Mongibello, he saw a great flame of sparking fire, more than usual, issue from that mountain. Summoning his staff, which was great and honourable, he said to them: "Surely some rich and powerful man is about to die, for I have seen the sign in the fire of Mongibello, which is waiting to receive him and throw him down to hell." It is customary in that land that when Mongibello does something unusual, like sending forth greater flames of fire, because the country folk say that it is one of the mouths of hell, people say: "Some great and terrible sinner is about to die, and Mongibello is preparing to receive him." And so, seeing the unusually large flame, he said what is usually said, not thinking that he was

---

54 In the *Homiliae in evangelia* [GA].

55 In the *Moralia in Job* [GA].

56 In "De abdicatione episcopatus," a letter addressed to Pope Nicholas II (1059–1061), but more likely direct from the *Alphabetum narrationum* [GA].

talking about himself, nor that the mouth of hell was being prepared for him. That night, lying down with one of his lovers, feeling happy and secure, he died in the act of sin by which he had lived for a long time, and he lost his life, and he who had gone to bed happy and healthy was found dead in the morning by his staff.

What we said above about the English knight and the count of Mâcon, and about the one who uselessly sought a delay until the next morning,[57] we can say here as well, according to St. Gregory. Scripture puts it well: *Nescit homo finem suum, set sicut capiuntur pisces hamo et aves laqueo, ita capiuntur homines in tempore malo* [Ec 9:12]: No man knows how he will die, but as fish are caught on a hook and birds with a net, so too are men taken at a bad moment. We call it a bad moment when a man becomes evil by sinning and doing bad things, or when he dies and is judged for his evil deeds. So you should not allow yourself to be deceived by this worthless and foolish hope by which many go to perdition, as the wise Ecclesiasticus says: *Repromissio nequissima multos perdidit* [Ec 29:24]: The promise that some incorrectly make of a long life, many have already lost. St. Bernard says of this: why, you wretched man, do you vainly make assumptions about the time to come, as if God had put it not in His but in your power and control, when He spoke to the apostles: *Non est vestrum nosse tempora vel momenta, que Pater posuit in sua potestate* [Ac 1:7]: Is it not yours to know the hour and the times that the Father has put in His power? Which means that someone who makes assumptions about the time to come does harm to God, who reserves unto Himself the power to arrange and apportion time.

Let worthless hope not deceive us, therefore, most beloved brothers, so that we indiscreetly and foolishly count on divine mercy for a long life. We said a great deal about this above, where we dealt with the uncertainty of death.

Fourth Chapter

Wherein we show how desperation keeps others from repenting.

The fourth impediment that keeps some from penitence is desperation. This happens in two ways. The first is when a man despairs of God's mercy; the other is when others despair of themselves, not believing that they can persevere in the work of penitence. And since each desperation keeps us from repenting, we want to talk about both here.

---

57 See p. 48.

The first desperation is when someone despairs of God's mercy. This usually happens when one feels that he has committed many serious sins and has fallen back many times, so that he does not hope that God will have mercy and pardon him, considering the seriousness of his sins. Cain, having killed his brother Abel only out of jealousy, despaired in this way, and considering the seriousness of his sin he said: *Maior est iniquitas mea, quam ut veniam merear* [Gn 4:13]: The evil of my sin is so great that I do not deserve pardon. He did not have respect for God's mercy, which is infinitely greater than his sin was, and which could pardon and make him deserve pardon. Likewise, Judas the traitor considered the seriousness of his sin, saying, *Peccavi tradens sanguinem iustum* [Mt 27:4], and by not humbling himself to ask for mercy and forgiveness, he despaired and went off to hang himself by the throat. St. Augustine says that he sinned more by despairing of God's mercy, which if he had requested with a good heart he certainly would have received, than he did by betraying Jesus Christ our saviour.[58] For this desperation there is the efficacious remedy of considering God's infinite mercy, which without comparison and equal surpasses every human evil and wretchedness. This is what the prophet David meant when he said, *Misericordia Domini plena est terra* [Ps 32:5]: The earth is full of God's mercy. Elsewhere he said: *Domini, in celo misericordia tua,* and *Misericordia eius super omnia opera eius* [Ps 35:6]: God's mercy is in heaven, and above all His works. And saying thanks for this, he said: *Misericordias Domini in etternum cantabo* [Ps 144:9]: I will sing of God's mercies forever without end. St. Paul calls God *Pater misericordiarum, et Deus totius consolationis* [2 Cr 1:3]: Father of mercies, and God of all consolation. We know of God's mercy especially in his passion, by which we are mercifully saved and redeemed; as St. Paul says: *Non ex operibus iustitie, que fecimus nos, sed secundum suam misericordiam salvos nos fecit* [Tt 3:5]: Not by the works of justice that we might do, but by His mercy did He save us. St. Bernard spoke of this,[59] and he says in the person of the sinner: I have committed a great sin, what will become of me? My conscience will be troubled by it, but it will not be perturbed (which means that it will be troubled by contrition, but it will not be perturbed by desperation), because I will remember my Lord's wounds, and I will see by the wound on his side the heartfelt love by which he redeemed me; the nails will be a key that will open the treasury of his mercy; there can be no sin so worthy of death that the death of Christ does not destroy and remove it, so I will not be afraid, fearing any grave illness,

---

58 In the *City of God* [GA].
59 In the sermon on the Song of Songs [GA].

since I have such an efficacious and virtuous medicine as the death of Christ. St. Augustine, speaking to God the Father, said:[60] Your one and only beloved son redeemed me with the price of his blood, so I do not fear my adversaries, since I think again about the price he paid. Not only did he redeem us with his blood, but he is forever our advocate, and he prays for us, as the apostle says: *Advocatum habemus apud Patrem, Jesum Christum iustum: et ipse est propitiatio pro peccatis nostris* [1 Jn 2:1]: Although a man sins, he must not despair, thinking that we have in Jesus Christ a just advocate before God, who defends us for our sins.

Although we often fall back into sin, we should not despair, because God is ready with mercy and forgiveness just as often as man is ready to fall and sin. Christ made this point in his statement to St. Peter, when he asked him how many times he should pardon him, and whether seven times were enough, and he said: not even seven, but seventy times seven, as is explained above.[61] In many ways and many times, in the Holy Gospel, he explained how merciful God is, as is shown by what he said to the Pharisees, that he had come to the world as a doctor to a sick man, and that they should remember in Scripture that God says: *Misericordiam volo et non sacrificium* [Mt 12:7]: I want mercy rather than sacrifice. And he shows that by many words and similes, like that of the pastor who looked for the lost sheep and, finding it, lifted it on his neck, and was happy and celebrated [Lk 15:4–6]. So too, the woman who found the lost drachma [Lk 15:8–9]. Likewise, that prodigal and wayward son who returned to his father, who, moved to mercy, received him kindly and made a great celebration for him, restoring him to his prior dignity [Lk 15]. Similarly of the servant, upon whose prayer God forgave the debt of 10,000 talents [Mt 18]. Explaining this, he said that he had come to call the sinners to penitence, and that there was great happiness for the angels when the sinner turned to penitence. He showed how merciful he was not only by similes and words, but even more by deeds and in fact, because he mercifully received all the sinners who came to him – as the Holy Gospel says: *Erant apropinquantes ad Iesum publicani et peccatores* [Lk 15:1] – and freely he pardoned them, not imposing penitence on them but saying: go, and do not sin anymore [Jn 8:11]. If you think about it, you will see that what I am telling you is true: how he received Mary Magdalene; how he forgave the woman caught in adultery; how he forgave the Canaanite; how he mercifully watched over St. Peter, who had denied him; how he called to St. Matthew; how he drew St. Paul to him, and how he set

---

60 In the *Confessions*, Book 10 [GA].
61 See p. 34.

the publican right; and how he easily saved the thief from the cross. Who is therefore so great a sinner that he flees from God and does not instead run to the kind and merciful Lord and sweetest Father, asking for forgiveness and mercy with the sure hope of it being granted: how were the great sinners named? St. Bernard speaks of that and says:[62] O good Jesus, by your mercy and your pity, which we preach, let us run in the odour of your oils, certain that the poor and the sinners do not disgust you. Indeed, the greater the sinners, the more He honoured and exalted them, as we see in David, St. Peter, St. Paul, St. Matthew, and in many others, in whom the greater the sin, the more abundant his grace.

Who will resist, who will be so hard, so pertinacious, so obstinate in evil? Who will be so cruel and pitiless about himself that he will not surrender to Jesus's kindness, not allow himself to be drawn to the charity of Christ the Redeemer? O sinners, o hardened ones, insolent and sleepy, wake up, come to your senses, open your eyes! Look at yourselves: Jesus, crucified for you, calls to you, his blood cries out and offers mercy and pity; his open side shows you the wounded heart of love, full of charity; his open arms, his bent head draw you to peace and to his friendship; his pierced hands and feet invite you with patience and with tranquillity. The cross is set before your eyes as an example of penitence and mirror of virtue and health, and as a ladder, by which one rises to the glory of God and to eternal happiness.

How temptations and tribulations are useful for the soul,
which wants to follow God.

The other despair that impedes penitence is when a person loses hope in persevering in the work of penitence, and this despair usually is born of the many and grave temptations that those who repent often face, more than others who live in a worldly way. St. Gregory says[63] they are more tempted because the devil does not tempt those whom he peacefully possesses, but he tempts more harshly those who rebel against him by abstaining from sin. St. Augustine says: we see from continuous experience that the enemy most cruelly persecutes those who flee from him and from the world. It is therefore a good sign to be tempted, and it follows very well from the presence of temptations. We should not fall into despair because of temptations. Indeed, we should have greater hope in God, and with greater trust ask for the help of His grace, which

---

62 In the sermon on the Song of Songs [GA].
63 In the *Moralia in Job* [GA].

comes more quickly and more widely where there is greater need, as St. Martin said when the assassin wanted to wound him with an axe and asked him: "Are you afraid?," and he answered that he never felt safer than at that moment, because he knew that God's help is more quickly ready when the man who trusts in Him is in greater danger.[64] Though He does sometimes delay obvious help so that others might better recognize their defect, and for other uses that we will discuss later.

We read[65] that St. Anthony was defeated by the demons in a tomb he had entered in order to sleep. As he was left for dead from the many wounds and blows inflicted by the demons with God's permission, there suddenly appeared a great splendour with much light, which chased away the demons and healed every wound. Coming to and feeling comforted, St. Anthony recognized the presence of God in that light, and he cried out: *Ubi eras, bone Jesu? Ubi eras?* (Where were you, good Jesus, where were you?). And Christ answered: "Anthony, I was right here; but I was waiting to see your skill in the battle the demons waged with you."

Now we should consider the usefulness of temptations for the soul, because of which one must not be sad or fall into despair.

The first benefit is that a man, recognizing his fragility, becomes humble and turns for help to God, whom he recognizes he needs. Speaking of himself, St. Paul says that he was tempted so that he would be humble and not arrogant about the great gifts he had received from God.

The other benefit that temptations provide is that they make a man diligent and test him, and they do not allow him to become neglectful and slothful, and they lead us to keep vigils, and to engage in prayer and fasting and other spiritual exercises that bring a man to the perfection of spiritual life. St. James says: Blessed is the man who endures temptation, because when tested he will receive the crown of life: *Beatus vir qui suffert tentationem; quoniam cum probatus fuerit, accipiet coronam vitae* [Jm 1:12]. And a man must have faith in God, that He will not let him perish or win, but will lend him the assistance of His grace, about which St. Paul says: *Fidelis Deus, qui non patietur vos tentari supra id quod potestis, sed cum tentatione faciet proventum, ut possitis substinere* [2 Cr 10:13]: Faithful is God, who will not let you be tempted beyond

---

64 The anecdote appears in the *Legenda aurea* [GA].
65 The tale appears in the *Vitae Patrum* but likely for Passavanti via the *Alphabetum narrationum* [GA].

your power, but with temptation will give you strength and help you to endure.

The other benefit that temptations provide is that they make the soul grow in virtue. St. Bernard says that when a man sees himself engaged in battle and, being tempted, looks for God's help, he often receives it. As the prophet says of Him: *Adiutor in opportunitatibus, in tribulation*: He is our helper in need and in tribulation. Faith in Him grows, hope takes comfort in Him, love blazes up towards Him, and so a man becomes virtuous, expert, and knowledgeable about many things that he was not before, as Scripture says: Who is not tempted, what does he know? As if to say, little or nothing. Through temptation man is also tested to see if he has any goodness, and how constant and firm he is, so that, since these are useful things, a man should not despair but be comforted and have greater hope. And one may speak likewise about other tribulations, that they are very useful to those who patiently endure them, because God allows them and has them come as correction and punishment of those whom He loves, as He says in Scripture [Rv 3:19]: Those whom I love, I correct and punish. It was also said to the holy Job [Jb 5:17]: Blessed is he who is corrected by God. St. Gregory explains this[66] by saying: If you are not among those who are corrected and punished, you will not be among those chosen to be saved. As St. Paul says [Hb 12:7]: What child is there whom the father does not correct and beat? About which St. Augustine says:[67] Do not be so puerile and childish in wisdom as to say: God loves so-and-so more than me, because He lets him do what he wants and grants him prosperity, and me He suddenly torments even though my mistake is small. Take pleasure instead in the torment of the whipping, because it is a sign that God corrects you here as a son and elsewhere holds an eternal inheritance for you. St. Gregory says[68] that continued prosperity in earthly things is a sign of eternal damnation, as shown by the example of the rich and the poor Lazarus of the Gospel, to whom it was said: *Recordare, quia recepisti bona in vita tua, et Lazarus similiter mala* [Lk 16:27].

We read in the legend of St. Ambrose[69] that once when St. Ambrose came from Milan, where he was archbishop, to Rome where he was born, while passing through Tuscany he came to a village named Malmantile[70] in the Florentine countryside. Arriving at an inn with his

---

66 In the *Regula pastoralis* [GA].

67 In the *Enarrationes in Psalmos* [GA].

68 In the *Moralia in Job* [GA].

69 As recounted in the *Legenda aurea* [GA].

70 Malmantile is west of Florence, about halfway to Empoli.

entire entourage, he started talking to the innkeeper, asking him about himself and how he was doing. The innkeeper replied that God had been very good to him, that for all his life he had enjoyed great prosperity, and he had never had any adversity. "I am rich, I am healthy, I have a beautiful wife, many children, a large household. Nor have I ever been injured, harmed, or hurt by anyone. I am revered, honoured, held dear by everyone. I have never known evil or wretchedness, but I have always lived happy and content." Hearing this, St. Ambrose was filled with amazement, and summoning his entourage he ordered that the horses be saddled and that everyone leave at once, saying: "God is not in this place, nor with this man, whom He has allowed to have so much prosperity. Let's get out of here, so that the wrath of God does not descend here upon us." His entire company left, and they had not gotten very far when the earth suddenly opened up and swallowed the inn and the innkeeper, his children, his wife, and his whole household, along with his equipment and everything he possessed. When St. Ambrose heard about this, he said to his entourage: "Now you see, children, how earthly prosperity leads to a bad outcome. Do not wish it for yourselves; indeed, fear it, as you would anything that leads souls to hell. Content yourselves with adversity and tribulation, as they are the path to paradise, when they are endured with a good spirit and with patience." As Christ said in the Gospel: *Ve vobis divitibus, qui habetis vestram consolationem hic!* [Lk 6:24]: Woe unto you, rich people, who have your consolation here!

The psalmist speaks of just men who are troubled: *Multe tribulationes iustorum, et de omnibus hiis liberabit eos Dominus* [Ps 33:20]: Many are the tribulations of the just, and God will free them from all of them. Indeed, He makes them very beneficial, as St. Gregory says:[71] Through temporal afflictions God tries to remove and purge the stains of sin among his chosen, so that He does not have to punish them for eternity. Elsewhere he says: Those evils that weigh upon and prick at us spur us and almost force us to turn to God.

Two other things are an effective remedy against the despair born of tribulation and temptation. First, if we consider the weakness of the enemy who tempts us, about whom the saints say that when he is defeated by us, which happens when we resist his temptations, he becomes cowardly and loses his daring, and thinks twice before tempting someone with that same vice for which he was already defeated. And we have the example of Jesus Christ, about whom the Evangelist

---

71 In the *Moralia in Job* [GA].

says: *Tunc reliquit eum diabolus* [Mt 4:11]: Then, when he had defeated him, the devil left him alone and did not tempt him anymore.

Here is an example of this.

We read in Caesarius that there was a knight in Saxony named Albert, prized and famous for his skill at arms, who once happened upon a place where there was a young girl possessed by the devil. The young girl began to cry out: "Here comes my friend." And as he entered the room where she was, she said, "Welcome to you. Make room for him, let me get close to him, for he is my friend." As the knight heard these words, which he did not like very much, he said, smiling: "Foolish demon, why do you torment this innocent girl? Come with me instead to the tourney." The devil answered: "Yes, I will come willingly, if you will let me enter into your body somehow, either through your saddle, or your reins, or some other way." The knight, feeling compassion for this young girl, said: "If you leave her, I will give you a piece of my clothing, on the condition that you must not do me any harm." The devil promised not to hurt him, and leaving the young girl, he took possession of the knight's piece of clothing, where he showed his presence by the strange movement that it made, and by his voice, which issued from it. From then on, when wearing the bedevilled vestment the knight was always victorious in tourneys, jousts, and battles, knocking anyone he touched to the ground. When he did not put it on, the devil complained and dragged him around the house, and it looked like he would tear him apart with his teeth. Once, when the knight was praying in church, he said: "Enough with the murmuring; let's get out of here." When the knight took some holy water, he said: "Look, be careful not to touch me." In the end the knight came to a certain place where the cross was preached, and while he was there, listening to the preaching, the devil said: "What are you doing here? Let's go!" The knight answered: "I want to leave you and serve God." The demon said: "Why do you want to leave me? What did I ever do to displease you? I never hurt you, I never denied you anything you wanted; indeed, I made you victorious, rich, and famous for your great valour." The knight answered: "I want to take the cross. Go away and don't ever come back, I order you in the name of the Jesus Christ crucified." The devil left, furiously tearing up the piece of clothing, and he never returned. The knight took the cross and spent two years overseas, and upon his return he founded a hospital where, using his own wealth to provide for the poor and the sick, and serving them personally, he lived in a holy way until his death.

You can see how the devil has neither strength nor power over a man if the man does not give it to him, and how he leaves when someone stands up to him and chases him away. St. Paul teaches us and says: *Nolite locum dare diabolo* [Ep 4:27]: Do not make room for the devil. Indeed, as the apostle says elsewhere: *Resistite diabolo, et fugiet a vobis* [Jm 4:7]: Stand up to the devil, and he will flee from you. For, as St. Gregory says, it is a weak enemy who defeats only those who want to be defeated.[72]

The second effective remedy against desperation is the virtue of penitence, which vigorously comforts and sustains those who adopt it. As St. John Chrysostom says,[73] there is nothing so serious that the virtue of penitence will not defeat it. Speaking of this virtue he says: O penitence, which forgives sins, opens paradise, heals the contrite, makes the wretched happy, brings the dead back to life, restores status, renews honour, reforms trust, recovers grace, untethers what is bound up, safeguards the untethered, mitigates adversities, clarifies and reveals confused and hidden things, makes fearful things safe: through you, o penitence, the thief on the cross went at once to paradise, David recovered his salvation after his error; through you Manasseh was received in mercy, Peter gained pardon, the prodigal son was received and embraced by his father, the city of Nineveh felt divine mercy! Why therefore, o man, do you fear penitence? There is nothing hard, harsh, or uncomfortable about it; indeed, it has great sweetness and soft delight, which those who fervently undertake to repent, and fervently persevere in it, will taste. Be not afraid, therefore, but always be most ready in process, prepared in deed, and fervent in love. Flee from laughter, hold your tongue, behave yourself, defeat your vices, love virtue, and pursue salvation. But because some deceive themselves about true penitence and do not produce fruits worthy of it, Chrysostom himself shows what true penitence must have, saying: Penitence disdains avarice, recoils at lust, chases away anger, holds love fast, tramples arrogance, closes the door to envy, holds its tongue, behaves itself, holds malice in contempt. Perfect penitence forces the sinner to suffer everything willingly. When provoked, he replies gently; when challenged, he does not defend himself; when bothered, he gives thanks; when whipped, he remains silent; in his heart there is contrition, in his mouth confession, in his deeds humility is always found.

It should greatly comfort and hearten the penitent to consider that through penitence he has received God's grace, which makes him a

---

72 *Moralia in Job*, but possibly via Aquinas's *In I–IV Sententiarum*, a commentary on Peter Lombard [GA].

73 Auzzas (Passavanti, 488–9) points to Pseudo-John Chrysostom's "Sermo de penitentia," though with a likely closer source in Domenico Cavalca's *Specchio de' peccati*.

participant in all good things that are done anywhere for any of the faithful, and that Jesus Christ and the Virgin Mary, and all the angels and all the saints in paradise, male and female, and all the just who pray in this world, pray for him. He should especially have faith in the Virgin Mary, who takes singular care of sinners who turn to penitence. She is called their advocate, as we can show through many examples, which we will not put here for brevity's sake. We will only give two examples, the first of which suggests how the Virgin Mary cares in general for all sinners and is their advocate, and the other, how she prays solicitously, especially for those who show faith and devotion in her.

We read in the legend of our father St. Dominic[74] that, having come to Rome for a council in order to ask for confirmation of his order, which he had just founded, and that it be called the Order of the Friars Preachers, he set about to pray in the church of St. Peter, and he prayed fervently to God and to the Virgin Mary, to whom he had special devotion, for the sinners of the world. He asked her to direct them on the path of truth and salvation, and to set the pope's and the cardinals' hearts so that they would agree to confirm the new order, which he had founded and organized to return the errant world and the sinners to the path of salvation. As the holy father saint prayed with great fervour, suddenly he was raised up and carried away in spirit, and he saw Jesus Christ aloft in the form in which he will come and judge the world, with three lances in his hand, and, thrashing about and aiming them at the ground, he pretended to throw them down and wound the people who lived there and to destroy the world. Then he saw the blessed mother Virgin Mary come out from the other side, and she asked her son what he wanted to do. He answered that he wanted to destroy the world and kill the sinners with those three lances, as they were corrupted by three vices, pride, avarice, and lust. She knelt before him, forming a cross with her arms, and begged him piously to temper the rigour of his justice with the gentleness of his mercy. He replied that he had put up long enough with the world, which had not corrected itself either through the prophets or by his presence, or through the apostles, or through the other saints who had followed, who had studiously tried to convert the world and return it to God. Full of piety and mercy, she still begged him sweetly: "By your love and grace towards me, may it please you to pardon those sinners once again, for the redemption of whom you wanted to be born of me, making me your mother, and you wanted to endure passion and death, and I offer to you a devoted

---

74 The narrative appears in the *Legenda aurea* [GA].

and faithful servant of mine, who with your grace, in word and deed, will convert the world and restore it to the path of truth." And as Jesus Christ said that he wanted to see whether he was up to and deserving of such a duty, the Virgin Mary, extending her hand straight over St. Dominic's head, showed him to Christ, who accepted and approved of him and commending him said: "And I, out of love for you, sweetest mother, forgive the world for now. And I set upon Dominic, a faithful servant, my grace and spirit, with which he and his descendants, by speaking throughout the world as evangelical and apostolic men, will uproot vices, plant seeds of virtue, and harvest the fruit of eternal life through preaching and action. But as I sent my apostles in pairs to the task of doctrine and preaching, so too is it good that Dominic have a companion in that same task." The Virgin Mary said that she had prepared for this. With her other hand she indicated St. Francis, who was then in Rome, praising the latter as she had the former. Accepting him for the same duty, the Virgin Mary made them companions, imposing on them to faithfully and diligently pursue the great task for which they had been chosen. St. Dominic, who was seeing this vision, waited, staring at the companion who had been given to him, and whom he had never seen; and just then the vision ended.

The next day St. Dominic ran into St. Francis and, recognizing him as the one he had seen in the vision, affectionately embracing him said: "You are my companion. Let's stay together, and no enemy will have power over us." From then on, with St. Dominic revealing his vision to St. Francis, they stayed together and conversed, conferring about how to fulfil the duty that had been given them. Once they also talked about creating an order together, but St. Dominic, having already founded his order and having ascertained, through his vision, that God accepted it and that the Church would approve it and confirm it (which it did, when the pope had the vision that St. John Lateran was falling down and that St. Dominic was coming from the other side and, by offering his shoulder, holding it up and putting it back in place), he continued with the order he had founded and created the Order of the Friars Preachers. Not long after that, St. Francis founded and created the Order of the Friars Minor. A companion of St. Francis saw the vision recounted above, of Jesus Christ and the three lances and the Virgin Mary who showed him St. Dominic and St. Francis, with all its process, at the same time that St. Dominic saw it. Then, seeing St. Dominic and St. Francis together and recognizing St. Dominic, he recounted to both the vision he had seen, and they praised the name of God, being careful to fulfil what they had learned from the vision, according to the plan already inspired in each of them.

The other example, which we read in Caesarius, was that of a young knight of noble lineage in the county of Louvain, who had spent his entire inheritance on tourneys and other useless worldly things. Coming into poverty, and unable to appear with other knights as was his custom, he became so sad and melancholy that he almost lost hope. One of his administrators, seeing this, comforted him and said that if he would follow his advice, he would make him rich and restore him to his earlier honourable state. The knight agreed, so one night he brought him to a forest, and using his necromantic art he summoned a demon who came and asked him what he wanted. He replied that he had brought along a noble knight who was his lord so that the demon would restore him to his previous state, giving him riches and honour. The demon replied that he would willingly do so, but that the knight first had to renounce Jesus Christ and his faith. The knight said he did not intend to do that. The administrator said: "So you don't want your riches and your status back? Come on! Why have you made me work in vain?" Seeing what was needed if he wanted to be rich, and also having a great desire to return to his prior status, the knight allowed himself to be convinced, and he followed his administrator's bad advice. Albeit unwillingly and with great trembling, he renounced Christ and his faith. At that point the devil said: "He still has to renounce the mother of God, and then he will get what he wants." The knight replied that he would never do that, and he turned his back and left. Along the way, thinking about his great sin of having renounced God, he entered a church feeling penitent and ashamed, and there was a wooden image of the Virgin Mary with her son in her arms. Kneeling reverently before it and sobbing, he asked for mercy and pardon for his great mistake. Just then another knight, who had bought all the possessions of that penitent knight, entered the church and, seeing the knight, whom he knew well, praying devoutly before the image and with painful tears, he was filled with amazement. He hid behind a column, waiting for the shameful knight's tearful prayer to end. As both knights were waiting, the Virgin Mary spoke through the mouth of the image, and each of them clearly heard her say to her son: "Sweetest son, I beg you, have mercy on this knight." The son, not responding, turned his face away from her. The gentle mother begged him again, saying that he had been deceived. He answered: "That man for whom you are begging has denied me. What should I do to him?" With these words the image stood up and, putting her son on the altar, fell to her knees before him and said: "Sweetest son, I beg you, as you love me, pardon this contrite knight for his sin." At this entreaty the son took his mother's hand and, lifting her up, said: "Dearest mother, I cannot deny you what you ask: I forgive the knight all his sins." The mother took her son in her arms again and sat back down, and the knight, certain of pardon because of the words of the mother and the son, left, feeling pained and wretched about his sin but happy and consoled by the pardon he had received. Leaving the church, the knight who had listened and watched what was said and done from behind the column secretly followed along and, greeting him, asked why his eyes were filled with tears. He replied that it was the wind. Then the second knight said: "Nothing that has been said and done for you is hidden from me, so by the grace that you have received, because of the love of the one who begged for it, I want to help you out. I have but one daughter, a virgin, whom I will give to you in marriage if you want. And all your great and rich possessions, which I bought from you, I want to restore to you as a dowry, and I intend to keep you as a son, and make you heir to all my possessions, which are many." Hearing that, the young knight agreed to the proposed marriage and, having received everything that was promised him, he thanked the Virgin Mary, from whom he recognized all the graces he had received.

Sinners, have reverence and devotion for such an advocate as the Virgin Mary, who unfailingly gets what she asks for, and does not allow those who have faith in her to perish.

Fourth Distinction.

Wherein we show what the parts of penitence are, and how many things are required for true penitence. And first we will talk about the main part, which is contrition.

The fourth thing to say about penitence, according to the order we adopted at the beginning, is what its parts are, and how many things are required for true penitence. The Master of Sentences says[75] that there are three parts without which, or without one of which, we cannot say that penitence is true or complete. The first is contrition of the heart, the second confession of the mouth, the third satisfaction by deeds. St. John Chrysostom speaks of these three parts of penitence in the *Decretum*[76]: *In corde contritio, in ore confessio, in opera tota humilitas: hec est fructuosa*

---

75 Peter Lombard, in his *Sentences*.

76 In the *De penitentia* section of the *Decretum* [GA].

penitentia: Contrition in the heart, confession by mouth, humility in all works of satisfaction: this is fruitful penitence. Those three parts correspond to the three ways by which we offend God, with the heart, the mouth, and the hand, and so we make up for them by repenting in three ways: with contrition, with confession, and with satisfaction. It is necessary to speak of each of these three parts in an orderly manner. First, we will speak of contrition, about which we will write four things: what contrition is; where the word "contrition" comes from; what things lead us to have contrition; and last, what is the effect of contrition.

First Chapter

Wherein we show what contrition is, and how it must have three conditions.

Contrition, according to our teachers, is a pain voluntarily felt for sins committed, with the intention of confessing and repairing them. This definition sufficiently includes what contrition is, both as an act having the virtue of justice (and therefore it says that it is voluntary pain for sins) and as part of the sacrament of penitence (and therefore it says with the intention to confess and repair).

This pain called contrition must have three conditions.

First, it must be general, i.e., someone generally feels pain for every one of his sins. This is what the prophet David suggests in the psalm, saying: *Lavabo per singulas noctes lectum meum: lacrimis meis stratum meum rigabo* [Ps 6:7]: I will wash my bed every night, and I will bathe it with my tears. By night he means the guilt of sin, so he says that he will cry for each sin, and he will cleanse his conscience with the tears of painful crying. This goes against many who, although they suffer the pain of vituperation and shame for some sins, do not suffer for certain others. Instead, whenever they think about them, they feel happy and content for having done them, and worse still, they praise themselves and boast about them, as for having acquired honour and status and wealth in an illicit way, for having had victories, taken revenge on enemies, acquired love children, and the like, for which they rarely repent well or suffer. Nevertheless, for one's own salvation it is necessary to feel the pain of contrition for all sins generally and each one specifically, i.e., for every mortal sin, since in every mortal sin the will is disordered, distancing itself from God and approaching the sin with pleasure. In like manner, one needs to be reformed and reordered in the opposite way, by separating from the sin (which causes pain) and turning to God (which love makes us do). The pain that comes only from fear does not make for sufficient contrition; it has to come as well from love of charity, like the pain of the Magdalene, of whom Jesus Christ said: Because she has loved much, many of her sins are forgiven [Lk 7:47]. St. Gregory says of this:[77] What shall we say love is, if not a fire? And sin, if not rust? Therefore, the more the heart burns with increased love, the more the rust of sin is consumed. And what is the pain that is born of love of charity? It is that a person suffers more from harming and injuring God than from any harm or punishment that he suffers. This is the pain that is born of love of charity, which one feels more for God than for oneself or one's possessions. But for sins we have forgotten, it is enough to have a general contrition, forcing oneself to remember them best as possible – also, because somebody might suffer from a forgetfulness that comes from negligence or some other defect.

The second condition is that this pain must be continuous, understood not in terms of real memory with real pain but as habitual displeasure. In other words, every memory of sin is displeasing, and it is never remembered without displeasure, even as it is often very useful to remember and suffer for it, because such pain is a type of satisfaction and always reduces the purgatorial punishment.

We will show through an example how it is useful to remember the sin with pain.

We read in the *Life of the Holy Fathers*[78] that at the time of the emperor Valentinian, there was in Greece a worldly woman who, in her youth, thanks to her dishonourable mother, had wed her body to sin. Her name was Thais, and as she was a very beautiful and famous prostitute, many came to her from various countries, and she was the reason why many lost their soul and their body. The abbot Pannuntius, a highly tested monk of great holiness, upon hearing of this sinner's fame, indeed infamy, felt badly about her damnation and that of those she drew into sin, and he thought about how to remedy such an evil. With great faith in God's grace and protection, he dressed up as a merchant, and he hung a purse full of money at his side. Coming to Thais's city, and soliciting sin from her, he then paid the price she asked for. He entered her room, where there was an expensive and well-made bed, and beckoned by her to the dishonourable act, the holy father asked whether there might be another, more secret place elsewhere in the house. She answered yes, but asked why he was looking for a more secret place, because if he feared the eyes of men, that place was shut

---

77 In his sermons on the Gospel [GA].
78 The *Vitae Patrum* but directly through the *Alphabetum narrationum* [GA].

up and hidden from the people, and if he feared the eyes of God, every place was obvious and open to God. The abbot said: "So, do you believe that God sees everything?" The sinner answered yes, and she believed there was paradise, and the kingdom of heaven where God would take care of the just, and hell where the damned would be tormented. Then St. Pannuntius said: "If you believe this, then why do you sin, for which you will be damned to the punishments of hell, and you are the reason for the loss of many souls, which you will have to explain, as well as endure punishment for their damnation?" At this the sinner, ashamed and tearful, threw herself at the holy abbot's feet, asking him for mercy and repentance. He first ordered her to burn, in the middle of the town square before all the people, everything she had gained by sinning; and it was done at once. Then, once she had made a general confession of all her sins, he shut her up in a little cell, locking it from the outside and sealing it with his ring. He ordered her not to leave there until he, who had shut her up, opened it. And he said: "You are not worthy of speaking God's name, but ask for mercy for your sins." The converted sinner spent three years locked up this way. After three years God revealed to the holy abbot that He had pardoned her for her sins; whereupon, opening the sealed door of the cell, the abbot asked her what she had done in these three years. She answered that she had continuously thought about all her sins, day and night, and as if bundling them up, she set them before her mind's eye and cried with great displeasure, suffering for the harm she had done to God; and then she said in prayer, "*Qui plasmasti me, miserere mei*": while never speaking the name of God, which the holy father had said she was not worthy to say, she said, you who created me, have mercy on me.

Although we can take many lessons from this example, what matters here is that we must often recall our sins and feel pain and contrition for them. The psalmist teaches us about this when he says: *Ecce ego in flagella paratus sum, et dolor meus in conspectu meo semper*:[79] Here I am, always ready to receive discipline and punishment, and my pain is always before me. Note here how a person should always feel pain and contrition when he remembers his sins, or any one of his sins, so that he would sin anew by thinking about his sins, or any single sin, with delight and pleasure. The human mind would fail to endure this continual pain, and could not bear it, if divine goodness did not mitigate and temper this pain with the sweetness and consolation that it gives to the mind that suffers for its sin. It derives pleasure from suffering, and

---

79 Psalms 38:17, the third of the seven penitential psalms.

trust is born in the soul and a certain hope of God's mercy and grace, which comforts and contents the soul. This is what the holy psalmist seems to have meant when he said: *Fuerunt michi lacrimae mee panes die ac nocte* [Ps 32:3]: My tears were bread to me day and night, meaning that he fed on his continuous pain and tears with pleasure, as a man does with bread. He put this more clearly elsewhere: *Cibabis nos pane lacrimarum* [Ps 80:5]: Lord God, you will feed us the bread of tears. St. Gregory says of this[80] that the soul feeds on its crying and its pain. Elsewhere he says:[81] After the rust of sin is purged, a faith is born in the soul, by which it certainly hopes, after the tears and the pain, to receive mercy and pardon, whereupon the soul can take delight and feed.

The third condition which this pain must have is that it be excessive: in other words, it must be very great, so that it can surpass every other pain that one might have or should have for any temporal or corporeal thing. Here's why. As we said above, this pain should come from and be born not of servile fear of torment or pain, but from the love of charity that we have for God. This love, according to the order of charity, should be the greatest love there is, because we should love God more than ourselves or anything of ours. It follows therefore that the pain we feel for hurting God, the love for whom should surpass every other love, must be greater than any other pain. Also, according to the order of charity, next to God we should love our soul more than anything else. As St. James says [Jm 1:15], sin, about which we should feel pain, is the death of the soul, and therefore we should feel greater pain about the death of the soul than about our own death or the death of others, or of the punishment, harm, shame, infamy, or any other evil associated with the body or a corporeal or temporal thing. St. Augustine says:[82] O Christian, have you no awareness? Have you no feeling of piety for yourself? You suffer and cry over the departure of the soul from the body, yet you do not cry over the soul's leave-taking from God. The true death is the one we do not fear, which is the separation of the soul from God, who is the blessed life of souls.

Now, we may ask if this pain of contrition could ever be too great. St. Thomas replies[83] that we can think about the pain in two ways. One is insofar as it is in reason and will, that is, displeasure about sin inasmuch as it is hurtful to God. Understood this way, it cannot be too much, just as the love of charity that we have for God cannot be too

---

80 In the *Moralia in Job* [GA].
81 In the sermons on the Gospel [GA].
82 In his *Sermons* [GA].
83 In the Commentary on the *Book of Sentences* [GA].

great. Indeed, the greater our love of God is and the more it grows, so too grows our displeasure and pain about sin, which has hurt God. Therefore, we said above that the pain is born of love, and the quantity of pain equals the quantity of love. The other way we can consider pain is by how it can be felt, as an afflictive saddening. And this could be too great, like fasting and other corporeal afflictions that we want to experience in such a way and to such an extent that life and salvation are preserved, and the flesh remains subject to the spirit and sensuality to reason. St. Paul showed this when he said: *Rationabile obsequium vestrum* [Rm 12:1]: Let your service be done with reason. It appears that this is what the holy prophet David meant when he said: *Potum dabis nobis in lacrimis in mensuram* [Ps 79:6]: Lord God, give us a drink of tears in equal measure, meaning that this feeling of pain, because of which one becomes wretched and cries, must be felt appropriately and to the correct degree. We could also understand this measure to correspond to the quantity of sins, for however great the sin is, we should feel great pain and displeasure. As St. Gregory explains:[84] the mind drinks as many tears of shame as it knows it has become arid and distanced from God through sin. And although it is said that we should feel the pain and wretchedness in just measure, still, since it is not in our power, like pain is, which is in will and reason, we cannot always measure it our way. So it often happens that someone wants to feel it in order to suffer for and cry over his sins, or to show compassion to his neighbour, or to share the passion of Christ, and he cannot feel it at all. Nevertheless, we can will ourselves to feel sufficient contrition, both loving compassion for our neighbour's suffering and a meritorious feeling and participation in the passion of Christ. Indeed, it often happens that no matter how little we show on the outside, we have all the more within, and however much we show on the outside, inside there is little left. Likewise, we often show more abundant pain and tears than we would like, so we would not criticize ourselves for not having it, or blame ourselves for having too much, were it not for the fact that we call the one or the other a defect or a fault.

To feel too much pain, as I take it, is not to be imputed to a fault, as an example will teach us.

We read in Jacques of Vitry[85] that there was once a young woman who, at the devil's urging, sinned carnally with her father. As the evil

---

84 In the *Regula pastoralis* [GA].

85 The *Alphabetum narrationum* attributes this *exemplum* to Jacques de Vitry (ca. 1160–1240), a canon regular and cardinal best known for his history of the Crusades. See Passavanti, ed. Auzzas, 491.

continued, her mother became aware of it and scolded her daughter about it, and the daughter, offended, poisoned her mother, who died. When her father got the news, he yelled at his daughter and felt contempt for her, and so one night, while her father was sleeping, indignant, she sliced open his veins. Taking from the house everything that was in it, she went to a faraway land and became a public prostitute. It so happened that one day at a festival she heard preaching. Among other things, the preacher spoke of how very great God's mercy is, and that He never rejected any sinner, no matter how evil; indeed, He stood with open arms to receive every sinner who sought repentance. When the preaching was done, the sinner, ashamed and contrite at hearing such words, threw herself tearfully at the friar's feet, asking for mercy and penitence. Once he had heard her confession, she asked him whether God's mercy was as great as he had preached, and when the preacher replied that it was infinitely greater, she said: "Now grant me penitence, for no matter how great a sinner I am, I have faith in God's mercy." The friar who, because of the many evil sins that she had confessed, did not think that he should grant her penitence at once, told her to come back after his second preaching, following the meal. Then the woman said: "I realize that you are despairing of my salvation, so you don't want to impose true penitence on me." "I am not despairing," said the friar, "indeed, I have great faith that God has forgiven you and will accept your good penitence. For the time being, wait and come see me after the second preaching." The woman waited for the confessor in the church, and in the meantime, as she thought about her sins, she felt stricken with so much pain, and so much sadness gripped her heart, so many tears overflowed, that she could not bear it: indeed, her heart burst and she fell dead. Told of what had happened, the confessor commended her with great compassion and grief to the people to whom he was preaching. When everyone was praying for her before she was buried, a voice came from heaven: "You do not need to pray for this woman, because she is in heaven before God, and she can better pray for you." Whereupon all the people gave praise to God, who because of His mercy saves sinners.

Second Chapter

Wherein we show where this word contrition comes from, and what the difference is between contrition and attrition.

The second thing to say about contrition is where this word "contrition" comes from. The doctors say that it comes from *conterere, vel conterendo*, that is, from *tritare*, to mince, as we see in body parts, of which something is said to be minced when it is divided up and broken into tiny parts, so that nothing solid remains of it. So too the sinner's heart, which sin hardens when it is whole and obstinate in evil, when feeling sufficient pain and displeasure about the sin almost breaks and gets minced in such a way that there is no space left for the sinner's desire. This pain is called contrition, to which the prophet Joel leads us, saying, *Scindite corda vestra* [Jl 2:13]: Cut your hearts up in tiny pieces with the knife of pain. The more the heart is broken and chopped up by this pain, the more God accepts it, and the more He solidifies it in order to put the treasure and gift of grace in it. Whereupon the prophet David says: *Cor contritum et humilitatum, Deus, non despicies* [Ps 50:19]: God, do not disdain the contrite and humbled heart. Indeed, He accepts and wants it; saying in His Scripture: *Fili, prebe mihi cor tuum* [Pr 23:26]: Child, give me your heart. Your heart is not yours while there is the desire for sin; indeed, it belongs to the devil, who owns it by means of his malice: and then God disdains it. But when the desire for sin is removed, which is what the pain of contrition does, then you get your heart back, and God accepts and wants it. It is worth noting that not every pain one feels because of sin is contrition, so that the saints say that there is a difference between contrition and attrition. Contrition, as we have said, is the perfect and voluntary pain born of the love of God's charity, and attrition is a lesser, diminished, imperfect pain that comes from servile fear, by which a man fears punishment or the loss of his reward; or else it is born of such tepid and defective love that it is not equal in measure to the seriousness of the sin. The meaning of the two words shows this. As contrition refers to a minute chopping up of all the parts together, done perfectly, with nothing left that is whole and complete, which makes the pain of sin intimate and the displeasure perfect, so attrition refers to a breaking into large pieces that are not perfectly chopped up, which makes the pain and displeasure about sin defective and imperfect. Such an attrition of imperfect pain does not lead to salvation.

We read in Caesarius that there was a well-paid cleric and canon in Paris who, while living a life full of vice and incontinence in the pleasures of the flesh, became seriously ill and asked devoutly for all the sacraments of the Church. Receiving confession and communion with extreme unction, having shown signs of his great contrition with many tears, he died and left this life. A few days later, he appeared before a companion of his in a dark and terrible form, painfully lamenting that he was damned. His friend, greatly aggrieved, asked why he was damned, since although he had been a sinner and lover of worldly things, still he had confessed and received the other sacraments of the Church and shown pain and contrition for his sins. He answered: "Woe is me! I lacked what I needed most, and without which nothing else has any value, that is, contrition of the heart, for although I cried and showed pain for my sins in my mortal sickness and when I confessed, that was neither true pain nor true tears. I was not crying because I had hurt God by sinning, nor did I feel the pain of contrition out of charity or love that I felt for God our saviour, nor did I have a firm intention, were I to survive, to stop sinning once and for all. Instead, I was crying out of fear of the punishments of hell, and I was pained that by dying I had to leave the things of the world that I had loved so much." Having said this, he disappeared with anguished lament.

Third Chapter

***Wherein we show what and how many things there are
that lead us to contrition.***

The third thing we have to say about contrition is what it is and how many things there are that lead us to it: and the doctors say there are six.[86]

The first is rethinking one's sins, of which the prophet Isaiah, speaking to God, said: *Recogitabo tibi omnes annos meos, in amaritudine animae mee* [Is 38:15]: I will think, and set before you, all my years, in the bitterness of my soul, that is, with bitter pain. The example written above about that most famous prostitute Thais leads us to this, as does the one about the woman whose heart burst from pain, and also the one about the knight who had denied Christ and his faith, although he did not want to deny the Virgin Mary.

The second thing, after thinking over one's sins, is shame. Solomon says in Proverbs: *Putredo in ossibus eius, que confusione res dignas gerit* [Pr 12:4]: May the bones of that person shatter who does things worthy of confusion and shame. The shattering of the bones signifies intimate pain, which softens the hardness of the feelings of sin, about which a man should feel shame and confusion. The prophet Habakkuk said: *Ingrediatur putredo in ossibus meis* [Hk 3:16]: May my bones shatter, i.e., the desires of the heart, if they are not harder and more solid against

---

86 Auzzas (Passavanti, 492) cites the *Summa* of Raymond of Penyafort, a thirteenth-century Dominican who compiled the *Decretals* of Gregory IX. He is today the patron saint of canon lawyers.

sin, so that I do not have to feel shame about them. The example given above about the monk who, when led to judgment before God, felt so much shame about his mother's scolding speaks to this.

The third thing that leads the soul to contrition is the baseness of the sin, which makes a man abominable and vile. The holy prophet Jeremiah spoke about this baseness and said to the sinning soul: *Quam vilis facta es iterans vias tuas!* [Jr 2:36]: Oh, how you have become vile, starting over every day! And the psalmist says of the sinners: *Corrupti sunt et abominabiles facti sunt in studiis suis* [Ps 13:1]: They are corrupt and made abominable in their studies, i.e., in their evil deeds, which they do studiously.

The fourth thing is the fear of God's judgment and of eternal punishment. St. Peter speaks of this and says: *Impius et peccator ubi parebunt?* [1 Pt 4:18]: On the day of judgment, the impious man and the sinner, where will they appear? (Almost as if to say: there will be no place for them to look good in the presence of the wrathful judge.) And how will they be able to endure the intolerable and eternal punishments of hell?

We read[87] that in the kingdom of France there was a nobleman who ate very delicate foods and was a lover of the world's vanities. One day he began to think about whether the damned in hell might be freed after 1,000 years, and he said not. Then he thought: or after 100,000 years? And he replied, never. Then he thought about whether their liberation would be possible after 1,000,000 years, and he said no. After so many thousands of years, as many as there are drops of water in the sea, could it be that they would come back out? And he replied to himself, never ever. Troubled and frightened by such a thought, the pain and tears of contrition overcame him, and abandoning the emptiness of the world and sin he said: "How foolish and miserable are worldly men, who for whatever small pleasure they want in the world go to punishment without end!"

The fifth thing that leads to contrition is the pain that one should feel for having lost the celestial city of paradise because of sin, and the pain of hurting God, whom we should obey because He is our Creator. We should revere Him as our celestial father and love Him as our redeemer and saviour who redeemed us with His precious blood, as St. Peter says [1 Pt 1:18–19]. And St. John in the Apocalypse: *Dilexit nos et lavit nos a peccatis nostris in sanguine suo* [Rv 1:5]: Jesus Christ loved us, and he washed our sins in his blood. It must lead to much pain and displeasure

---

87 The tale appears in Jacques de Vitry's *Exempla*, likely known to Passavanti through the *Alphabetum narrationum* (Passavanti, ed. Auzzas, 492).

about sin to consider that the soul is washed and purified in the blood of Jesus Christ, and that others have dirtied and muddied it in the filth of sin.

The sixth thing that leads us to contrition is the hope of forgiveness for sins, and of grace, by which we can function well, and the hope of glory, to which God finally will lead us. As the psalmist says: *Gratiam et gloriam dabit Dominus* [Ps 83:12]: God will give His grace and glory.

Above all the other things that are valuable for perfect and sufficient contrition is devout and fervent prayer, through which God gives the soul the gift of contrition. Since it cannot be perfect without God's grace and charity, a man cannot obtain this by himself without a special gift of grace, which faithful prayer makes possible. Anyone who desires such grace should therefore pray; otherwise there is no salvation. He should live so that his prayer is worthy of being answered, always begging God to let him live well and pray worthily.

Fourth Chapter

Wherein we show the effect of contrition.

The fourth main thing to say about contrition is what effect it has. The saints say it is through contrition that a man reconciles himself to God, whom he hurt by sinning, and he is purged of the stain of guilt, which his soul contracted through sin. Contrition does this both because it is an act of virtue, as we said above, and because it is part of the sacrament of penitence. The pain of contrition, and the love of God's charity, from which said pain proceeds in the mind and the heart, could be so great as to remove not only guilt, which is its principal effect, but also the punishment due for sin. Nevertheless, confession and satisfaction are required, completing the penitence as ordered or taken, both because of the command of the Church and because of uncertainty. For no man is certain, about himself or anyone else, of having sufficient contrition to cancel all punishment for his crimes: in other words, all the punishment to which one is obligated because of his sins. True and perfect contrition must therefore be accompanied by the intention to make confession and satisfaction, when possible. So if someone had the opportunity to confess and make the required penitence and did not want to do so, no matter how sufficient and perfect his contrition was at first, his sin would not be pardoned, with regard to both guilt and punishment. Even if, once pardoned in contrition, the sin did not return, still he would acquire a new mortal sin which would send him to damnation: that of not obeying the Church's commandment, and not keeping the sacrament of penitence whole, but of having diminished and reduced it. As St. Ambrose says:[88] No one can truly be set right from sin if he does not first confess. St. Jerome, speaking of true penitence, says:[89] Let the sinner cry for his own sins; that is contrition. He continues: Let him enter the Church, which he had left because of his sins; entering the Church signifies confession, by which others are represented, on order of the Church, to the one who is the vicar of Christ in the Church. He then adds: Let him sleep in sackcloth and ashes, hoping for an austere life, so that he may compensate for his past pleasures with which he hurt God; and this is what satisfaction means. St. Augustine spoke with this understanding and said:[90] Repent, as is done in the Holy Church. No one should say: I do it in secret in my heart, and God sees me and pardons me for my sin. That is not enough, he says. What would Christ's word to the apostles have meant: What you undo on earth will be undone in heaven? For what purpose were the keys given to St. Peter? Almost as if to say, uselessly, if something other than contrition of the heart were required for true penitence. But confession and satisfaction are required, by which true and perfect penitence are accomplished, and the use of the keys and the apostolic authority of the Holy Church for that purpose. This is what Jesus Christ meant when he brought Lazarus back to life. Alive thanks to Christ's voice, he came out of the tomb, where he had lain dead, but he came out with his hands and feet tied, and with his face covered with a handkerchief. Jesus ordered the apostles to untie him and let him go, meaning that God is the one who, by His infinite power and measureless virtue, which no creature has or can have, brings back to life the sinner who lies dead and buried in the tomb of his stinking and bothersome heart: in other words, in the tomb of his hardened and obstinate behaviour. God does this in the secret place of his heart, giving the grace of painful contrition. This is what it means to resuscitate Lazarus in his tomb; but to come out of it alive but tied up means that even though the sinner is set right and brought back to life before God through contrition, still he remains bound and obligated to the external judgment of the Holy Church. The apostolic hand, i.e., the authority of the prelates of the Holy Church who stand in for the apostles, has loosened this knot; and they use this authority in the judgment of confession, absolving sinners who humbly and truly confess their sins by virtue of the keys that were

---

88   In *De Paradiso* [GA].
89   In his commentary on Joel [GA].
90   In his *Sermons* [GA].

given, and at their discretion they impose certain acts of satisfaction, as the confession of the sins and of the sinners requires. This is Lazarus being untied by the hand of the apostles and being set free, according to Christ's command to them: *Solvite eum et sinite abire* [Jn 11:44]: Untie him and let him go. Having said this both literally and figuratively, he said it again to those same men spiritually and truly, giving them ordinary jurisdiction and power, when he said: *Quaecumque solveritis super terram, erunt soluta et in celis* [Mt 18:18]: Everything that you untie on earth will be untied in heaven. But if it so happens that a truly contrite person could neither confess nor satisfy, as he had set his heart to when God gave him the grace of contrition, either because of sudden death or because he did not have a confessor, or because of some other legitimate impediment, then contrition alone would be enough to set him right and save him. As said above, it might suffice to remove the sin completely as far as both guilt and punishment are concerned, so that whoever dies in that state would fly off to eternal life without any impediment. Or if it were not enough to remove everything, it would send the soul to purgatory in order to satisfy whatever was lacking for sufficient satisfaction.

This is shown by the example, given above, of the sinning woman who, instead of receiving penitence from the friar, because of the great pain of contrition that she had, had her heart broken instead. We also read in Caesarius that there was a scholar in Paris who, because of his obscene and grave sins, was ashamed of coming to confession, even though he was in great pain. One time, when the pain overcame the shame, he went to confess to the prior of the monastery of St. Victor. Sitting at the priest's feet, so great was the pain of contrition in his heart, so many sighs in his chest, so many sobs in his throat, so many tears abounded in his eyes, that he lost his voice and could not form any words with which to confess his sins. Seeing this, the confessor told him to go and write down all his sins. Having done that, and wanting to try again to confess by mouth by reading out loud, he was similarly impeded as before. Whereupon the prior said: "Give me your paper." Having received it and reading the great and unspeakable sins, and not knowing himself what penitence to assign, he asked the scholar's permission to talk it over with his abbot, who was a well-read man. Having received permission, he asked the abbot's advice, and he handed him the paper whereupon all the sins of that contrite sinner were written. Unfolding it, the abbot found that the paper was blank, without any writing whatsoever. He said to the prior: "What am I supposed to read, since not a word is written on this paper that you have given me?" Seeing it, the prior said: "Truly, Father, all of that scholar's sins were written on this paper, and I read them; but as far as I can tell merciful God wanted to show the virtue of contrition, and how He has accepted that young man's contrition, and therefore He has dismissed and forgiven all of his sins." And both the abbot and the prior told the scholar what had happened, and he, happy about the pardon, thanked divine mercy.

It is shown to be true that contrition alone is enough where we cannot have confession and satisfaction, while nevertheless having the intention to confess and satisfy, in those words of the holy prophet David, who said in the psalm: *Dixi: confitebor adversum me injustitiam meam Domino, et tu remisisti impietatem peccati mei.*[91] Cassiodorus explains this: *Dixi*, which means: I proposed to myself and decided; *confitebor adversum me*: to confess against myself; *iniustitias meas*: my injustices, that is, my sins, which I unjustly committed, or which, by committing them, made me unjust; *Domino*, to God; because what we confess to a priest we confess to God: or directly to God when we cannot have a confessor. And he continues: *et tu remisisti impietatem peccati mei*: And you, Lord God, forgave the impiety of my sin. Great is God's pity, for He pardons sins on the promise alone, and receives the will as He would the deed. St. Augustine, explaining the above statement, says:[92] Even when he does not confess the sin out loud, but promises to confess it, God forgives him; because the heart's declaration is an open confession before God, who sees the heart. It is not through a voice coming from the mouth that a man can hear confession, and God hears from the intention of the heart. This is what the prophet appeared to mean when he said, speaking for God [Ez 33:15–16]: Whenever the sinner converts and cries, I will no longer remember any of his sins. In other words, He will not remember to punish him, because He has already forgiven him. He did not say, whenever the sinner confesses by mouth, but when he converts with his heart and cries with the pain of contrition, meaning that even when the mouth is silent, the guilt is forgiven because of contrition and because of the heart's intention. This is what was meant in the Holy Gospel [Lk 17] about those ten lepers who ask Jesus Christ to be cured, and he tells them to go before the priests, who stood in for our priests; and along the way, before they reached the priests, they found that they were cured and healthy. Which shows that before we appear before the priests and open our mouths for confession, to show them the leprosy of sin through contrition, with the intention of confessing,

---

91 Psalms 31:6. This is the second of the seven penitential psalms. The gloss appears in Peter Lombard's *Sententiae* (Passavanti, ed. Auzzas, 493).
92 In his commentary on Psalm 31 [GA].

which is still to come, we are cleansed and cured of sin, as was said above. Likewise, what happened to Lazarus, as explained above, means that before the sinner is brought back by God from the death of sin to the life of grace in the secret of the conscience – which is done in the contrition of the heart – may the apostolic hand untie it (which is done in the absolution of sacramental confession by mouth); the ministers of the Church, who stand in for the apostles, make use of the virtue of the keys they have been given.

Fifth Distinction.

Wherein we deal with the second part of penitence, namely confession.

Following our order, we now come to the second main part of penitence, which is confession. It is necessary to write about it diligently and in an orderly manner, because the principal intention of those at whose request the author undertook to write this book was to learn how to confess well. In general people do this poorly, because they are impeded either by ignorance or negligence or shame or by a certain malice. Ignorance does not let them know and recognize their sins and their reasons, and their types and differences, or their circumstances, or to discern their gravity, and therefore they don't know how to confess them according to the type of sin. Negligence often keeps them from pondering their sins, from feeling pain and regret about them, and from recalling them in order to recount them discretely and completely. They delay confession out of fear of having to trouble themselves with the work of penitence that confession imposes, and out of fear of not being able to persevere in doing well. It feels hard to abstain from the delights and pleasures of the flesh, which they pursue in line with their concupiscence, and to stop doing what they are used to doing according to their own judgment and the appetite of their own will. Shame keeps them from daring to name their unspeakable and abominable and dishonourable sins, for which they believe they deserve dishonour, vituperation, and blame. Because they arrogantly want to be deemed good and seem good, but not be good, they keep silent out of shame about what they corruptly and shamelessly do, which they could usefully show with fruitful shame. Malice keeps them stubborn and perversely wilful, and because of a vicious and corrupt disposition to evil, they neither suffer not repent, and they do not take it to heart to behave themselves from then on. Indeed, given the disorder of their sinful desires, they want the chance to fulfil their evil intentions, and therefore they do not take the medicine of confession. Thus, I shall say everything regarding confession that God will grant us, usefully and fruitfully teaching and instructing those who faithfully and devoutly read this book how to make a good confession. I shall do this so that they cannot make excuses by claiming ignorance, which only makes matters worse, and so that they will not be filled with negligence but instead be driven with studious solicitude, and so that shame does not deter them out of cowardice of spirit, but instead sure readiness with the hope of pardon drives them forward, and the obstinate malice that hardens them in sin does not keep them in vice. I shall speak principally of seven things: first, what is confession; second, when and by whom confession was ordained; third, what is its effect and usefulness; fourth, who and what the confessor who hears the confession should be; fifth, how the sinner who goes to confess should arrange and compose himself; sixth, how you should make confession and how many things are required for it to be done well; seventh, what the confession should consist of, that is, what sins you should confess. Once these seven things are set forth in an orderly manner, what must be said about confession will be sufficiently addressed.

First Chapter

Wherein we show what confession is.

It is first necessary to say what confession is. St. Thomas says, and St. Augustine adds:[93] *Confessio est per quam morbus latens, spe venie, aperitur*: Confession is speech through which the hidden sickness of sin is revealed with the hope of pardon. Or, according to the teachers:[94] *Confessio est legitima coram sacerdote peccati declaratio*: Confession is a legitimate declaration of sin before a priest, with the hope of pardon. They really are saying the same thing and include everything required to perform a good and legitimate confession. As St. Thomas says, the act of confession takes place by and large in speaking, which is revealing through speech what was hidden. This tells us that, as the other sacraments have a special and specific material, like water for baptism and oil for extreme unction, so too does confession, as part of the sacrament of penitence, have a specific act, which is the language and speech by which the sin is made manifest. So, when you can speak for yourself,

---

93 The source is Pseudo-Augustine, *Speculum virginum* (Passavanti, ed. Auzzas, 494).
94 Here, Aquinas, *Scriptum super IV libros Sententiarum* (Passavanti, ed. Auzzas, 494).

it is not enough to confess in writing or through signs or through an interpreter. That would be enough if someone were a mute and did not have language or was impeded in some way, so that he could not make his sins manifest with his own tongue.

What can we say about those who do not state their sin on their own but ask the confessor to ask them, and answer yes or no? According to the wise men, it would be a better and more legitimate confession if one were to state one's sins himself without being asked. Still, if contrition and the other things required for confession, which we will discuss later,[95] are there, it is enough for the sinner to answer the confessor's questions. However, if the confessant, before he might be led to state the sin himself, leaves the confession, it would not suffice just to be asked and to answer. Later on, where it will fit better, we will say what and how the confessor should ask. That a person should state his sin himself, God says through the prophet Isaiah: *Dic tu iniquitates tuas, ut iustificeris* [Is 43:26]: Speak your iniquities and your sins, so that you might be set right. He does not say, let the confessor or someone else speak for you, unless you cannot or do not know how, as happens to many people, and especially women, who get lost or fall short out of shame or fear, forgetting the sins they had first thought to say. When that happens, the confessor must reassure sinners and help them, reminding them of the sins he believes might have hurt God, while still discreetly asking, as the confessor will be taught in due time, along with the other rules he should follow.

St. Augustine's definition of confession includes what confession should do, inasmuch as it speaks of *morbus latens*, the "hidden sickness," namely sin, which is called a sickness of the soul, which the holy prophet David asked to be cured of when he said: *Miserere mei, Domine, quoniam infirmus sum, sana me, Domine*:[96] Lord God, have mercy on me; because I am sick, heal me. It says that the sickness is hidden because although sometimes the work of sin is visible, the evil will, which is the root of and reason for sin, is hidden. Therefore, no matter how evident the sin may be, we still want to confess it privately to the confessor priest, as to a judge, both because the bad will is hidden and because as a man he knows the sin which is evident, and that must be stated to him, as God's vicar and judge set above the sinners. Therefore, Augustine gave the second definition above, *coram sacerdote* (it should be made to a priest), because when they are ordained, priests receive the power and authority to hear the confessions of sins, to absolve of guilt,

---

95 See pp. 45ff.
96 Psalms 6:3. This is the first of the seven penitential psalms.

and to prescribe a certain punishment, as we will detail later. The confession must be legitimate, that is, done in a lawful and orderly manner; because not every priest can absolve every sinner, nor of every sin. We will say what the Holy Church allows in due order over the course of the treatise.[97] The given definition also contained the reason for and effect of confession, as it said *cum spe venie*, that one who confesses should have hope of pardon, for without hope, which should move the sinner to confess, one would not have pardon, which is the effect and fruit of confession.

We will say elsewhere how the priest pardons sin, and how far the virtue of the given keys extends.[98] Here it is enough to tread lightly, suggesting what confession is by explaining its definition, which is the first thing that we proposed to say about confession.

Second Chapter

Wherein we show by whom and when confession was ordained, and that there are several ways to confess a sin.

The second thing to say about confession is by whom and when it was ordained. Here you need to know that the sinner can confess his sin in four ways. The first way is to confess it in his heart to God, and to admit his error in having hurt Him, and ask Him for forgiveness and mercy, as the prophet Isaiah says: *Recogitabo tibi omnes annos meos in amaritudine anime mee* [Is 38:15]: I will rethink before you all my years in the bitterness of my soul. And St. David: *Tibi dixit cor meum* [Ps 26:8]: To you, God, my heart spoke. More explicitly elsewhere it is explained: *Dixi:confitebor adversum me iniustitiam meam Domino* [Ps 31:6]: I will confess to God, accusing myself of the injustice of my sin. This confession is and was always necessary, and without it we cannot have salvation, for law and natural reason command it. Even in the time of the law of nature, before the written law was given to Moses, it was necessary to make this mental confession to God, recognizing one's own sins and regretting them, just as now it is also necessary and done in contrition. Its necessity during the time of the law of nature is shown by the fact that Adam and Cain, who were not subject to another law, are scolded for not confessing their sins.

The second way of confessing sin is in judgment, when someone accused of some excess, or by another judicial means according to the

---

97 See pp. 100ff.
98 See p. 102.

order of reason, appears before a legitimate judge and, when questioned and examined by him, confesses the truth, notwithstanding his fear of any punishment or harm. Otherwise, by lying to the judge, denying or excusing the sin committed, he sins mortally, even as the sin is already so hidden that it is not the judge's job to look for it.

The third way of confessing sin was what was done under the old law of Moses, where that mental recognition before God, as was done in the law of nature, was not enough. Instead, it was necessary, by God's commandment, to confess one's sin by some external sign, indicating that someone was a sinner. This was done through sacrifice and through the offer of the host for the sin, which was a specific sacrifice according to the law, and someone who had sinned was supposed to do it; and sometimes it was done on behalf of the whole people, and other times for individuals.[99] Thus the priests who received the offering and made the sacrifice understood that those who asked for it, and who brought the offering, were in sin. Not only could the ministers of the temple see that, but everyone, by hearing or by seeing, knew that such a sacrifice was being made for such people. They did not, however, have to confess their sins or their circumstances individually, as we must do today under the new law of Jesus Christ.

The fourth way by which sin is confessed, which we mainly have to talk about, is when the sinner, recognizing his sin, submits to the ministry of the Church, i.e., to the priest, who has to dispense the sacrament of penitence, through which remission for sins is given by virtue of Christ's passion, from which all sacraments draw their efficacy. The sinner does this by humbling himself before the priest and confessing his sin shamefully and completely. Through this confession, done secretly and sacramentally, the priest, as judge, recognizes and discerns all the sins, which should all be stated individually so that the priest can judge them and, by imposing the punishment that will satisfy them, can absolve the sinner once he has confessed his offences with his own mouth. It was not necessary to practise this type of confession under the law of nature, nor under the written law of Moses. However, those practices were an allegory[100] and signifier of our confession, which is done now in the time of grace, as the most perfect thing. Our saviour Jesus Christ ordained it, along with the other sacraments, which are remedies and medicines for the infirmity of sin. He appeared to do this

---

99 For details on this practice see Leviticus 4–5.

100 Passavanti here applies the common practice of figural allegory to pre-Christian texts, particularly the Old Testament, seeing in it a prefiguration of what is fully realized in the New Testament.

when he said to the apostles: *Accipite Spiritum Sanctum, quorum remiseritis peccata, remictuntur eis* [Jn 20:22–3]: Accept the Holy Spirit, by virtue of which the sins of those whom you will pardon will be pardoned. Similarly, when he gave the keys to St. Peter, he said: *Tibi dabo claves Regni Coelorum: et quodcumque ligaveris super terram, erit ligatum et in celis: et quocumque solveris super terram, erit solutum et in celis* [Mt 16:19]: I will give you the keys of the kingdom of heaven, which represent ecclesiastical power and jurisdiction, by which what you commit to on earth will be committed to in heaven, and what you fulfil on earth will be fulfilled in heaven. In other words, it will be approved, if the keys do not err. After Jesus Christ rose to heaven and sent the Holy Spirit, who confirmed the apostles in grace and reaffirmed all authority and power that Christ had given them, so that they would be legitimate promoters of Christ's law, they gave the commandment of confession and had it obeyed in the primitive Church. It spread from there to the Holy Church of Rome, which commands every faithful Christian to confess sacramentally if he wants to be saved, as the apostles ordained, and they had it published by St. James, who says in his epistle: *Confitemini alterutrum peccata vestra et orate pro invicem, ut salvemini* [Jm 5:16]: Confess your sins together and pray for one another, that you may be saved. Here we see that confession is necessary for salvation either in action – i.e., when a man in fact confesses – or in vow – i.e., by intention – if he has the opportunity and ability to confess. St. Ambrose says no one can truly be set right if he does not first confess his sins.[101] Then the Holy Church, and the general councils of the Holy Fathers and pastors of the faithful, taught and instructed by the Holy Spirit, which governs and rules the Holy Church and does not allow error in those matters regarding the substance of faith, ordained how confession should be done, the time and the manner and the minister, requiring confession at least once a year. It is a deadly sin to violate that rule, because a commandment of the Church imposes an obligation like a commandment from God, who said to the pastors of the Holy Church: *Qui vos audit me audit: et qui vos spernit me spernit* [Lk 10:16]: He who listens to you listens to me, and he who disdains you disdains me.

There is another way of confessing sins beyond those given above, i.e., by general confession, which the priest does when he starts the mass and the preacher when he has completed his preaching: the value of which, and which sins are pardoned through it, we will explain later in the proper place.[102]

____

101 In *De paradiso* [GA].
102 See p. 149.

Third Chapter

Wherein we show what the benefit and effect of confession are.

The third thing to say about confession is what its benefit and effect are. St. Ambrose says:[103] *Confessio a morte animam liberat: confessio aperit paradisum: confessio spem salutis tribuit: quia non meretur iustificari, qui in vita sua peccata non vult confiteri*: Confession frees the soul from death, confession opens paradise: confession gives hope for salvation: and he who does not confess his sin during his life does not deserve to be set right. With these words, St. Ambrose shows that there are three effects of confession. First, it frees the soul from death, in other words, death from sinning. Confession does this, as St. Thomas says, through penitence, which being a special sacrament has its perfection in confession, because through confession a man submits to the ministers of the Church, who are dispensers of the sacraments. Also, confession must include a vow of contrition, i.e., an intention, otherwise it would not be valid. Satisfaction similarly is levied and imposed in the judgment of the priest to whom one makes confession, so that penitence, as far as all its parts are concerned, receives completion and perfection in confession. Through the sacrament of penitence God infuses the soul with grace, giving remission for sins, which kept the soul dead, and through grace, with death opened up, life is given to the soul. Whereupon it follows that through confession and absolution death is removed from the soul and life restored to it.

Some might now wonder, since, as we said above, the guilt and death of sin are removed through contrition and the life of grace is given (as shown in the figure of the resuscitated Lazarus before he emerged from the tomb and was untied by the apostles): How can we say now that life is given to the soul and death is removed through confession? If the life of grace is first given in contrition, how is it then given in confession? We answer that for grace, through which sin is removed, to be given in contrition, there must be confession either in act or at least in vow, i.e., in intention; otherwise contrition would not be valid or sufficient for grace. Therefore, it is true that through confession the soul is freed from death and restored to a life of grace. Also, if contrition were not sufficient before confession, one is often granted in confession the grace necessary to have sufficient contrition. But if someone has sufficient contrition by intending to confess, before confessing he is surely freed from the death of sin, and the life of grace is rendered unto him.

---

103 In his sermons [GA].

Then, as he has been set right in this way through grace, let him confess. What is the effect of such a confession? St. Thomas replies[104] that grace, first acquired through contrition, grows in the soul by means of confession because of the humble obedience shown to the Holy Church, and by virtue of the keys that the Church's minister, i.e., the priest, uses in absolution. Thus, remission of sins would take place, if not at first in defective contrition, if there were sufficient pain of contrition in the act of confession, or after confession.

The virtue of confession frees the soul not only from the death of sin but also from bodily death.

We read in Caesarius that in the city of Arras, in the kingdom of France, there was a young man who was a poor clerk, and who because of his poverty often did bad and obscene things. One time he went to a goldsmith he knew, and he said that he wanted to share his wealth with him and nobody else. He said that a rich merchant had come to his house seeking to buy a great quantity of gold and silver dishes, and that the goldsmith should come with him and bring some along for him to see. The goldsmith, looking to make money, took many dishes, then told his family that he was taking the merchandise to the clerk's house, and off he went. Arriving at the house, no sooner did he step inside than the clerk killed him. Hiding all the dishes, he called a sister of his to help him, and having dismembered the murdered goldsmith they threw his body into the latrine. When he was late in returning, the goldsmith's family, who knew where he had gone, came to the clerk's house asking after him. As the clerk denied that he had been there, the goldsmith's family became suspicious, and they went to the police, who, coming to the clerk's house, arrested him and his sister. When they could not deny that they had committed the evil act, they were both sentenced to burn for homicide and theft. Then the sister said: "My brother, this is happening to me because of you, but since we cannot escape bodily death, let's at least try to avoid the death of our souls. Let's confess our sins, and God will have mercy on us." The clerk did not want to confess and dug in, but his sister confessed all her sins with much contrition. Set afire and tied together to the same post,[105] the desperate clerk burst into flames and burned up, while the woman left the fire safe and sound, and only the ropes by which she was tied to

---

104 In the *Scriptum super IV libros Sententiarum* (Passavanti, ed. Auzzas, 495).

105 Note here Passavanti's use of *hysteron proteron*, the inversion of the sequence of events, which by its seeming illogic draws attention to the central feature of this *exemplum*.

the post were burned. Out of reverence for the miracle of her life being given back to her, she behaved in a holy way from then on.

The second effect of confession is that it opens our way to paradise. St. Thomas explains this,[106] for although paradise opened by virtue of Christ's passion (as Christ said to the thief on the cross: "Today you shall be with me in paradise" [Lk 23:43], and so it came to be; and St. John the Evangelist, as he says in the Apocalypse, saw the open door in heaven [Rv 4:1]), still it closes because of original sin and because of present and deadly sin. The virtue of Christ's passion, which first opened it, is used to reopen it. This virtue is located in the sacraments, all of which draw their efficacy from the passion itself. Baptism is said to open the door of paradise in the face of original sin, and in the face of present sin, for whoever might have it. Penitence opens it against present sin, so that, since confession with absolution, as was said above, especially contains the virtue of penitence, which removes present sin, which shuts off paradise to us, it follows that confession opens the door of paradise.

The third effect of confession is that it gives hope for salvation and remission of sins. St. Thomas says[107] that since all hope for our salvation and for remission of sins is from Christ and through Christ, and that by confessing a person submits to the keys of the Church, which have virtue and efficacy because of Christ's passion, therefore confession gives hope for salvation, not only because it is a meritorious act but also because it is a sacrament, or one of the parts of penitence, which is a sacrament.

How confession has this virtue of pardoning sins and opening heaven is told in one example among many.

Legend tells us[108] that there was a woman who while confessing often left out just one sin, through either shame or forgetfulness. While promising to confess it whenever she could and still putting it off, she fell deathly ill, and while confessing her other sins she still did not confess that one, and so she died. While her body was still in the church, during the mass her soul returned to it, and opening her eyes she made a signal to one of the priests who was nearby, and when he approached the casket, she said she wanted to confess. The people in the church, both clerics and laypeople, watched and awaited the outcome, atremble with wonder, while the woman confessed and said to the priest: "I truly did die, and was put in a dark and harsh prison, and was told not

---

106 In the *Scriptum super IV libros Sententiarum* (Passavanti, ed. Auzzas, 495).

107 In the *Scriptum super IV libros Sententiarum* (Passavanti, ed. Auzzas, 495).

108 The *exemplum* appears in the *Alphabetum narrationum* (Passavanti, ed. Auzzas, 495).

to hope for salvation or to go to heaven, because I had not made a complete confession of my sins. But because St. Francis, to whom I had been devoted, prayed for me and said that my omitting that one sin alone had come from simple-mindedness rather than malice, the grace was granted to him that I might return to my body and confess the sin I had omitted, which I now confess to God and to you, Father. Once I receive absolution, my soul will leave my body, and in hope of salvation and of going quickly to paradise, it will go to purgatory." Thus it happened: once she had received absolution from the priest and said *amen*, the woman put her head down and died. They continued with the mass and entombed the body, and her soul went on to salvation.

Beyond the three effects of confession set forth by St. Ambrose and explained by St. Thomas, St. Thomas[109] says that confession has another main effect, namely, it frees a man from the punishment due him because of sin, or it lessens it. Confession is understood, together with absolution, in two ways. First, as a confession not yet made but still held as a vow, that is, in intention, by a contrite person. As it removes the stain of guilt, so too does it remove the offence, that is, the obligation of eternal punishment, to which a man is subject because of deadly sin. But he remains obligated to temporal punishment, which, like a purgative medicine, he must endure in purgatory. Now, punishment in purgatory is not proportional to the strength of the living person, because a living person could not endure punishment in purgatory, which, according to St. Augustine,[110] surpasses every punishment that one might endure in this life. So divine mercy has found a way for the minister, i.e., the priest who holds the keys of the Holy Church, to mitigate and temper that punishment, making it proportionate to the strength of the living person, who can thus be purged and satisfied of all that punishment that he was supposed to suffer in purgatory by enduring those painful works that the priest imposes in confession, absolving him. The other way that confession diminishes and reduces punishment is through blushing, that is, through the shame that one feels confessing one's own sin, which is painful, especially for many shameful people who would want to suffer any other punishment than shame. That painful shame and shameful pain take the place of satisfaction, like the other painful deeds of penitence. The saints say that it is useful to confess a sin many times and to many confessors, because by renewing the shame and punishment the debt of punishment is reduced. The punishment of the pain of contrition and the punishment of shame, voluntarily endured

---

109 Passavanti continues to draw here from the *Scriptum super IV libros Sententiarum* (Passavanti, ed. Auzzas, 495).

110 In his commentary on Psalm 37.

out of love of justice and charity, could be so great that there would be no punishment left to suffer in purgatory for one's sins. God explains through a few comprehensible examples how confession takes away and reduces the punishment.

We read in Caesarius that in the French city of Arras certain heretics were arrested by the inquisitor and, fearing death, they denied their heresy. Being highly suspect of error, they were put to the judgment of the hot iron, as was customary in that place, and because they were evil heretics, the burning iron burned all their hands, so they were all sentenced to burn. One young man among them, of refined blood, was urged by a cleric to abandon his heresy. When he answered that he knew very well that he had erred but that it was too late for penitence, the cleric said true penitence was never late. The priest therefore was called, and the young man began to confess. As he began to recount his sins, the burning decreased, and as the confession continued, so too did the pain, little by little, and the black colour of the fire disappeared. Having completed his confession and received absolution, all the pain and the burning and every sign of fire left his hands, as if he had never touched fire. Appearing before the judge, he, as a faithful Christian, was freed, whereas all the others had been sent to the fire.

At the proper time, we will speak about how useful it is to confess the same sin more than once, and how it should be done, if it is sometimes necessary to confess the same sin several times.

Another effect of confession is that the sin made manifest in confession is covered, hidden, and forgotten first of all by God, who does not see it, and it is said that the sin is hidden and forgotten by God, who does not see it and does not remember to punish it. As God says through the prophet [Ez 18:21–2]: If the sinner will convert and leave his sins, I will not remember all his sins. Likewise the psalmist: *Beati, quorum remisse sunt iniquitates et quorum tecta sunt peccata* [Ps 31:1]: Blessed are those whose evil deeds are forgiven, and their sins are covered and hidden. The confessed sins are also hidden from the devil, who cannot accuse someone of them later; for, as many examples prove, the devil shows that he writes down a man's sins as he sees them when they are done, and he keeps them in mind and reminds him about them at the time of his death, when he faces God's judgment. He cannot do this with confessed sins, which are hidden, and he forgets about them. We find one example of this among many.

We read in the legend of St. Constance,[111] archbishop of Canterbury, that as he was saying mass a young monk who had sung the Gospel

---

111 The source of this tale appears to be the *Alphabetum narrationum*. Auzzas
    (Passavanti, 496) relates that the tale is associated with St. Dunstan of Canterbury.

in that mass, perhaps with deadly sin, was seized by the devil. Among other things, the devil said that unless the monk confessed his sins, he would expose them, while openly scolding others, despite their having been committed in secret. Many, fearing shame, confessed before they came before him, and some who had been shamed by him, not having confessed, confessed. How great is the virtue of confession! To those who had confessed he first said nothing, and those whom he had first shamed for not having confessed, he did not acknowledge when they returned after confessing. Instead, he said: "To them I say nothing other than: bravery and honour."

We must understand what was said about the virtue of confession, that the confession is made legitimately, as it should be, with contrition and the intention of not committing the sin again, because otherwise it is not valid. And here is a beautiful example of that.

We read that in Bramante, according to Caesarius, there was a bedevilled person who scolded everyone he saw for sins committed but not confessed. One man wanted to see and hear him but feared being scolded for his sins, so before he came before him, he went and confessed all his sins, though he felt no contrition, nor would he set his heart to abandoning them. Having thus confessed, he appeared before the bedevilled one, who, seeing him from afar, cried out: "Welcome, my friend! You certainly are well washed and laundered." And he began to say terrible things to him and scold him for many of his sins, about which the man felt great shame and confusion. Feeling wretched and pained, he left and went to his own confessor, telling him what had happened, and when the priest asked him what the reason might be, he found out that the confession had not been valid. On the confessor's advice, having confessed all his sins again with pain and contrition, he returned to the bedevilled man, who said nothing to him. One of those who were around the possessed man said, "Here is your friend, to whom you earlier said so many terrible things with so much scolding," and he answered: "I never said anything to him, nor do I know anything but good things about him." Because of this, those who were listening to him, and who had heard him earlier, judged that the devil had lied when he spoke before. And so, through confession, the man who at first had been vituperated recovered his good name.

Fourth Chapter

Wherein we are given to understand who the confessor should be who hears the confession.

The fourth thing to say about confession has to do with the confessor who should hear it. Properly speaking, he should be a consecrated and ordained priest, according to the way and rite of the Holy Church, because God has given the power and authority to unloose and to bind only to priests, as the *Decretum* says, adding what Christ says in the Gospel: *Quorum remisteritis peccata, remictuntur eis* [Jn 20:23], as was explained above. With these words Christ gave power and authority to the apostles in the person of all the priests, who would be duly and truly ordained to such a ministry by the apostles and by their successors, the bishops. As the priests alone are ministers of the Church, and their ministry is taken up on the true body of Christ, which they must consecrate, so too are they ministers to dispense the other sacraments, in which grace is given, which descends from the head to the limbs, i.e., from Christ. Speaking of him, St. Paul says [1 Cr 12] that God has given him as head of the body of the Holy Church of all the faithful, who are members of this body and this head, as the apostle says that all the faithful are one body, and each one is a member of this body. Therefore, since grace is given in the sacrament of penitence, which is properly carried out and fulfilled in confession, only the priest is minister of this sacrament, and to him alone, as to a minister of the Church, should we make the sacramental confession.

Where necessary, if a priest is not available to the sinner, he could confess to a layman. I say where necessary, meaning when there is the possibility or danger of death. And I say that he could confess, not that he must do so, because where no priest is available, contrition is enough for salvation, with the desire, if possible, to confess and with the intention, if one survives, to do so. Still, if someone had the faith and devotion to want to tell his sin to a layman with humility and shame, wishing for a priest if he could have one, this confession is valid, even if it cannot properly be called sacramental, because the proper minister of such a sacrament would be lacking. Nevertheless, when he is led to confess to a layman, such a confession has some efficacy, because of the humility that leads the sinner to recount his sins to someone like him and almost to submit to his judgment, and given the shame of showing his sins, and the good will and intention in his heart that, if there were a priest, he would confess to him.

We read in Caesarius that in a villa in the countryside of Toulouse there was a priest who became friendly with the wife of a local knight, and the two were led to sin. As this went on for some time, it was reported to the knight, who at first did not want to believe it, albeit he was not without suspicion. Not saying anything to the priest or to the lady, nor signalling any suspicion at all, one day he asked the priest to accompany him to a certain place for a secret meeting. He took him to a villa, where there was a bedevilled man who scolded all those he saw for their sins, no matter how secret they were. The priest, who had heard about what the bedevilled man was up to, correctly assumed that the knight had brought him there so that the demon would expose the adultery he had committed with the wife. Having heard that a confessed sin is hidden from the devil, but there being no priest around, he dashed into a stall where the knight's horse and servant were. Throwing himself at the servant's feet, he diligently confessed his sin, and as he asked for penitence the servant said: "Do that penitence that you would give to another priest who confessed a sin similar to the one you have committed." The knight then went with the priest to the bedevilled man, and the latter, while scolding the knight and the others for their sins, said nothing to the priest. Whereupon the knight said: "You have nothing to say to the priest? Think it over: what do you have to say to him?" He answered: "I have nothing to say about this man." He said these words in German, which the knight alone understood, and he also said in Latin: "He was set right in the stall," which only the priest understood. And seeing the grace of his escape and the virtue of confession, he gave up his sin and became a monk of the order of Cîteaux.[112]

It is worth noting here that if someone who confesses to a layman survives, as soon as possible he should kneel before a priest and again confess all the sins he had told to the layman. Then the sacrament will be perfected and the sinner will have remission of his sins by virtue of the keys of the Holy Church (of which the priest alone is minister), and he will have obeyed the commandment that the Holy Church makes about confession. The layman is required always to conceal the sins that he has heard in confession, as the priest must do.

Although it is said that the priest should be the one who hears the confession, that does not mean that every priest can absolve every sinner, and of every sin, except when there is the possibility of death. To be precise, it must be a priest who has power and jurisdiction over the man whom he has to unloose and bind, and can order him to do those things necessary for his salvation. So a priest is specifically called for who has ordinary care of the soul, like the pope of all Christians, the legate of those who are in his legation, the bishop in his bishopric, the priest in his parish; i.e., he takes care of the souls of those who live within the boundaries of the church that he has to lead. Such priests do not have to absolve their parishioners of every sin, because the Church reserves certain more serious sins for the bishop; and the bishops reserve them for themselves and for their vicars, as they deem, and can do. Parish priests cannot involve themselves with sins that are reserved to the

---

112 I.e., a member of the Cistercian order, an offshoot of the Benedictines.

bishop, or that the Church reserves to bishops, and even less so those that are reserved to the pope, unless by special assignment.

The sins that are reserved to the bishops are shown in a decretal of Pope Benedict XI,[113] which begins *Inter cunctas*. No matter their condition, confessors must know which cases are reserved to the bishops for canonical reasons, and the others that the bishops keep by their authority or by provincial or synodal constitutions, so that they do not get mixed up in them. Whoever might absolve the sinner of any of the reserved sins would first of all sin mortally if he did so on purpose, knowing that he could not do it, and ignorance would not be an excuse; also, he would deceive the sinner, who would believe himself to be absolved. Though ignorance would perhaps excuse the sinner, it would not excuse the confessor, and if he were accused of it, it would carry a serious punishment. I say "perhaps" about the sinner because there could be such a person and such a sinner and such an ignorance that it would not excuse him. If someone were wise and learned, having frequented church and sermons, he should have heard and read about going to a confessor who can absolve these sins, and that not every priest can absolve for every sin, as was said above. So if someone feels that he has committed such sins that he wonders whether he can receive absolution from that priest to whom he turns if he does not have the authority to absolve him, then he is not excused. Also, if the person knows or believes that the confessor is either senile or forgetful, because of sickness or a natural condition, or stupid, or a foolish chard-eater, or an unrefined, unlettered person, and he still wants to confess to him so as not to feel too ashamed, or because he asks nicely, or because it's worth his while, and he can have another confessor who is sufficient, and he does not want him and does not go looking for him, then he is not excused if that confessor cannot or does not know how to absolve him.

What should the confessor do with someone who confesses sins reserved to the bishops, which he cannot absolve? He should diligently hear the confession of all the sins, then he should tell the sinner that there are one or two sins for which he cannot grant absolution. He should then do one of two things: either go in person to the bishop or his vicar for authority to absolve for those reserved sins, without saying the name of the person who has confessed, or he should tell that person

---

113 The Benedictine Nicola Boccasini, born in 1240, ruled as pope for nine months between 1303 and 1304. The *Inter cunctas* was a new Dominican constitution, drafted by Benedict, which addressed questions pertaining to confessions heard by Dominican friars.

to first go and have himself absolved by someone who can absolve him because he has permission to do so, then eventually absolve him for those sins for which he can grant absolution. In a case involving excommunication, the person must first be absolved and then come back to be absolved of his other sins.

An excommunicated person cannot receive the grace of absolution or the benefit of any sacrament until such time as he is reconciled with the Holy Church, which happens through absolution from excommunication. The one who absolves says, *Absolvo te a vinculo scommunicationis, et restituo te Sacramentis Ecclesiae*: I absolve you of the bond of excommunication, and I restore you to the sacraments of the Church. It is almost like saying: you were first bound up, and I unloose you; you had disappeared and were deprived of the sacraments of the Church, and I restore and render them to you.

Although I said that the confessor should eventually absolve the person for those sins that he can, while sending him to one who has a greater authority to absolve, like bishops and their vicars, or the confessors of Rome, still I prefer, as more orderly, if he first sends the person to the confessor to have him absolved of those sins that he cannot, and then has him return to him, as I said about excommunication.

There are some who, when the sinner comes to confess, before they hear the other sins, ask whether he has committed any of those sins that are reserved to the bishops, which they cannot get mixed up in. Hearing yes, they send the sinner away, saying that they cannot absolve him and that he should go to a confessor who can absolve him of all his sins. Likewise, there are some who, at the beginning of the confession or in the middle, hear some sin for which they either cannot or should not grant absolution (such as taking someone else's things, or committing adultery, or taking revenge, or not being disposed to not commit the sin again, and so forth). They do not allow the sinner to continue, saying: "Say no more, because I would not absolve you of any of your sins," and they send him away, not letting him finish the confession. These confessors do no good in any of the individual cases, because a sinner sent away in this fashion goes away scorned and unhappy. Because of his disdain, he may lose hope and not go to confess to another confessor, and he may hold the confessor who chased him away in contempt and speak ill of him, and abandon the Church's commandment of confession and fasting, or certain other good things that he had set his heart to do when he decided to come and confess. Perhaps by completing the confession he would have had that grace of contrition that he did not have before. The discreet confessor should therefore listen patiently to the sinner and be loving and kind towards him. He should first send him to someone who has greater authority, and he should lead him with words of affection and compassion, mixing in the fear of God's judgment where necessary to provoke contrition and departure from sin. He should send him away without anger and with the hope of God's grace, telling him to come back and beg God to grant him contrition, and saying that he will also pray for him and the like. Still, the confessor should be careful lest he absolve the person of those sins that he cannot, out of pleasure or indiscreet courtesy, and not be so presumptuous, if he cannot tell how serious the sins are, as to judge if they are reserved or not. If he does not know, he should ask someone who knows better, or else advise the sinner that some cases are difficult to understand and that he should see a confessor who is better prepared. In other words, he should not get mixed up in what he does not know, getting in the middle, involving himself and others. There are certain cases that even many wise and learned men wonder about and unwillingly get involved in, such as usurious contracts, of which there are many, and you can find some all day long which you can barely understand. Some write them off or excuse them in terms of exchange, or interest, as deposits or reserves; some call them purchases and sales or earnings on risk and investment. Many others say they involve rentals, companies, partnerships, ventures, and many other things, leaving out simony, barratry, and dishonourable gains. There are difficult cases like marriages, dispensations, commutations of pledges, restitutions, wills, executions, guardianship and the raising of women, arbitration, judgments, advising, procuring, lawyering, revenge, pawning, excommunication, irregularities, interdictions, suspensions, removals, and many other things that we cannot teach here, much less account for very well, but we mention them in order to teach confessors to be cautious, and to learn not to put themselves and others at risk by being so presumptuous as to do what they cannot do or don't know how to do.

And although it has been said that a person must confess to his own priest, still there are several cases in which it is permitted to confess to someone else.

Here we show how in certain cases a person could confess to someone other than his own priest.

First of all, every lay and secular person, man or woman, no matter their status and condition, can confess to the Friars Preachers and the Friars Minor, who by a special privilege of the pope and the Church of Rome can hear confessions, absolve, and impose salutary penance, with a certain service and reverence which must be shown by the prelates of said orders to bishops or archbishops in whose cities and dioceses, in the bishoprics where they might hear confessions, as is contained in the Clementine Constitutions: *De sepulturis. Dudum.*[114] They do not, however, have the authority to absolve for sins reserved to the bishops that parish priests might hear about, unless the bishops have already given them a special commission; nor can they hear confessions in a bishopric other than the one in which they serve. This service lasts for as long as that bishop lives whom they once served. Once he is dead or removed from the bishopric, it also lasts until another bishop is elected and confirmed, and he or his vicar is present in that city. Then they must serve him as they did his predecessor, and they can hear confessions without permission of the parish priests, even if they oppose it.

For communion one should turn only to the parish priests, or to those to whom they have given permission. The pope has ordered that no one else should give it and, according to some, the person who might receive it on purpose from someone else, without permission from one's own priest or bishop, would mortally sin. So a person should not dare to say that he has permission if he does not have it. For this reason, at least once a year, i.e., for the Easter of the Resurrection, when all faithful Christians are commanded to take communion, everyone should confess to their own priest, who should give them communion and who should know the condition of his subjects like the pastor his sheep, and he must give them extreme unction, i.e., the holy oil, in case of death and a church burial, if a burial site was not chosen elsewhere already. If someone still does not want to confess to his own priest, and especially if there were some defects in him, as will be set forth shortly,[115] he is not required to do so; but he must appear at the time of communion and tell him in faith how he has confessed to another priest, a religious, or another man who had authority or governance over him. The priest should believe him and give him communion, unless it is a case of excommunication, and then the priest must ascertain that the person who had been excommunicated and asks for communion is legitimately absolved. Otherwise, if he was notoriously and openly excommunicated, he should not give him communion.

Although it was said above that the Friars Preachers and the Friars Minor have authority from the Church to hear confessions, this does not, however, prevent other religious men from hearing confessions,

---

114 The Clementine Constitutions, promulgated by Pope Clement V, were enacted at
   the Council of Vienne (1311–1312).
115 See p. 109.

either by special privilege of the pope, as with Augustinian friars and the Carmelites, or by special permission of the bishops in their bishoprics, as certain other religious men have. But those two principal orders were named, Preachers and Minor, because typically those two are mentioned in the old and the new and the common decretals and in certain special privileges.

The other case in which one may confess to a priest other than one's own is when one's own priest is a heretic, schismatic, excommunicated, or someone base, a promoter or inducer of evil, fragile and inclined towards those sins that a person might confess to him. This would be the case if he were lustful or an adulterer, and a woman had to confess similar sins to him, so she might think that he, hearing about her, might ask her or induce her to sin. Or if someone realistically believes that he would disclose the confession, or if the sin that someone else might confess had been committed with the priest, or against the priest, or if the priest were so wholly ignorant that he could not discern sins or make absolution. In these cases, and in any other in which there might be danger for the priest or the person who confesses, one may confess to a confessor other than one's own priest.

If someone wanted to confess to the Friars Preachers or Friars Minor, or to other religious men who might hold a privilege from the pope and the Church or permission from the bishop in his bishopric, no other permission is necessary. However, if he wanted to confess to other priests, he should seek permission from the bishop, or from his vicar, or from the priest himself. If he cannot get permission, he should act as if he did not have his own confessor, in which case one may confess to any available priest and also to a layman. We should note here that, when the bishop or his vicar gives permission to confess to someone other than one's own priest, one need not also have the permission of one's own priest, nor do the sins confessed on the basis of such permission need to be confessed again later to one's own priest. The same holds true for those who confess to religious men who hold a privilege from the pope and the Church. No harm is done to the parish priests by doing this, because such authority and power to hear confessions is not granted in favour of priests or confessors, but rather for the good of souls, in favour of the people and in God's honour. Therefore, the major prelates, if they see the good of souls and God's honour, can and should give such permission, and the parish priests themselves should be happy about it and allow it, considering that it is done better and more sufficiently by someone other than themselves. If they were to create an impediment they would sin gravely, because there are many who would give up confession before they would confess to their own priests, for one reason or another.

The other case of confessing to someone other than one's own priest is that of necessity, such as the possibility or risk of death, or if a man had to go into battle or out to sea and did not have his own priest at hand, he could confess to any priest, or even to a layman, as we said above. The other case is of pilgrims to Rome and elsewhere, and merchants who go to different countries and places who, when they leave home, must ask their priest's permission, or that of the bishop or his vicar, to confess and receive the sacraments of the Church in those places where they are supposed to go. If they don't do this, they cannot confess, except when necessary. Of those pilgrims to Rome and elsewhere, it is said to be enough if they take a walking stick and purse, as is the practice, from their own priest. By that it is understood that they may confess anywhere along their pilgrimage route. Should it happen that pilgrims to Rome or elsewhere, merchants, or other wayfarers confess along the way, not having permission as we said, when they return home, they should come before their own priest or another confessor who has authority to absolve them, as we said above, as soon as possible and diligently confess again all those sins they had confessed during their trip or pilgrimage. If by chance the wayfarer runs into his own bishop, or his vicar, or his own parish priest during his trip, he can confess and be absolved by each one of them as he could have done at home.

To the pope's confessors in Rome and at court, everyone can confess without any other permission and be absolved of those sins, as permitted, because they cannot absolve for every sin. The same is true for legates and their confessors within the terms of their mandate. The priests of the various parish churches must, with the bishop's permission, general or particular, tacit or explicit, confess to one another, whether they are priors or chaplains of the same church, or rectors or chaplains in different churches. They do not together have greater authority to absolve than do parish priests over their lay subjects, unless by special commission of the bishop. Monks, canonicals, friars, religious of any cloth and order should confess to their prelates, or to one another of their order, and absolve of sins to the extent that said prelates are allowed to. The prelates can absolve and allow their other subjects, when they are allowed by their rule which is approved by the Church, or by special privilege of the pope or a legate with authority over them, or by permission of the archbishops or bishops to whom they are subject. Convent nuns who are subject to bishops must confess to those confessors whom the bishops provide to them, either chaplains in continual service or others to whom the bishops give special permission to hear them, or others whom the abbesses of the convents, with permission of the bishops, can call for, either for themselves or for the sisters, one or more times. Those women who are subject to monks or other religious can confess to the abbots or prelates of those orders, or to those who might be granted to them. Hermits, both male and female, may confess to the priests in whose parishes they have their hermitage, or to others with their bishop's permission. The pope can choose as his confessor whomever he wants. Cardinals, if they are legates, similarly can choose their confessor. If they are at court, they should confess to the pope or to the confessor, or with the pope's permission choose a confessor. Chaplains and the other courtiers, if they are in the pope's household, ought to confess to the pope's confessor. If they are in a cardinal's household, they should confess with permission of their lords, who look after them, either with the pope's permission or that of the highest confessor. Patriarchs, archbishops, bishops, and exempt minor prelates may all choose their own confessor. The other minor prelates who are not exempt must confess to the bishops or, with permission of the pope or the bishops, choose their confessor. Emperors, kings, princes, and secular lords may choose their confessor with the pope's permission. Otherwise, if their primary residence is in one city more than another, they can confess to the bishop of that city or to the parish priest. But if they have a residence and houses in different places, and it is not clear which is the main one, they may confess to the priest of the parish where their residence is; but it is better and safer to choose a confessor with the permission of the bishop, or bishops if they have residences in many bishoprics. Those who spend part of the year in one parish and part in another must confess to that priest in whose parish they intend to reside. Those who move from parish to parish must confess to the priest of that parish where they go to live.

Another case when a person needs to be absolved by someone other than his own priest is when he commits some excess outside of his parish for which he was excommunicated. In this case, he must seek absolution from the prelate who excommunicated him, whether he has been excommunicated by name or in general, the latter in the case of robberies and the like where the evildoer is not known.

Having said who should be the confessor, we must say how and what he should be.

Here we show how and what the confessor should be.
First of all, he should be of a mature age, not too young, so that he is revered and there is no suspicion of dishonourableness. This is why bishops are ordered not to ordain priests younger than twenty-five. Much more importantly, the care of souls should not be entrusted to

them. The confessor must not be illegitimate, neither servant nor slave, nor a leper, paralytic, epileptic, or apoplectic; not blind, deaf, mute, crippled, lacking a hand, or shrunken; and he should not have given help, counsel, or assistance in any way, legal or illegal, in someone's death. He may not have had two wives, nor a wife who first had another husband, out of reverence for the sacrament of the body of Christ, which he has to consecrate. He may not be a drunk, a tavern-keeper, a gambler, a highway robber, or a deceiver, not quick to fight, not a buffoon, not a courtier, not worldly, not avaricious, not a troublemaker, not importunate, not outside the law, not litigious, not ruled by anger, not insane, not a flatterer, liar, slanderer, swearer, defamer, blasphemer, arguer, gossip, falsifier, simoniac, speaker of worthless words, not supercilious, effeminate, a trickster, not cruel, not a thief, not a vagabond, not disloyal, hurtful, impious, envious, undisciplined, presumptuous. He must be sober, clean, chaste, modest, gentle, pious, benign, affable, generous, patient, faithful, a keeper of secrets, silent, pacific, quiet, truthful, charitable, continent, honest, expert, and not guilty of any bad behaviour. Anyone who wants to know how one should be who has care of souls should read St. Paul's first epistle to Timothy, the chapter where he says: *Oportet episcopum inreprehensibilem esse*, etc. [1 Tm 3:2]. This chapter, as St. Ambrose and St. Augustine explain it,[116] as is contained in the Decretal, and while it appears that the apostle is talking about bishops, that rule is meant for all those who are ordained as priests and take care of souls. Woe unto that priest to whom is entrusted the care of souls, and who has to consecrate the body and blood of Christ and distribute the sacraments of the Church, if he does not have enough of what is required for such a duty, and for the holy life and good behaviour, and wisdom and knowledge, with the necessary discretion! What makes a priest especially unworthy of the holy office is dishonesty and bodily incontinence, considering with how much reverence the sacraments of which he is the minister and distributor should be treated, and especially the body and blood of Christ. In this regard, a beautiful miracle once happened.

We read in Caesarius that in France there was a priest who, one Christmas night, while passing from one town to another to say mass, ran into a woman who was alone, and with whom, defeated by her incontinence, he sinned carnally. Fearing human shame more than divine justice, having said matins, he prepared for the holy mass and sang it solemnly. After he had consecrated the body and blood of Christ

---

116 Auzzas (Passavanti, 496) points instead to Raymond of Penyafort's *Summa*.

and shown it to the people and laid it on the altar, a dove, white as snow, suddenly descended from heaven, put its beak in the chalice, and drank all the blood. Looking at the priest, it also removed the consecrated host from the altar and flew away. The priest, completely stunned and not knowing what to do, and fearing shame if the truth should come out, proceeded to finish the mass, appearing to take communion. Being daring and presumptuous and not wanting to reveal the truth about himself, he celebrated the second and third masses, as is usually done on such a holy day. At each mass, as God did not want him to take the sacred sacrament with a sinful and dirty conscience, the dove did as before, carrying away the venerable sacrament. His duty done, the priest came away thinking about his sin and the miracle that had happened. Ashamed, he went to an abbot of the order of Cîteaux, and tearfully confessing his sin he recounted the miracle that had happened. The abbot, seeing the priest's contrition, ordered him as penitence, among other things, to say the Christmas mass, which he had done badly three times. The priest did this fearfully and with many tears, and when he was about to speak the words of consecration over the host and the chalice, the dove came to the altar with three hosts in its mouth and, putting them onto the plate it emptied into the chalice all the blood-wine it had drunk at the three masses, which it held in its throat. The priest took communion with one of those hosts and drank some of the blood, saving the rest as proof of the beautiful miracle. Returning full of happiness to his confessor and telling him what had happened, he asked humbly to be received into the order. His wish granted, he abandoned the world and took up the habit of the holy religion, where, living in a holy way, he lived out the days of his life.

*Here we show how the confessor priest should have discretion with
    knowledge, especially about four things.*

Among the other things that are especially necessary for the confessor to have, there is knowledge with discretion. He should have knowledge and wisdom, if not excellent then at least sufficient for him to do his job. Inasmuch as he has to recite the mass and other divine offices, he should know as much Latin as allows him to offer and stress the words well, especially the sacramental words. Also, he should know what he says and reads, at least by the letter. As a minister of sacraments, he should know the required content of each sacrament, what its requisite form is, and how the sacraments should be distributed. As a teacher, he should at least know what the articles of faith are, the sacraments of the Church, and the commandments of the law. As a judge of conscience, he should know how to distinguish among sins. And, as was said above, he should have knowledge with discretion, because he should have discretion about four things regarding the sinner who confesses.

First, he should know how to tell one sin from another, which one is grave, which is venial, and which is deadly. He should know how to discern and recognize the reasons for sins, in order to teach others to confess and eschew them: because some sins are committed out of ignorance (and sometimes ignorance is an excuse, other times not), some out of a certain malice, some out of fear, some out of violence, some out of poverty, some because of bad company or opportunity. He also should have discretion in knowing how to scold the sinner, both softly and harshly, as the person's sin and condition require. Likewise, he should be discreet in knowing how to comfort, console, counsel, and teach as the subject and the need require, and have compassion for the sinner, and not be pitiless or cruel, as someone was whom we read about in Caesarius.

There was a monk of the Cistercian order who, already an ordained priest, left the order and became a ne'er-do-well and a roadside bandit. Once, during a siege at a castle, he was mortally wounded by an arrow. Begged by many to confess, although at first he rejected the idea, once the priest was called he began to tell his sins. At this point God gave him so much contrition that so many painful tears overflowed that, struggling to breathe and speak, he could not recount his sins. In the end, taking a few breaths, he began to confess, saying that he had been a great evildoer and a faithless sinner: "I am an apostate, a highway robber, a killer of many men. I burned many homes. I raped the wives and daughters of other men, and I have done many other evils in my life." The stunned priest, hearing the evil and grave sins, turning with indignation towards the sinner said: "You are the devil's son: so many and such grave sins could never be pardoned, and I will not give you penitence." The sinner replied: "What are you saying? I am a cleric: and I know that Scripture says that whenever the sinner converts and cries over his sin, God receives him in mercy, no matter how great a sinner he is. I beg you by God's mercy to assign me some penance." As the priest was saying that he did not know what penance to impose, because he was lost and damned, the sinner said: "Since you do not want to impose it on me, I shall assign it to myself, and I impose upon myself to remain in purgatory for 2,000 years, after which may God have mercy on me. I only ask you to write down my sins and present them to a bishop who is my uncle, so that he might pray to God for me." Having said this, and as the priest promised to do it, he died. Upon receiving the list of his nephew's sins and news of his death, the bishop cried and said: "I loved him in life, and I will love him after death." He ordered masses and prayers to be said for his soul for a whole year, throughout his bishopric. Once the year was over, the nephew, thin and pale, appeared before his uncle and thanked him, for because of what he had done for him 1,000 years of penitence had been forgiven; and he said that if he would do the same for a second year, as he had done the first, he would be delivered. The bishop did for the second year what he had done the first, and at the end of the year the dead man appeared before the bishop, while he was saying mass for him, in a surplice white as snow, and with his face fresh and clean, saying to him: "May God reward you for me, my father, since through your goodness I am delivered of the punishments of purgatory, and I am going to paradise."

In imposing penitence, the confessor should also be discreet as the greater or lesser sin requires, and according to the condition of the person, because one person can do and stand one thing that another cannot, and therefore he should discreetly consider whether the person is healthy or sick, young or old, rich or poor, free or servant, bound in matrimony or obedience, or unloosed, and if he has fallen repeatedly into the same sins. If he does not find the person to be well-disposed to carry out the necessary penitence, he should not let him hurry off without penitence, but he should lead him to accept the due penitence. And even if he cannot bring him around, he should give him some penance, indicating the penance that pertains to his sins, and that what he does not do in this life, he will do more harshly and gravely in purgatory; and he should not excuse him from penitence.

We read an example of this.

It is written in the Book of the Seven Gifts[117] that certain pirates, i.e., sea thieves, at one time being in a great tempest at fortune's beck and call and fearing death, made a vow that were they to survive they would confess and leave sin behind. Freed of danger, they went on to fulfil their vow. Among other things, their leader and captain went to confess to a hermit. Hearing the many and serious sins he had committed, the hermit scolded him harshly, saying that he would not absolve him of those sins and impose penitence on him, but that he needed to go to the pope. The evildoer said that he was not prepared to go to the pope and begged the hermit for penitence, saying he had faith that it

---

117 As Auzzas points out (Passavanti, 171–2), the source of this tale is not the so-called *Libro dei sette doni* (Book of the Seven Gifts) but the *Libro de dono timoris*, the Book of the Gift of Fear, authored by the French Dominican Humbert of Romans (1200–1277), though likely through the mediation of the *Alphabetum narrationum*. A section in Humbert's treatise addresses the seven gifts, and this likely led to the confusion.

would be valid before God. The hermit did not comply, so the pirate, fully outraged, picked up a knife and killed him. Still wanting to fulfil the vow, he went to another priest, and when he confessed his sins and the murder of the hermit, the priest got angry and said that for that homicide alone, leaving aside any other sins, he would have to go to the pope, and that he himself would neither absolve him nor give him any penitence at all. Outraged, the evildoer swore that since the priest did not want to give him penitence, he would give it to him, and that if he still had to go to the pope, he would go on his account as well, and so he killed him. He came to a third confessor and confessed his old and new sins, whereupon the confessor, hearing that he had killed two confessors, said to himself: "You will not kill me." Speaking to him gently and hearing his confession, he only imposed that, as penitence, when he should see a dead person, he should accompany him all the way to the grave and help bury him and think about death. The sinner received the penitence willingly and went away happy. At one point, while doing the assigned penitence very faithfully, he developed a horror of death and, ashamed about his situation, left for the desert, and taking the habit of religion he lived in holy penitence until his death.

We should not want to impose any penitence at all on the sick, but rather insist that if they recover, they should return within a certain period to receive their orders and worthy penitence.

> *Here we show how the confessor should make absolution both for those excommunicated and for other sinners.*

For those who were excommunicated with a greater excommunication, when absolving them in the Church's way with the psalm and the whip and with prayer, the confessor must ask them to swear they will obey the orders of the Church and then say: *Ego absolvo te a tali sententia excommunicationis.* Finally, he should order them never again to fall into such folly for which they were excommunicated, and he should impose a proper penitence if they are fit. If they are sick, following the said format, he should order that if they survive, they should return to him to receive penitence. Someone who has the authority to absolve from greater excommunication, when absolving others, should be careful not to stray from the Church's format in any way, because he would sin gravely. The format and manner of such absolution is this. First, the excommunicated sinner should humbly kneel before the one who is to absolve him. Before anything else, the priest, before doing the other three things, should make him swear, while putting his hand on the missal or some other holy book where the Holy Gospel is written, that he will continue to obey the commandments of the Church.

Having done this, he should recite the psalm: *Miserere me Deus*, or the *De profundis* if he is in a hurry. While he says the psalm, he should beat the excommunicate on the lower back with some whip or club. Having finished the psalm with *Gloria Patri*, he should add: *Kyrie eleison. Christ eleison. Kyrie eleison, Pater noster*. And he should say the entire Our Father clearly, beating him all the while. And having said: *Sed libera nosa a malo*, he should say: *Salvum fac servum tuum, Deus meus, sperantem in te*. And if there are several who need to be absolved, he should say: *Salvos fac servos tuos*, etc. Then he should say: *Dominus vobiscum*, and having heard the reply, *Et cum spiritu tuo*, in order to have a companion who answers him, he should add: *Oremus. Deus, cui propium est miserere semper et parcere, suscipe deprecationem nostrum, et quem (vel quos) delictorum catena costringit miseratio tuae pietatis absolvat. Per Christum Dominum nostrum. Amen*. Then the priest should say: *Ego autoritate qua fungor et mihi commissa, te (vel vos) absolvo a vinculo (seu sententia) scumunicationis, quam incurristi propter contumaciam (vel aliam causam, eam exprimendo), et resituo te sacramentis Eclesie. In nomine Patris et Filii et Spiritus Sancti. Amen*. Then he should impose penitence, according to the sin and the person's condition, ordering him to take care not to fall again into an error like the one for which he was excommunicated.

The confessor should not ask for sacrament from other sinners, nor a promise to do or not to do something. It is enough to say that they have the intention to do penance, alms, restitution, or something else that they have to do, and not to commit sin, injury, usury, and similar things. Then he should absolve the sinner, all the while insisting that if he does not do as instructed, he will not have the fruit of confession and absolution.

The priest who can absolve for other sins can absolve for a minor excommunication, which happens when someone participates in conversation or eats with an excommunicate. And the form of absolution is: *Ego absolve te a vinculo scumunicationis, et restituo te Sacramentis Ecclesiae.*

The format for absolution for sins that a man confesses sacramentally to a priest is this. Having first made the general confession, and the priest having said, in lieu of a prayer, so that the effect of the absolution does not impede the confessant, *Misereatur tui omnipotens Deus*, etc., the priest should then say: *Auctoritate qua fungor ego absolvo te (vel ego te absolvo) a vunculo excommunicationis, si teneris, et resituo te sacramentis Eclesie*. Absolution should come first because someone who is bound by minor excommunication cannot receive absolution for his other sins or any sacrament. Then the priest should add: *Ego absolvo te (vel ego te absolvo) ab istis peccatis et ab omnibus aliis quorum memoriam non habes.*

There are some who mix certain words into the form of absolution which are not substantive and therefore are not necessary, but when they are said they should be said as a prayer, such as: *Misereatur tui omnipotens Deus et Filius Dei (vel Dominus Iesus Christus) per misericordiam te absolvat.* Some add: *Passio Domini nostri Iesus Christi et merita Beate Verginis et omnium Sanctorum,* etc., which is also said as a prayer. Sometimes the priest says: *Bona que fecisti et intendis facere sint tibi in remissione peccatorum tuorum,* etc. The good that is done through these words spoken by the priest, when he holds the keys, has some greater efficacy to satisfy for the sins than they might otherwise have. Some put their hand on the head when they absolve, and that is not good, because this sacrament, unlike some others, does not require the laying on of hands. It is better to make the sign of the cross, to signify that by virtue of the blood of Christ's cross this sacrament, of which the priest alone is the minister, is being used and is effective.

The fourth thing about which the confessor must exercise discretion is in interrogating and searching the conscience of the confessant. If he sees that someone, either out of ignorance, or shame, or fear, or forgetfulness, does not state his sins as the confessor judges or believes he should have done, he should reassure him and remind him of the sins and ask him: "Have you offended in this or that way?" St. Thomas says that the confessor should probe the sinner's conscience, like a doctor the wound, which he could not heal if he did not first understand its quality and its damage, and like the judge the case, which he could not adjudicate or settle if he did not first know the truth of the event, and therefore he investigates and examines it. The priest confessor should do the same, as he is doctor and judge, who has to treat and judge the sick sinner and evildoer. But he should do that with great discretion, and he should follow three rules.

Here we show the procedure the confessor should follow in questioning the sinner who confesses.

First, he should ask the confessant about the sins that people of that state and condition usually commit, so he should not ask the knight about the sins of a cleric, nor the merchant about the sins of a lawyer, nor the woman about the sins the rectors of the commune commit.

Second, he should not ask specifically and openly about sins that are not commonly manifest in everyone. He should keep his distance, so that if the person has not committed them and does not know about them, he does not start wanting to do them, and they do not occur to him. He can ask explicitly about common and obvious sins, like theft, homicide, adultery, and the like. Certain hidden sins, which many people do not know about and do not do, he should either be silent about or hint at so carefully, and at such a distance, that he does not teach an evil that is not already known. When the priest, like a doctor, must take care of a wound, he should not do it in the way that once happened, according to Caesarius.

In a convent in Cologne there was a young girl of seven named Beatrice, placed there by her father and her mother. She grew up in the convent, and having become a woman and ordained a nun, she once made a general confession to a priest who was not very wise and even less discreet, and who, when asking her about the sins she might have committed in her situation, among others he asked whether she had ever sinned carnally. She answered no, because she had entered the convent when she was a girl of seven and a man had never touched her. "Therefore," the confessor said, "are you a virgin?" The woman replied: "You know perfectly well that I am, since a man has never approached me." The priest said: "A woman can sin without a man and lose her virginity." "I can't follow," said the nun, "unless you speak more precisely." Then the stupid priest, who should not have gone further, asked her about certain specific things that are better left unsaid. Having finished the confession and granted absolution, the confessor left. The woman, returning alone to her cell, thought about what she had heard from the priest, and with one thought leading to another and awakening in her the innate concupiscence of the flesh, strong temptations tugged at her heart and lit up the mind's desire, which was anxious to try and taste what she had never tried or tasted. Inflamed by the devil, the troubling temptation grew day by day, and the nun, suffering from it, could not resist and was finally defeated. Out of desperation she decided to leave the monastery and live in a worldly way, dishonourably following the appetites of her fragile flesh. One day, at her wit's end, she took the keys of the sacristy, where she had been in service for some time, and threw herself before the altar of the Virgin Mary, where her image was, saying: "My lady, I have kept these keys of yours safe for many years in the service of the sacristy, serving you day and night. Now I am fighting an unusual battle, one so difficult that I don't know how or whether I can defend myself at all: and you are not helping me. And so, I surrender to you the keys of my office. I give up." Leaving the keys on the altar, she left the convent and lived with a clerk for some time. After he left her, she so lost her way that she became a common and open sinner. After fifteen years of sin, one day she came to the door of the convent where she had been raised, and she asked the doorkeeper: "Did you know a nun who was once the sacristan of this convent, named Beatrice?" "I know her well," said the doorkeeper, "and she is a wise and honourable religious woman, and from her childhood up until this day she has lived in this convent in a holy way and with common grace." The sinner did not understand the man's words, but she turned and went away. The Virgin Mary, from whom she had taken her leave when she had left, and to whom she had surrendered her keys, then appeared before her and said: "I have done your job for the fifteen years since you left the convent, in your habit and your person, and there is no one alive who knows anything about your sin. So come back to the convent and do your duty, and repent of your sin. You will find the sacristy keys on the altar, where you left them." Ashamed at seeing God's mercy and the Virgin Mary's grace, Beatrice returned to the convent and lived in penitence and holiness until her death. No one ever knew of her error, except that she confessed it in penitence to the priest, telling why and how she had lost her way and the grace she had received, and that she wanted it recorded as an example and teaching for confessors and sinners, and in praise of the mother of Jesus Christ, defender of sinners.

The third thing the discreet confessor should do, when asking about sins, and especially the carnal ones, is not dig into details. As St. Thomas says,[118] the more you think about and focus on the things that delight the flesh, the more concupiscence they provoke, so they could hurt the confessor and the person who confesses. The confessor should be especially careful about this when he hears the confessions of women. He should not ask confessants to name the person with whom they have sinned, because just as the confessant should safeguard the reputation of others and not confess the sins of others except in certain cases, so too should the confessor not ask about the sins of others.

With regard to when you should name the person with whom you have sinned, this should be done when you cannot be clear about the sin and its gravity without naming the person. If a woman has sinned with her father or her brother, it would not be enough to say, when confessing, "I have committed a sin with a man," because to sin with your father or your brother is incest, which is much more serious than fornication or adultery. So she must call the sin what it is and name her father or brother. She should take care to have a confessor who does not know them. Still, if in this case or any other during confession someone else's name should be mentioned with whom you have sinned, or someone else should be named not to defame him but so that the

---

confessor might pray to God for him or admonish him, or stop him from doing evil, this would not be a sin but mercy.

The confessor can remind the confessant that he knows about the sin or sins when he sees that he does not confess them, out of either ignorance or fear or shame.

Here we show how the confessor should keep hidden what he hears about in confession.

Above all else, the confessor must be careful to keep hidden and secret what he hears in confession, which he is not permitted to disclose in any way. If the confessor were questioned about them by any civil or ecclesiastical judge, even by the emperor or the pope, he should not disclose them, and if he were asked by any judge under oath, he can safely swear that he knows nothing about them: meaning that he does not know as a man or in such a way that he should or can speak. The judge who questions him would sin gravely by attempting to find out things that do not pertain to his job. But if the confessor knows what the judge is asking about in ways other than through confession, he can speak of it, while not saying however that he learned it in confession. At the same time, if he doesn't have to say it, he should be as careful as possible to keep it to himself, so that no scandal should arise from it, since others might think he had revealed what he had heard in confession. Likewise, what a man learns in secret and under seal of confession should be kept hidden. Nevertheless, the person who confesses a sin or says something in secret can give the confessor permission to speak if necessary. Said permission should not be used except in cases of great need, especially when one fears that a scandal might arise. And the person who hears, with the confessant's permission, what was said in the secret of confession must keep it secret unless it is the confessant's wish that he reveal it. The importance of keeping the secret of confession hidden, both out of reverence for the sacrament and because of the great punishments that the law imposes on someone who reveals the confession, is shown by the *Decretum* and the Decretal,[119] and so that people do not withdraw from confessing out of concern that their secret sins might become public: because no matter how great the danger, it should be allowed to happen before someone reveals a confession. The discreet confessor can attach some remedies to the dangers heard in confession, either by removing those who have confessed from their bad intention or their bad endeavour, by telling them to stop doing the

---

119 Gratian's *Decrees* and the *Liber extra* of the *Decretals* [GA].

bad thing in some appropriate way, or by saying to the relevant person, the prelate or rector or individual who might be coming upon great danger, that they should take great care and be alert and make themselves very safe, and so forth, not saying anything however about what he might have heard in confession.

Here we show which sins the confessor should ask the sinner about, and how many circumstances there are that the confessor should ask about.

As need be, if he cannot or dare not speak of them himself, the confessor should ask the confessant about the eight principal and capital vices – arrogance, vainglory, avarice, anger, envy, sloth, gluttony, and lust – and the vices and sins that arise from them. We will speak more specifically about each one later in the chapter, where we deal with which sins and how a person should confess. The confessor should ask not only about sins but also about their aggravating circumstances, which the sages say are eight and are contained in a single verse: *Quis, quid, ubi, per quos, cur, quotiens, quomodo, quando*: and the other verse follows, which is said to the confessor: *Quilibet observet, anime medicamina dando.*

We'll explain the said circumstances here for the benefit of confessors.

The first circumstance that the confessor should ask about, if the sinner does not say it himself, is *quis*. In other words, the confessant should state whether he is a prelate or a subject, cleric or layman, educated or not, old or young, bound in matrimony or free, because, as St. Augustine says,[120] the same sin is aggravated or lightened according to the status, job, and condition of the person.

The second circumstance is *quid*, what sin was committed. It is not enough to speak in generalities: I have sinned by gluttony or lust, or I have been injurious towards my neighbour. The person who confesses must speak explicitly and specify by what type of sin he has offended. If he has sinned by gluttony, eating and drinking too much, or wanting things that are too delicate, or not waiting for mealtime; in lust, whether by fornication, or adultery, or a sin against nature, or something else; in being injurious towards someone, what the injury was: if by words, what words (threats, scolding, defamation); if by deeds, what the deeds were: whether to things or possessions, or towards someone; if there were blows, with what (an iron, a club, a stone, a fist); and who the person was whom he offended (father or mother, prelate or others); and if damage came of it, or danger, scandal, or shame. He should also ask

---

120 Pseudo-Augustine, *De vera et falsa poenitentia* [GA].

what he wanted or intended to do; because oftentimes one sets one's heart on doing something very bad, like homicide, betrayal, or the like, and it is not done, and one should confess bad will and evil intention.

The third circumstance is *ubi*, where did the bad thing happen: in public or private, because a sin committed in public is more serious because of the bad example and shameless daring; and if it was in a sacred place, where the sin is greater because of irreverence towards God, to whom the place is sanctified and deputized. With great indignation, Jesus Christ chased from the temple those who sold and bought therein.

The fourth circumstance is *per quos*; with what help and company did he commit the evil act, because often a man, in order to carry out a vendetta or to attain some goal, will require help and company in doing evil; and he will have all the evildoers together with him, whence it is the reason for their sin.

There are those who, in order to achieve some purpose, either gain or pleasure, make use of the help or counsel of demons, or evil enchanters, or soothsayers, which are very serious sins.

The fifth circumstance is *cur*: why, for what reason did someone commit the sin, because the reason makes the sin more serious. It is a greater and graver sin to steal out of avarice and for the pleasure of doing harm to someone else than to do it out of poverty. It is a far more serious sin to injure someone out of a desire to do harm or because of one's own arrogance than out of indignation over an injury received. It is a greater sin to provoke concupiscence and nourish temptation and ill will than it is to allow strong temptation to win because of fragility. It is a greater sin to sin on purpose and out of a certain malice than out of ignorance or sickness.

The sixth circumstance is *quotiens*, how many times has someone committed the sin. The second time is more serious than the first, and the third more than the second, because it appears that he disdains and holds the goodness and gentleness of God, who sustains him, in contempt, especially when he falls back on that same sin of which he had been absolved before. With the seriousness of the sin there is ingratitude for grace received, and there is the breaking of the peace and the pact made with God to not do Him harm. In order to show how serious it is to return to sin, Jesus Christ always said to those whom he absolved: *Vade ed amplius noli peccare* [Jn 8:11]: Go, and don't do it anymore. When someone gets sick again, it is more dangerous than the first time, and to cure it requires greater diligence from the doctor. So too the confessor, who is a doctor to the soul, should know if a sinner has fallen back into the same sin, and how many times, so that he might better know how give the medicine of penitence and advise him to be careful in the future.

The seventh circumstance is *quomodo*, how did the man sin. If he says, against another, he should be asked how: by usury, stealing, theft, gambling, or by keeping the product of someone else's efforts. If he says that he struck someone else, he should be asked if the blow was soft or hard, with an empty hand or some other way, and if he did it out of betrayal or to carry out a vendetta. Here and in other cases, he should examine the sinner about the ways that worsen the sin. Nevertheless, as we said, he should do so cautiously and discreetly, so that the person might state the sin and how, if he did it; and if he did not do it, so that it does not occur to him, as was said above.

The eighth circumstance of sin about which the confessor must ask is *quando*, when: when he was young, and if the sin is old or new, if it was on a holiday or in a time of penitence, like Lent and the four holy periods,[121] or if it was when mass was being said, or when someone was preaching, or when ordinations of clerics or processions happen, or when one should be dispensing or receiving the sacraments of the Church, or when others were about to go off to sea or to battle, because the sin is so much worse and shows a worse disposition when someone should be better disposed.

The other verse that is said to the confessor: *Quilibet observet*: Everyone should obey, i.e., the things said above: *anime medicamina dando*, giving medicine to the soul, or of the soul, which the confessor does, who is, as said above, the doctor of the soul.

Fifth Chapter

Wherein we show how the sinner who wants to go and confess should prepare himself, and what he should do to confess well and fruitfully.

The fifth thing that we should say about confession, according to what we promised above, is how the man who wants to go and confess should prepare himself. Here we must consider that the person

---

121 Passavanti here appears to refer to the four liturgical seasons: Advent, which runs
     until Christmas Eve; Christmastide, beginning on Christmas Eve and ending
     with the Feast of the Baptism on 13 January; Lent, from Ash Wednesday to
     Holy Thursday; and the Season of Easter, from Easter Sunday to Pentecost. The
     remainder of the year is known as Ordinary Time.

who wants to confess well, and have a fruitful confession, has to do three things.

First, he must completely account for all his sins with all the aggravating circumstances, as said above. To do that, the person should have his sins in mind; otherwise he could not, nor would he, know how to state them. Therefore, several times over several days before coming to confession, he should examine his conscience and recall the sins committed, the ways and reasons and times. If it had been some time since he had confessed, and he was worried about not remembering well at the time of confession, when many people forget out of shame or fear, he could make a written list, which he could then read at the priest's feet. If the person could not recognize or discern the sins and therefore could not state them and offer them distinctly, he should seek instruction and ask the confessor, not before he begins the confession, but saying what he knows and remembers about some sins. If he believes or is worried that he has sinned in one way several times or offended in several ways that he does not recall or cannot state, and the confessor does not enquire, he should not proceed to the other sins but say: "With this sin that I have told you about now, I believe that I have offended in several ways and several guises; so that I am guilty of this sin among others, and I know that I do evil and then don't know how to put it in words. I ask you, out of love for God's charity, to question me, so that there is nothing left to say because of my forgetfulness or ignorance." He should do the same for each vice and sin, where he might believe that he has offended more than he remembers and doesn't know how to say it. Understanding readers who remember what was said above, and what will be said later in this book of ours, and especially in the seventh chapter on confession (this being the fifth), will not need to be asked by the confessor, because they will themselves be able to recognize and state everything about the vices and sins that might have caused offence.

The second thing that someone who wants to confess fruitfully should do is to strive to feel contrition and pain about his sins, without which the confession will not be fruitful. In order to feel contrition, it is worthwhile to rethink the sins committed, by which a person has offended God, harmed his neighbour, made the devil happy, saddened the angel, put his soul in danger of eternal death. Carefully considered, these things give you cause and reason to feel displeasure and pain about the sins committed. To feel contrition, you need those things that were stated above, where we dealt in an orderly way with contrition and the things that pertain to it. Above all else, prayer affectionately offered to God is useful and necessary, because it is a gift and grace of

God to feel the pain of perfect contrition, and it cannot be had except from God, but it can be had with studious prayer. While everything else has to do with removing impediments or preparing the soul for the pain of contrition, only grace concedes or gives it, for which prayer is necessary. This is as the prophet says, having spoken of contrition and of the intention of confession: *Recogitabo tibi omnes annos meos in amaritudine anime mee; Dixi: confitebor adversum me iniustitiam meam Domino, et tu remisisti impietatem peccati mei* [Is 38:15], as explained above.[122] He then adds: *Pro hac orabit ad te omnis sanctus in tempore opportuno*: In order to have this, i.e., the bitterness of contrition by which sin is relieved and forgiven, every saint will pray in a time of need.

The third thing that someone who wants to confess well should do is to set himself at the feet of the priest, pained and repentant of all his sins, ready and prepared to obey his commands. He should choose him if his own priest is not sufficient, according to the form and the rule stated above. Coming to him reverently, as to God's vicar, and with shame, as the evildoer should do before the judge who has to judge him, he should throw himself humbly at his feet, either sitting or kneeling, in such a way that he is at his side leaning backward more than forward. In particular, if the confessant is a woman, she should position herself so that her face and eyes cannot meet those of the confessor. She should do this out of a sense of honour, so that she can declare her sins more securely and openly. St. Mary Magdalene offers an example of this. St. Luke says of her in the Gospel: *Stans retro secus pedes eius* [Lk 7:38], i.e., coming to Christ, she stayed behind, next to his feet. The sinner, therefore, sitting humbly and shamefully at the confessor's feet, should first make the sign of the holy cross and say: "I, wretched sinner, confess to God and to the Virgin Mary, and to all the saints, male and female, in Paradise, and to you, Father, all of my sins, in which I have offended my Creator. First, I give myself up in guilt, and accuse the sin of arrogance"; and he should then proceed with this sin and the others according to what he will find written in an orderly manner in the next two chapters, where we will show what the confession should be, and how, and what sins it should consist of. Having completed the confession, the confessant should say: "In these sins, and in many others that I either don't remember or perhaps do not recognize, and which I have confessed other times, and then fell back into and offended my Lord Jesus Christ, I declare my guilt in all of them, and I beg you, Father, to pray to God for me, and to absolve me."

---

122 See p. 88.

Sixth Chapter

Wherein we show how we should make confession, and how many things are required for it to be done well.

The sixth thing to say is how the confession should be done, and how many things are required for it to be done well. The teachers say that there are twelve things. St. Thomas says that there are sixteen, or really seventeen:[123] and they are contained in certain verses, which he explains in an orderly manner in the fourth book of the *Sentences*. Following him, we will put those verses here and explain extensively what he says briefly: *Sit simplex, humilis confessio, pura, fidelis, / atque frequens, nuda, discreta, libens, verecunda, / integra, secreta, lacrimabilis, accelerata, / fortis et accusans, et sit parere parata.* These verses include all the conditions that the confession should have, both as an act of virtue and as one of sacrament. Some of those things are required out of necessity, some for perfection.

First, *sit simplex*: the confession should be simple, i.e., without a crease, it should be open, it should not have duplicity or the twisting of words which might hide the sin. Nor should the confessant have a corrupt intention that diverts him from straightforwardness and simplicity, but simply intend to accuse himself and correct his sins. Thus did the holy King David say to the prophet Nathan, whom God sent to scold him for his sin, *Peccavi Domino* [2 Sm 12:13]: I have sinned before God, I do not excuse myself, I do not hide it; and therefore he deserved pardon, so that the prophet said to him: *Dominus transtulit peccatum tuum*: God has taken away your sin. Many do the opposite of this, when in their confession they do not intend to accuse and correct themselves, but to praise and justify themselves and appear good and devout, so that people will praise them and trust them; and they do it to achieve standing: all of which are creases that corrupt and vitiate the confession.

The second condition is *humilis*: someone who comes to confess should be humble, and humbly state his sin, and know himself to be wretched and a sinner, and want to be judged that way. Not only should the sinner accuse himself with words, but with his heart, and if the confessor scolds him about his vices, he should bear up patiently. There are many who, in order to be held humble and just, oftentimes blame themselves, but if someone else scolds them or says the same thing about them that they were saying, they do not take it well and become

---

123 On the varying numbers see Passavanti, ed. Auzzas, 498. Thomas proposes his list in *In I–IV Sententiarum*.

indignant towards the scolds. This is a sure sign that they are not as humble as they showed in their words. As St. Gregory says, explaining the holy Job's statement: *Peccavi et vere deliqui et, ut eram dignus, non recepi*: He who is truly humble and humbly confesses his sin patiently endures everything that is said or done to him, so that patience stands with humility, anger and impatience with arrogance.[124]

Not only should a confessant be humble in his heart and show humility in his words, but also in his bearing and outward appearance, to be a good example to others. Since, according to Solomon's doctrine, external acts and behaviours show what a person is inside, vain and arrogant women who come to confession primped and dressed up in their finery and other ornaments, as if to a banquet or a wedding, betray a lack of humility every day. To recount their faults, their follies, their vanities, the ugly things they have done, their defects, their foolishness, their regrettable acts and their excesses, they should come with their head covered, their face covered, their eyes tearful and cast down, with sighs, crying, lamentations, and with undesirable and lowly clothes, which would be an indication of their contrite and humbled heart, of their soul repented and pained for the sin they have committed. And the confessors should scold them and teach them about that and have no other concern but for their salvation and correction. Any confessor who thinks about anything else may expect to be harshly judged and punished by God, because, as Scripture says, the one who does the work of God fraudulently is damned.

The third condition which the confession should have is *pura*: it should be pure, which means that it is not mixed with other news or stories, because someone who is truly contrite about his sins is not inclined to other things but is intent only on stating his sins. And it should not be mixed with falsehoods or excuses for one's sins, or with talking about others' sins, unless it were the case that one should not or could not be silent, as was said above.

The fourth condition that confession should have is *fidelis*: it should be faithful. In other words, it should be made to a faithful confessor and faithfully according to the rite and order of the Holy Church, and it should be made with faith and hope to have the effect and fruit of confession, which is remission and pardon for sin. Without this faith and hope confession is fruitless, as St. Ambrose says, who gives the example of Cain and Judas, who confessed their sins but, having no faith in God's mercy, despaired and lost the fruit of confession.

---

124 Job 33:27. Gregory's comment appears in the *Moralia in Job* [GA].

The fifth condition is that it should be *vera*: a person should not be silent about the truth out of shame, nor excuse the sin out of arrogance, nor speak ill of himself out of foolish humility, saying what is not true, as some people do, men and women alike, who say: I am the worst man in the world, I am the most evil woman on the face of the earth, I have done and said every evil thing. And then it turns out not to be true, so that, just as we should not be silent about what someone else has done, so too should we not talk about what others have not done.

The sixth condition that the confession should have is *frequens*, i.e., it should be made often. This can be understood in two ways. First, people should often confess the venial sins they commit, so that they don't forget their sins by delaying confession. Also, so that, by virtue of the keys that are used whenever the priest absolves, either contrition happens if it is not carried out well or grace for contrition received grows, and also the punishment due for the sins decreases, thanks to the humility of confession and the shame there is in confessing, which is painful. The commandment of the Holy Church (which we should obey for reasons of salvation, and the pope cannot give dispensation to any person who has not confessed, although he could give dispensation for the time beyond a year that someone has waited) also obligates us to confess every year, for the Easter of the Resurrection, when every faithful Christian, man and woman who is of age, should take communion. Still, there are other times when a man should confess, such as if he has become gravely ill, or if he has to go to sea or off to do just battle, or go to a far-off, uncertain land, or has to risk death, or, in the case of ministers of the Church, has to give or receive any sacrament, to laymen and clerics alike. Beyond these instances, a man is not held by need of salvation to confess, but it is useful for the reasons stated above. As Scripture says: *Omnia in confessione lavantur*:[125] all sins are washed, indeed, the soul is washed of its sins in confession, so that, as a man is careful to wash his hands, his face, his head, his clothes often, so should he wash his soul, which is stained and dirtied obscenely by sin, even more often. Those who do not do so signal that they attach little value to the nobility and cleanliness of the soul. Christ says of them in the Gospel, *Vae vobis* [Mt 23:25]: Woe unto you who leave dirty what is inside, you are like tombs that are scrubbed white on the outside, and on the inside are full of stinking carcasses. There are some, and in every state, who are beautiful on the outside and dirty and filthy inside.

---

125 As Auzzas points out (Passavanti, 173), this phrase appears not in the Bible but rather in St. Bernard's "Sermones in viglia nativitatis Domini."

The second way to understand that confession should be done often is that those same sins might be confessed again, and this is not necessary if someone has made a good confession the first time, has been contrite and absolved and made penitence. But if the person knows, or believes, or wonders about whether he has made a good confession the first time, he should confess again.

Here we show that there are four cases in which someone should confess all over again from the beginning.

In order for people to be well-instructed on what to do, they should know that there are four cases in which someone should confess again.

The first is if the priest cannot absolve them, either because it was not their own priest, or if he did not have the authority of the Church or the bishop, or if he was not authorized to absolve for serious sin, or if he had been excommunicated or suspended or deprived, or if he did not legitimately hold the benefit of the Church. If someone knows that there were any of these defects either at the time he confessed or later, he should confess those sins again from the beginning to a priest who can absolve him. Therefore, before he confesses, a person should seek such a confessor who makes the confession valid and who can absolve him. Still, if he did what he could and was not negligent and believed that he had a legitimate confessor, good faith in this case helps him, and the highest priest, God, fills in what was missing in the defective priest. However, if at some point the person finds out that his confessor had some defects, he should confess again from the beginning to another legitimate confessor.

The second case in which it is necessary to confess again is when the confessor does not have the knowledge to discern and judge the sins, which were serious and which light, which deadly and which venial, or if he did not know how to make absolution according to the format set by the Church, nor impose due penitence for the sins. For the confession not to be in vain, the person should procure a confessor who can discern and judge, unloose and bind, using the two keys given to St. Peter in the name of all the ministers of the Holy Church. But there are many men and women who go looking for savage confessors, foolish and crude, who lack understanding, are unlettered, do not understand what is said to them, and who by asking indiscreetly say what the person should say in shamefully admitting his errors, and who do not know how to unloose and bind souls, which is a subtle art, but they barely know how to untie their own shoes. In this case the confessant, believing himself unloosed, remains doubly bound, and the confessor, thinking that he has unloosed someone, remains bound, and so the word of the Gospel becomes true for them: If the blind leads the blind, both fall into the ditch [Mt 15:14].

The third case is when the confession was not complete, when out of either shame or fear the person has purposefully been silent about some deadly sins. In that case he should confess again, from the beginning, all the sins that he had stated, plus the ones he kept to himself, admitting his guilt for the offence done to God and to the sacrament by not making a full confession.

The fourth case is when someone has not made penance and has forgotten about it. In this case, the person should confess again, so that the confessor knows what penitence to impose on him. This should be done when someone goes to a different confessor, but if he were to go back to that same confessor who had given him penitence and remembered the penitence that he had given him, it will be enough to recall the forgotten penitence, imposing that he do it, without restating the other sins. Were the confessor also to forget the penitence, if he remembers the sins for which he had imposed the forgotten penitence, he should impose the penitence again at his discretion. If he has forgotten the sins and the penitence, then there is no other remedy save for the sinner to confess again from the beginning and suffer punishment for his negligence and forgetfulness and receive penitence. Some would say that it is not necessary to confess again if the penitence was not done or forgotten, as long as the confession had been done completely and with contrition and according to the other conditions of sufficient contrition and confession. However, it would suffice to confess not having done the penance imposed and to receive new penitence for the negligence or forgetfulness, or for not having wanted to do the penitence imposed, with the forgotten penitence reserved for purgatory in the other life. I do not like this option, and it is not as certain as the first.

Of those who sin mortally before they begin to make penance, or, having begun it, before they complete it, and do the penance imposed along with the deadly sin, we say that such penitence is not valid to atone for the sins. Anyone who does such a thing should immediately be contrite about the sin committed and intend to confess it or go without delay to confess it, and then go and complete the penitence. It is not necessary to confess the other sins again from the beginning, although it might be a good idea to do so. At least in general you should say: "I, wretched sinner, give myself up in guilt and admit to falling back into sin before I completed the penitence that you gave me (or: that was assigned to me by my confessor), after I confessed and received the grace of absolution for many serious sins; yet I was ungrateful and did not recognize the benefit received."

In the above-mentioned case, when someone should confess again if he has forgotten the penitence, if he were to remember the penitence there would be no need to confess again, but he should make penance and confess his negligence in not having made penance.

There is yet another case where a man should restate his confessed sins, and this is when he cannot or does not want to do the assigned penance and asks for it to be changed. In that case, he should tell his confessor the sins for which the penitence that he wants to change was given. Another case, according to some, is if he was not contrite about his sins when he confessed, or if he did not suffer or did not repent for all of them or did not have the intention to stop sinning. This person was stuck; he did not have that internal disposition required for the external act of confession. Therefore, he did not receive the benefit of confession. Also, if he confessed all his sins and submitted to the keys of the Holy Church, by leaving behind the fiction, i.e., feeling the contrition he did not feel when he confessed, others say that he does not have to confess again from the start. But surely it is necessary to confess the fiction, because he did not come to the confession contrite, as he should have.

Of those who fall back into those same sins which they had confessed before and for which they had been absolved, some say that they should confess again from the beginning. But those with greater understanding think this is not necessary and that the sinner need only say: "I confessed before – or for a similar sin – what I confess now, and I was absolved, and then, like someone ungrateful for the benefit received, I fell back into it."

Now, although I said above that one need not repeatedly confess his sins, except in certain cases, St. Thomas nevertheless says, in the fourth book of the *Sentences*,[126] that it is very useful to confess those same sins several times, and to many confessors, both because of the blush of shame that comes with punishment, so that you are in a place of satisfaction, and because of the efficacy of the keys and the penitence that the priest imposes, which always diminishes the punishment. You could confess so many times that the entire punishment, reduced a little every time, would be removed, and there would be nothing left to do, either in this life or in purgatory.

We might well ask whether rethinking and repeatedly confessing certain sins to which someone had been or is very drawn, like sins of

------

126 *In I–IV Sententiarum.*

dishonour or carnal sins, is harmful or dangerous to the person who often restates them, or to the confessor who hears them again and again. Those things, when imagined, pondered, discussed, and heard, have to provoke concupiscence and incline the senses and the mind to delight and pleasure, so someone who might worry about that should not put himself at risk or in danger.

What would be very useful and certain, which every person who can do, should do, would be to have an understanding and discreet spiritual father and expert confessor, to whom he can confess all his sins in general one time, laying open his whole life and opening his conscience up to him, turning to this man for instruction and counsel in cases of need and sparing him with due reverence when there is no need. He could confess generally to him once a year, or when he had to take communion, or when he was sick. He could easily do this, not specifying every sin in particular, as he did the first time, but saying: "I confess to God and to you, Father, that, as I said when confessing before, I was a great sinner and caught up in many vices, for I was arrogant and haughty, pompous and vainglorious as I told you then; I was quick to anger and disdainful, impatient and angry in many ways and guises, as I showed you specifically then; and now I confess it to you in the same way." He can speak in this way about other vices and sins too. Also, if he wanted to go into specifics, so as to feel more shame, or to make clear that he had confessed well, he could do that. But he should always be careful about the risk, as said above,[127] about the details of the carnal sins, about which it is better to keep to generalities once they have been confessed well.

The seventh condition of confession is *nuda*: it should be naked, i.e., manifest and open, and you should not cover up or hide any of your sins, no matter how obscene or abominable. Just as someone does not hide his sickness and wound from the doctor, no matter how unspeakable it is or if it is in a shameful place, so that the doctor can cure it and heal it, so too should we show the wound of sin to our confessor, who is the doctor of the soul. There are those who do the opposite when, either by denying the sin or excusing it or blaming someone else, they do not show their sins just as they are. This is what Adam and Eve did, because Adam put it on Eve, and even on God, saying, *Mulier, quam dedisti mihi sotiam, dedit mihi, et comedi* [Gn 3:12–13]: The woman whom you gave to me as a companion gave some to me (i.e., of the forbidden fruit), and I ate it. And the woman said: The serpent deceived me.

---

127 See pp. 116–17.

St. Gregory says:[128] It is a normal vice of the human generation to easily commit sin, and by excusing it to increase and multiply it.

The eighth condition that the confession should have is *discreta*: it should be discrete, i.e., it separates the more serious and greater sins from the lesser and lighter ones, and so a person confesses them with greater seriousness and more weightily than the light sins, which also should not be made worse by lack of distinction.

The ninth condition that the confession should have is *libens*: it be voluntary, neither compelled nor forced, but one should willingly admit his sins, out of love of truth and justice. The prophet David did this when he said: *Voluntarie sacrificabo tibi et confitebor nomini tuo, Domine* [Ps 53:8]: Willingly will I make a sacrifice to you and confess to your name.

The tenth condition that the confession should have is *verecunda*: it should be shameful; the person should shamefully admit his sin. St. Jerome says there is the hope of salvation when shame follows sin.[129] There is the example of the publican in the Gospel who, ashamed of his sin, did not dare to lift his eyes, but while shamefully confessing his sin beat his chest and said: "God, have pity and forgive me, a sinner" [Lk 18:13]. Explaining this, Origen[130] says it is good at first not to do anything confusing, but because we are men and often sin, it is a second good to be ashamed of the evil we have done and, casting our shame-filled eyes to the ground, not shamelessly defend the evil. This Mary Magdalene did when she shamefully trailed behind Jesus Christ [Lk 7:38]. But the shame does not have to be so great that someone might avoid doing what he should say or do. Rather, the sinner should feel a shameless shame, as St. Gregory says of the Magdalene:[131] when she saw the stains of her filthiness, she ran to the fountain of mercy to wash herself, and because of her great shame within, she did not care about showing shame on the outside. As St. Augustine says, this type of shame that one feels in confession is counted among the other painful acts of contrition.[132]

The eleventh condition that confession should have is *integra*: it should be whole. You should not be silent about any deadly sin, and

---

128 In the *Moralia in Job* [GA].

129 In the Commentaries on Ezekiel [GA].

130 The scholar and theologian Origen, born in 185 AD in Alexandria, Egypt, was the author of more than 2,000 treatises. The source of this argument, attributed by Passavanti to Origen, is uncertain.

131 In the Homilies on the Gospels [GA].

132 Pseudo-Augustine, *De vera et falsa poenitentia* [GA].

you should not divvy up the confession, stating some of your sins to one priest and some to another, because by doing so not only would the fruit of confession not follow, but a new deadly sin would be acquired. Nevertheless, if someone were to forget a sin and not remember it for some time, it is forgiven together with the others when he does what he can to remember. If he does remember, he should go at once and confess it, and it is good to have the same confessor. If not, he should confess to another, saying, "When confessing many other sins I forgot about this one, which I confess now to God and to you." It should also be whole in the sense that a person should not diminish the quantity and quality of the sin by excusing himself and blaming someone else. And it should be whole in the sense that the sin is confessed along with all those circumstances that make the sin worse. We have said enough about those circumstances in the chapter where we showed what the confessor should ask the confessant. And you should not believe that the confession is whole just because you confess several times and at different times to the same confessor for a legitimate reason, or because you cannot state all of your sins at once, which happens especially when making a general confession, either because you forget some sins or because of other impediments, either on the part of the confessor or of the sinner. The same holds true when the confessor does not have the power to absolve some sins and sends the sinner to someone else who can absolve him, as was said above.

In the next chapter, when we will discuss which sins should make up the confession, we will state whether venial sins should be confessed.

The twelfth condition that the confession should have is *secreta*: it should be secret, because the judgment of confession is of secrets of the conscience. Sins should be made manifest in secret to the confessor, who is the judge of secrets, and the secrets shown should be secretly confessed and secretly judged. If the priest had seen or heard the sins of the person who confesses, he still should not absolve him if he does not confess them secretly by mouth. The priest can very well remind him of them if the confessant did not say them, out of either shame or forgetfulness.

The thirteenth condition that the confession should have is *lacrimabilis*: it should be tearful and painful, as we have in the examples of St. Peter and St. Mary Magdalene, who cried very bitterly over their sins, with very painful tears. St. Gregory, explaining the prophet's statement:[133] *Potum dabis nobis in lacrimis in mensuram*, explained above,

---

133 In the *Regula pastoralis* [GA].

says: The amount the pain should be proportional to the size of the sin, so that you should drink as many tears of shame as you became arid and dry before God because of sin. Many disagree, and when they confess, they talk as if they were telling a story, without any pain or tear of shame. The holy Job did not do this; he said: *Loquar in amaritudine anime meae* [Jb 10:1]: I will speak of my sin in the bitterness of my soul. St. Gregory explains this,[134] saying the pain must open up and push out the voice of confession, so that the vice, within which it willingly hides others, does not stink and make you dangerously dirty. We spoke above, in the treatise on contrition, about how great and of what nature the pain of sin should be.

The fourteenth condition that confession should have is *accelerata*, i.e., you should confess just as soon as the sin has been committed and not put it off. This is so that the sin is not forgotten, it does not multiply, and the devil loses the alacrity and daring he has over someone when he does not let him confess his sin. There are many other reasons for removing every danger that can happen by delaying confession, as was said above in the chapter where we said that penitence should not be delayed. Although the Church orders us to make confession once a year, nevertheless, someone who has a greater need should do it more often, especially in the cases cited above. And someone who does not confess presently and in fact more often at the very least should always have the intention of doing so. Such intention, like contrition, is necessary for salvation, because one is always supposed to feel pain and displeasure about sin when thinking about it, and thus should have the intention of confessing.

The fifteenth condition that confession should have is *fortis*: you should be strong, so that you do not leave the confession, out of either shame or fear of the punishment that you must endure to atone for the sins, either by abstaining from the usual things or through the tribulations or temptations that you might expect.

The sixteenth condition required for confession is *accusans*: the confessant should accuse himself, not others, and he should not excuse himself or praise himself or boast about any worldly vanity, as those do who easily admit to vile or carnal sins but praise themselves uselessly for having carried out a vendetta, or for having had a victory or done some brash deed, or for having figured out clever ways to gain or acquire honour, even by sinning.

---

134 In the *Moralia in Job* [GA].

The seventeenth condition that confession should have is *et sit parere parata*: the confessant should be disposed and prepared to obey everything required of him. As St. Augustine says, the sinner should throw himself at the mercy of the judge, i.e., the confessor, ready and willing to do for the life of the soul, which is immortal, what he would do for the life of the body, which still has to die.[135]

Seventh Chapter

Wherein we show what sins we should confess, and that there is more than one way of sinning.

The seventh and last thing that we should say about confession is what sins a person should confess. There are three ways of sinning: original sin, venial sin, and deadly sin. And we could add a fourth, which is any sin for which there is uncertainty over whether it is venial or deadly.

Here we show what original sin is, and how every man and every woman who is born, according to the common course of nature, brings it with them.

Original sin is not present as a sin that someone might wilfully commit. On the contrary, it is the sin of the corrupt human nature of the first father of human nature, which was transfused into all those who are conceived and born through the seed of natural generation. Outside of Jesus Christ, who is not of human seed but was conceived by virtue of the Holy Spirit from the most pure blood of the Virgin Mary, all men and women who were born, are born, and will be born participate in and draw the infection and stain of original sin from corrupt nature, disordered and filled with vice by Adam, who sinned and lost the original justice that God had given him. St. Paul says: *Per unum hominem peccatum intravit in mundum* [Rm 5:12]: Through one man (i.e., through Adam, who was the beginning of human nature, which descends from him by seminal generation) sin (i.e., original sin) entered into the world. Elsewhere St. Paul says: *In quo omnes peccaverunt* [Ep 2:3]. Speaking of the first man, who disordered nature by sinning, he says *in quo*, i.e., through whom (Adam) all have sinned, drawing original sin from him, through which all of us, as St. Paul says, are born as children of anger;

---

135 Pseudo-Augustine, *De vera et falsa poenitentia* [GA].

i.e., we deserve God's anger because of a sin committed not by us but by the first father. As we all draw our natural being from him, so too do we draw original corruption, contrary to original justice, through which the whole sinning mass of human nature reasonably and justly is condemned. But God, who wants to save all men if they do not create an impediment to their salvation, out of an abundance of mercy always found a remedy for original sin, first through sacrifices and offerings, then through the sacrament of circumcision, and now, in the time of grace, through baptism, which draws its efficacy from the passion of Christ precisely in opposition to original sin, although it would also remove every present sin if a baptized person had it.

We surely do not find that any man or woman, conceived according to the common course of nature, by a male father according to seminal virtue, was protected or safeguarded from this sin of corrupt nature, originally transferred and derived from the beginning of nature. However, we do find a few saints who, because of the singular excellence of the duty for which God chose them, were cleansed of original sin in their mother's belly and sanctified before they were born into the world. We read about the prophet Jeremiah, who was chosen by God to foretell the passion of Christ more explicitly – both with doctrine and with his life and death, which he endured from the people, and from his people, the Jews – than any other prophet, so that God said to him: *Antequam exires de vulva, sanctificavi te* [Jr 1:5]: Before you came forth from your mother's belly, I sanctified you. Likewise, of St. John the Baptist, who was the chosen precursor and announcer of the coming of Christ, baptizer of his redeemer, preacher of penitence, the angel Gabriel said to Zachariah, his father: *Spiritu Sancto replebitur adhuc ex utero matris suae* [Lk 1:15]: He will be full of the Holy Spirit while still in his mother's belly.

We find nothing more explicit by anyone in Scripture.

Here we show whether the Virgin Mary had original sin.

Although Scripture does not speak of it explicitly but through certain similes and figures, still it is held by all that the blessed and glorious Virgin Mary was sanctified before she was born and full of the Holy Spirit in her mother's belly. And although we do not have clear and explicit authority in Scripture, there is the reasoning and authority of the Holy Church, indeed of the Holy Spirit which rules the Church, which makes a feast of her nativity. This feast was created not long ago, but by certain revelations and miracles a solemn feast was ordered, to last fully eight days. It is therefore certain that she was born holy, since solemnity and feast are made of her nativity, because, as St. Bernard says, we would not make a feast of her birth if she were not born holy. As we said, the reasoning is through the excellence and dignity of the duty for which God chose her. If Jeremiah and the Baptist were cleansed of original sin and sanctified in their mothers' bellies, then how much more, and more perfectly and excellently, did the Virgin Mary have the gift and grace of sanctification, she who was chosen for the most worthy and sovereign duty that any creature, angelic or human, ever was or ever can be, i.e., to be the mother of God? St. Anselm and St. Bernard also use this reasoning in praise of the Virgin Mary.[136] In addition, some say that the Virgin Mary was protected from original sin, because if she were to have the greater gift of holiness than Jeremiah or the Baptist, how would she have more if she had been also sanctified and cleansed of original sin like them? In order for her to have more than they, as she deserved, it was necessary and reasonable not only that she be sanctified before she was born, but that she be conceived as holy and protected and safeguarded from original sin.

This is not the place to debate the question, which has not been decided by the Holy Church, and no one knows anything about it. We do not find that God ever revealed it to either a prophet or an apostle or an evangelist, or to any saint worthy of faith who might have said or written something with certainty. But some doctors who speak about it give their opinion, and just as nobody affirms St. Mary's assumption in soul and body, so too does nobody deny this, because there is nothing about it in authentic scripture.[137] However, St. Jerome and St. Augustine, and the other doctors who speak of it, state their opinion and what should reasonably be the case, leaving the truth to God, who knows it and who, not without good reason, wants to keep the conception or assumption of His mother hidden from the world. No faithful Christian should doubt that God, if He wanted to, could protect the Virgin Mary and safeguard her from original sin, as He could do every day for any man or woman who might come into this world. If He formed a man or a woman from earth or another element, from a flower, a piece of human flesh, or a bone, that person would not have original sin, which, as was said above, is infused and transferred with the seed with which the father generates the child, which seed would not here be sown. So,

---

136 In Bernard's epistles and in Anselm's *De conceptu virginali et originali peccato* [GA].

137 Passavanti's reference here to "authentic scripture" may allude to the fact that the only scriptural record relating to the birth of the Virgin Mary appears in the apocryphal Gospel of James.

if Adam had not sinned, even though Eve did, original sin would not have been introduced into their descendants and human nature would not be corrupt; because the woman does not inseminate the child but receives the seed of the father within her, like the earth the seed of grain. With His infinite power God could also miraculously cause a woman to be impregnated, without the operation of a man, and the man who would be born would not have original sin. And so, if He wanted, He could, and in infinite ways beyond all our understanding, protect the Virgin Mary from original sin; but we cannot be at all sure whether He did so or not, and therefore we should not affirm that this was done. It is better to be unsure about something when there is no danger in not knowing than to presumptuously affirm what we do not know for sure. With regard to the reasoning given above, by which some want to affirm that otherwise the Virgin Mary would have no advantage over Jeremiah or the Baptist, we could reply that in other greater things God could, and in fact did, give an advantage, and gracious gifts, to the mother over all the other saints, without protecting her from original sin. The greater gift was to protect her from present sin, deadly or venial, and to fill her with the Holy Spirit, and to affirm her in grace in such a way that she could not sin, and to infuse love of God and of her neighbour most excellently in that soul with all the other virtues.

Moreover, to be conceived in original sin does not diminish the virtue of the Virgin Mary, because original sin is not the fault of the person but rather a condition of corrupt nature. Nor would it follow, however, that God must have given other greater gifts and graces to her than to all others because He had protected her from original sin, which He does not do for others. Being protected from original sin, assuming it were possible, and cleansed and sanctified before birth, which surely has been done for some, does not necessarily mean that one should be given, or was given, greater grace and glory than those who might be or who were conceived and born with original sin and then cleansed and sanctified by baptism – indeed, sinners set right by worthy penitence. Leaving aside the others, one could offer as proof the example of Jeremiah, who was sanctified in his mother's womb, in comparison with the apostles – we are talking about St. Peter, St. Paul, and St. John the Evangelist – who were not sanctified before they were born. They were purged of original sin and of their present sins through baptism, and some of them committed grave and deadly ones, like St. Peter and St. Paul and St. John, who were absolved, at least of the venial ones, through worthy penitence. It is not therefore the case that they have a lesser or greater abundance of grace and more copious fullness of the Holy Spirit, and greater perfection of charity and greater clarity of glory, than Jeremiah, even if he was sanctified in his mother's womb and they not.

It is not my judgment that the above-named apostles and the others surpassed all the other saints of the Old Testament and the New both in grace and glory, but rather that of St. Augustine and the other doctors, who speak about this in many places.

This is not, however, to diminish God's grace, nor to diminish the Virgin Mary's excellence and honour, but instead to suggest that people should not stubbornly affirm or deny something they do not know. There is no danger from not knowing, nor is it a problem if the thing is true or not, but the vice of presumption could be involved. Her being protected from original sin, as some believe, does not increase the honour and dignity of the Mother of God, nor does her having been conceived with the original defect decrease her sanctity. This is a vice of nature and not of the person, whom a gift of blessing and grace overtook, both before and after birth, greater and more abundant than that of any other saint. Herein lie the dignity and excellence of the Virgin Mary over all other saints, although God, who can do what He wants, and is *benedictus in saecula saeculorum, Amen*, could also, if He wanted, give the gift and advantage over all other saints of protecting her from original sin, which came from our saviour Jesus Christ.

To conclude the main argument, because original sin is not a present sin voluntarily committed but a vice of corrupt nature transferred by seminal generation, a person is not held to confess it but to receive the purification of baptism, which is ordained by God as a remedy for original sin, as penitence is a remedy for present sin.

Here we show what the second type of sin is.

The second type of sin is venial sin. We will consider three things about it: first, we will define what sin is; next, we will state the difference between a venial sin and a deadly sin; third, we will say whether one should confess venial sins.

Here we show what sin is.

First, it is necessary to say what sin is. St. Augustine says: *Peccatum est omne dictum vel factum, vel concupitum, quod sit contra legem Dei*:[138] Sin is everything said or done, and everything desired, against God's law. St. Thomas, explaining St. Augustine's statement and showing how he

---

138 In *Contra Faustium* [GA].

has sufficiently defined sin, says that sin consists of two things.[139] The first is what we do, or what we produce. This is shown by what he says: "everything said," which is an act made or produced with speech, and "done," which is the act produced and made with the hands or with any other part of the body, or "desired," which is an act of will, produced in the heart. The second part of sin is a defect of direction, i.e., of right reason, which has to direct human operations and acts to their due end. The due end of human actions is eternal beatitude. What directs men to eternal beatitude is God's law, which orders and regulates reason and human actions, which are defective, to their final goal, which is eternal beatitude. So, by acting according to God's law, man arrives at beatitude, which is the final goal of the rational creature, i.e., of man. But by acting against God's law, which is to commit a sin and fall short by defect of what a man should do, man is directed away from his ultimate purpose. Therefore, by saying what sin is, we reasonably add that it is against God's law. St. Ambrose, wanting to show what sin is, says:[140] *Quid est peccatum, nisi prevaricatio legis divine et Celestium inobbedientia mandatorum?*: What is sin, if not a trespass of God's law and disobedience of the heavenly commandments? In this we see how a lack of that which directs to the goal, i.e., to beatitude, is part of sin, and this is suggested when he says that it is a trespass of divine law. It is also a disordering and misdirection from said end, and we see that when he says that it is a disobedience of the heavenly commandments, by which, if we obey them, we arrive at the beatitude of eternal life – as Christ answered in the Gospel to the person who asked what he should do in order to have eternal life, saying, *Si vis ad vitam ingredi, serva mandata* [Mt 19:17]: If you want to enter into eternal life, obey the commandments.

It is therefore understood, as the Master of Sentences says,[141] that sin consists of both external acts, such as speaking badly and acting badly, and internal acts, such as thinking bad thoughts and wanting bad things and desiring bad things. Bad will, which is committed within and without, is specifically the root and reason of every sin.

Here we show the difference between venial and deadly sin.
The second thing to see is the difference between venial and deadly sin. Deadly sin takes its name from death, because it leads the soul to death, as St. James says: *Peccatum cum consumatum fuerit, generat mortem*

---

139 The discussion is found in the *Summa* [GA].
140 In *De paradiso* [GA].
141 Lombard in the *Sententiae* [GA].

[Jm 1:15]: Sin, when carried out, generates death. Death is a privation of life, and life of the soul is the love of God and one's neighbour. Every sin therefore that removes love of God or of one's neighbour leads the soul to death. This sin is called a deadly sin, for as St. Thomas says, a deadly sin is one that takes spiritual life away from the soul, which life comes from love.[142]

Now let's consider how and when sin removes love of God and of one's neighbour, so that we can know what deadly sin is, and by comparison and with respect to what venial sin is. Charity makes us love God above all things and our neighbour as ourselves. Christ said in the Gospel: *Diliges Dominum Deum tuum ex toto corde tuo et ex tota anima tua et ex omnibus viribus tuis et ex omni mente tua et proximum tuum sicut temetipsum* [Lk 10:27]. St. Augustine explains:[143] Love the Lord your God with all your heart, i.e., with all your thoughts and with your whole soul, i.e., your whole life, with all your mind, i.e., put all your intention in love of God, from whom you have what you have, and let there be no part of your soul that is not given to God, and let there be no room in it for the love of any other thing that does not refer to God. St. John Chrysostom says:[144] To love God with all your heart means that your heart is not inclined to the love of any other thing more than to love of God; to love God with all your soul means having a very certain disposition to the truth and being firm in your faith. Love of the heart is one thing; love of the soul is another. Love of the heart is in some ways about affection for the flesh and sensuality, according to which even God can be loved, but which we cannot feel unless we separate ourselves completely from worldly and carnal things. While this love of the heart is felt in the heart, love of the soul is not felt but understood, because such love is in the judgment of the soul. Those who believe that all goodness is with God, and that outside of Him there is no true good, love God with their whole soul. To love God with one's whole mind means that all feelings, both inside and out, are focused on God, so that the person whose intellect rises to God, whose thoughts address God's things, whose memory recalls God's good things, loves God with all his mind. Explaining this, Origen says: To love God with all your heart, i.e., according to all your memory, according to all your thoughts and all your actions, to love him with all your soul, means that you are ready to give your soul for the love of God, in all his mind, that you will think

---

142 In the *Summa theologica* [GA].

143 In *De doctrina christiana* [GA].

144 Auzzas (Passavanti, 501) locates this gloss by John Chrysostom, as well as the following one attributed to Origen, in Aquinas's *Catena aurea in Matthaeum*.

or say nothing except what is about God. St. Basil explains:[145] When it says with all your soul, it means that God is loved fully and without division; because the love you put in creatures reduces your love for the Creator, in whom you should put all your love. It is just as if some vessel full of liquid has a hole through which said liquid exits or seeps out, and by exiting it reduces the fullness of the vessel. So too is one's love for God reduced according to how much love you invest in illicit things, and so much could seep out, either through one hole or many, that nothing would remain, and the vessel would be left worthless. So it is with the love of God. Therefore, we want to sew up the holes in our heart, which are the feelings and intentions and affections that are open to creaturely pleasure. The venerable doctor Maximus, explaining this passage, says: The law teaches us to love God with all our heart, with all our soul, and with all our mind; so that He will draw us back from the love of earthly things. The gloss explains that we should love God with all our heart, i.e., with all our intention; with all our soul, i.e., with all our will; with all our mind, i.e., with all our memory, so that we might not want, or feel, or remember anything that is contrary to God.

You should therefore love God with all your heart, i.e., with all your intention, without error; with all your soul, i.e., with all your will, without contradiction; with all your mind, i.e., with all your memory, without forgetting. To this we add: with all your strength, which means that, as was said, a man must force himself to love God with all his power and give studious effort to it with diligence and attention, not tepidly and softly but fervently.

The second commandment is about love and charity towards one's neighbour, where it is said: Love your neighbour as yourself. Speaking of this, St. Augustine says that a person should love himself in three ways: either because he is just or so that he might be just, and he should love himself to have the prize for just living, which is the beatitude of eternal life. Likewise, he should love his neighbour, who is every person. First, he should love the goodness and justice that is in the person, no matter his condition, friend or enemy, and so he should hate evil, malice, and vice. He should love that someone is and becomes good and just by living in a just and correct manner, and he should love that one arrives at the beatitude of eternal life by living well and in a just and correct manner. This is what it means to love one's neighbour as oneself. This love of one's neighbour is also understood in the sense that, because of the love that one has for oneself, a person wants his needs

---

145 Here, and for the succeeding reference to Maximus of Tyre, Passavanti appears to rely on Aquinas's *Catena aurea in Luca* (Passavanti, ed. Auzzas, 501).

to be supported, and so too should he support his neighbour's needs. As someone wants the injuries done to others to be forgiven, with no vendetta, so too should one want to forgive the injuries suffered and not want to carry out or witness a vendetta. As a person wants to be accepted with all his defects, so too he should accept the defects of others. And as a person does not want to be judged for things kept hidden, so too should he not judge others. In brief, those good and licit and honourable things that he might want done to him, he should do to others, and those evil, harmful, or shameful things that he would not want done to him, he should not do to others. In this way a false love, with which you should not love yourself or others, is removed, about which Scripture says, *Qui diligit iniquitatem odit animam suam* [Ps 10:6]: He who loves sin hates his own soul. Which means that you should not love or desire what is harmful and damaging, either to yourself or to others, as sin is. So that whenever someone sins, believing that he loves himself, he would not be loving himself, he would be hating himself. Such love, which is to do one's own will and not that of God, to follow one's own concupiscence or malice and not the straight path of reason and virtue, leads a person to sin, and sin leads to eternal death, which is the greatest evil there is and can be. A person should not feel such love for himself or for his neighbour, because it would not be love but hate, it would not be charity but impiety, it would not be loving someone else but hating.

St. Augustine explains[146] that you should love your neighbour as yourself in another way, saying: you should love yourself not for yourself, but for God. In other words, God, as the highest and most perfect good and beatitude and the ultimate end to which your love should be ordered and directed, should be the object of your love, so that you can have the good and take pleasure in Him without end. You should not love yourself for you, i.e., you should not make yourself the goal, for you are neither so good nor so perfect or sufficient that you can make yourself blessed and content by taking pleasure in yourself. Only the highest and most perfect good, which is God, and nothing other than God, can do this. Love for oneself is a corrupt love, source of and reason for every vice and every sin, and it is called self-love. St. Bernard says:[147] Remove your self-love, and you will not be in hell. St. Augustine says[148] that self-love, by which a man disdains God, builds the city of hell, just as the love of God, by which a man disdains himself, builds the city of

---

146 In *De doctrina christiana* [GA].
147 In the Easter sermons [GA].
148 In the *City of God*.

heaven and of eternal life. This seems to be what Jesus Christ meant in the Gospel when he said, *Qui amat animam suam, perdet eam, et qui odit animam suam in hoc mundo in vitam etternam custodit eam* [Jn 12:25]: He who loves his soul, i.e., following his own will, which is nothing other than loving oneself with one's own love, will thus lose it; because by sinning and living corruptly, which self-love makes us do, one loses one's soul. But the person who, while living in this world, hates his soul, i.e., his own will, which love for God makes us do, will save and protect it in eternal life.

O human, you should not love yourself for yourself, but for God, as was explained. And so, you should love your neighbour not for yourself, i.e., not for your own utility or delight,[149] nor for the one who is the object of your love, but for God, whom you should love, and for whom you should love both yourself and your neighbour. You should also endeavour to make your neighbour love God with all his heart, with all his soul, with all his mind, and with all his strength, as you should love and do love, and then you will love your neighbour as well as yourself. If you think about it, you will see clearly that one and the same love, and one and the same charity, is the one according to which we love God and our neighbour. What Scripture says therefore follows, and the holy doctors explain it, that you cannot love God without loving your neighbour, nor your neighbour without God. As well, a person cannot love God or his neighbour if he does not love himself, nor can he love himself if he does not love God and his neighbour. It is one charity and one love. Therefore, Jesus Christ, saying in the commandment, love the Lord your God, etc., added the second commandment, like the first, and your neighbour as yourself. The first commandment contains the love of God as the thing most worthy, and the second the love of one's neighbour and oneself.

All the law and the prophets are reduced to these two commandments, as they follow the words of Christ, as St. Augustine explicitly explains,[150] proving it about both the Ten Commandments of the tablets of Moses, which are called the Decalogue, and the other prophetic, evangelic, and apostolic scripture. And Rabanus[151] says, in his

---

149 Passavanti here alludes to two of the three Aristotelian categories of friendship, both understood as imperfect: friendship based on pleasure, and friendship based on utility.

150 In Epistle 155, glossing Matthew 22:40 [GA].

151 The ninth-century Benedictine Rabanus Maurus, author of the encyclopaedia *De rerum naturis* as well as commentaries on various books of the Bible. Here Passavanti is referencing his commentary on Matthew [GA].

commentary on the Holy Gospel, that the whole of the Decalogue of the law is reduced to these two commandments. The commandments of the first tablet have to do with love of God, those of the second with love of one's neighbour. St. Paul says that the end, that is, the final perfection of every commandment, is charity; and elsewhere he says, *Qui diligit proximum, legem implevit* [1 Tm 1:5; Rm 13:8]: He who loves his neighbour has fulfilled the law. St. Augustine says:[152] since one loves God and one's neighbour with the same love, oftentimes Scripture mistakes the one for the other, as the apostle says: *Diligentibus Deum omnia cooperantur in bonum* [Rm 8:28]; and elsewhere: *Omnis lex in uno sermone impletur: "Diliges proximum tuum sicut te ipsum"* [Gl 5:14]: For those who love God, all things work towards the good; and then: The whole law is summed up in one statement: Love your neighbour as yourself. And the apostle concludes, *Plenitudo ergo legis est dilectio* [Rm 13:10]: Therefore, the fulfilment of the law is love, with which you should love God for Himself, as the final and perfect good, and your neighbour and yourself to God, in God, and for God.

Enemies are not excluded from this love, not because they are enemies, but because they are part of God and are creatures made in His image and saved with His blood; we should love them out of love for Him. All the other things that are less than God and less than man, we should love less. Indeed, they should be loved so temperately that they do not remove or impede or diminish the love of God and of oneself and of one's neighbour, which are one and the same. When it happens that someone loves something as much as he does God, or in opposition to God, or more than God, then he perverts the degree of charity that we should feel for God, and we sin mortally. When we do to our neighbour that which he would not want done to him, we pervert the love of charity towards our neighbour, and we commit a deadly sin.

So we should not think that every little injury and light offence that one does to one's neighbour is always a deadly sin. As we will state later, in order to fully understand what we said about the love of God and the charity that we should have towards Him, to which no other love should be equal, as we already said in part above, God is the highest good and the ultimate end and final beatitude of the rational creature, i.e., of man. Therefore, all love, all desire, all affection must be gathered up and directed towards Him, and every other thing should be loved in relation to God. In other words, we should love things in such a way and to the extent that they help and lead us to love God and do God's

---

152 In *De trinitate* [GA].

will, which is shown to us through those things that God commands of us, so that our love and final intention should all be directed at Him as the object. Other things should be loved as things ordered to that end, and then love and charity are properly organized. But if someone perverts this order of love and, pursuing concupiscence, greed, vanity, and the pleasure of his own will, loves things for themselves, as if they were the end, and delights and lingers on them with love and affectionate desire, making of them his end and postponing the intention with love of the ultimate end, then he sins mortally, because charity, which was the life of the soul which ordered it to its final purpose, is extinguished, and the love of one's own will, which divides the soul from God and from death, finally resides in Him.

It should therefore be clear what a deadly sin is. It has its origin in the will perversely shifted away from the ultimate end of God by love of creatures, which become the end, as if they were the final end. Then the sin proceeds from the internal act of disordered will to external acts – seeing, hearing, speaking, touching, and using the feelings and limbs of the body – as perverse will commands and moves, and each act to which such a will moves is a deadly sin, as it is produced and comes from a mortal beginning. When bad will is linked with an external act it is also a deadly sin, but when there is some interval of time between bad will and the act or undertaking, then there are two deadly sins: one is of bad will, with agreement and deliberation set on wanting the bad thing; the other is the external act or undertaking to which bad will leads and moves. It can happen, indeed it happens all the time, that before someone arrives at the external act of a deadly sin, such as homicide or adultery or the like, he first commits a deadly sin many times, because however many times the will, with reason's consent, after deliberation agrees and wants to commit a sin or arrive at the act of sin, or accepts and agrees to take pleasure in the thought or fantasy or memory of sin, either one already committed or one deemed possible to commit, even though he may not want to commit it, then he commits a deadly sin. The confessant, therefore, should not only recount his sin and when they were committed through external acts and undertakings, but also the bad desires with deliberate agreement that came before the act of sin, or that happened without ever arriving at or wanting to arrive at the external action or at the commission of sin.

A venial sin is one that is light and worthy of pardon, i.e., it is easily pardoned, because it does not remove the grace and charity towards God and towards one's neighbour, which is the reason for remission and pardon. Indeed, grace and charity remain with it in the soul, while deadly sin does the contrary, so that there is no place or reason for pardon, because it seals the soul off from grace and charity, without which pardon is not given. But venial sin does not exclude and extinguish love and charity for the ultimate end, God, nor does the will position itself to perversely love creatures as if they were the ultimate end, although it may remain somewhat fixed on them out of a stronger will than is needed to arrive, according to the order, at the ultimate end. The excess that stays with the intention and love of the ultimate end is called venial sin, which we commit whenever the soul, more than is necessary, resides in creatures with desire and with excess pleasure, loving them, but nevertheless always preserving the main love and charity of the Creator, who is the ultimate end, and is blessed in *secula seculorum. Amen.*

Although we have shown what deadly sin and venial sin are, according to the doctrine of the holy doctors, and the difference between them, nevertheless, because the material is difficult to understand, and not only for laypeople, who are uneducated (for whom this book is especially written), but also for educated clerics, next we will offer an example, or simile or parable, by which it will be easier to understand the difference between a deadly sin and a venial one, which will be delightful to the ears and pleasant and gratifying to the understanding, and it will be the adornment and perfection of our whole book.

Here we show whether one should confess venial sins.
Now is the time to say what we promised above, in the seventh chapter, about confession, where, having said what sin is and what the difference is between venial and deadly sin, we promised to say whether you should confess a venial sin. According to the saints, venial sins are not the proper material of confession, which is to say, it is not necessary to confess them; they can be pardoned just through contrition in the heart. Nevertheless, someone who wants to confess them is to be praised, and such a confession is meritorious and has an impact.

This raises a question.

Let's assume a person who has committed no deadly sin but only venial ones. It is the commandment of the Holy Church that every faithful Christian confess at least once a year and take communion, and that he do so for the Easter of the Resurrection. Is the person who has committed only venial sins, which he does not have to confess, obligated to the commandment of the Church, since there are no deadly sins, which one is required to confess, but only venial ones, which one is not required to confess? Some say that in this case, in order to fulfil the Church's commandment, the person should confess his venial sins at least once a year. Others say that it is enough if once a year, when he should take communion, this person appears before the priest and says that he does not know of any deadly sin that he should confess, and the priest should believe him and receive him for communion. They say that the Church's intention is not to obligate someone unless he has sinned mortally, so that, if we were to find by God's special grace someone who had sinned neither mortally nor venially, like the Virgin Mary, he surely would not be held to that commandment.

Although this second response is put well and subtly, still I like the first one better, as more certain, and especially because of the concern one might have about whether he is in deadly sin or not, because oftentimes a person who is not free of them believes himself to be without deadly sins, especially those that are hidden in the heart, in desires, and in mental affections, and we find few with good discernment, who know how to safeguard themselves well. So the prophet prayed to God and said, *Ab ocultis meis munda me, Domine, et ab alienis parce servo tuo* [Ps 18:13–14]: Lord, cleanse me of my hidden sins, and pardon your servant for those of others. By the sins of others, he means those which gave someone else cause for sin, either by bad example or in some other way. It is certain that, according to the doctors' judgment, a man is supposed to confess the dubious sins, i.e., those about which there are questions as to whether they are deadly or not, and it would be a deadly sin not to confess them. The person who confesses dubious sins does not, however, have to be certain that they are deadly, but just say what he did and let the priest decide whether it was a deadly or a venial sin. Since, therefore, a man is supposed to confess dubious sins and it is hard to know for sure, if you had not already received a revelation from God as to whether the sins we commit every day with our thoughts and agreements and undertakings are deadly or venial, in order to be sure, the better advice is to confess all your sins, whether deadly or venial or dubious, not just once a year but more often, and especially in certain cases which are given above. Nor should you hold venial sins to be base, because, although many venial sins do not erase grace and charity, which only deadly sin erases, still they weaken it, and they dispose someone to deadly sin. This is because the more a man gets used to venial sins, the more easily he falls into a deadly one. Therefore, you should forbid them as best you can, and not commit them or many of them, or once they are done, whether many or few, find remedies so that they can be pardoned.

With His benign mercy, God has found many remedies against venial sins, and there are eight, which are contained in two verses, which go like this: *Confiteor, tundo, conspergor, conteror, oro, / Signor, edo, dono: per haec venialia pono.*

First, venial sins are pardoned by *confiteor*, i.e., by general confession. General confession can be understood in two ways. The first is when a man confesses his venial sins to the priest in secret, according to the sacraments, stating certain sins that he specifically remembers, either because they are serious or because someone else thinks they are serious, and then all of his sins generally. They are then pardoned together with the others by virtue of the confessant's contrition, because of the humility of confession, or because of prayer that the priest makes in absolution, and by virtue of the keys that the priest uses in granting absolution as a minister of the Holy Church. The other means of general confession is what someone does in the open before many people, like what the priest does when he arrives at the altar to say mass, and what is done by clerics at matins and compline. Venial sins are also pardoned through this confession, and through both not only the venial sins but also the deadly ones, which somebody might have completely forgotten.

You should note here that venial sins are not pardoned in any way without the deadly ones, because venial sins cannot be pardoned while a person remains in a state of deadly sin. So either a person must not have any deadly sin, or the remedy must be such that it erases the deadly and venial ones together.

The other way in which venial sins are pardoned is *tundo*, which is to say, by beating one's chest, admitting guilt for one's sins. The third is *conspergor*, throwing holy water on oneself with faith and devotion. The fourth is *conteror*, feeling contrition and displeasure for having offended God. The fifth is *oro*, through devout prayer, and especially through the Our Father, which is the prayer that Jesus Christ taught. The sixth is *signor*, i.e., through the bishop's benediction; some say also through that of the priest. The seventh is *edo*, through communion. The eighth is *dono*, by forgiving injuries or by giving alms to the poor. Some say that they are pardoned also through extreme unction and through any good meritorious deed, done in a worthy manner and with charity, and they are pardoned all the more completely and efficaciously the greater the fervour of charity is.

Here we show what sins people should confess, and the treatise on the deadly sins, and on those sins that are born from them, begins.

Having seen that people do not need to confess original sin, and what you should do about venial sins and those that are unclear, we are left now to examine what we promised principally to discuss in the seventh chapter about confession, i.e., what sins people should confess.

According to the holy doctors, deadly sins are the ones that we should confess, not in general, but each one specifically and distinctly, with the circumstances and conditions we set forth in an orderly way above. In order for us to do this well, we will next show what and how many vices and deadly sins there are, and the ones that are born and descend from them, and how and what order the confessant should follow. Some doctors say that there are seven deadly sins; others say there are eight. Those who say that there are seven do not count pride among the capital and principal ones; those who say that there are eight do count it. Everyone is right, but in different ways. In an effort to settle the apparent dispute among the doctors, St. Thomas says that pride can be considered in two ways.[153] First, as a special vice in and of itself, distinct from the others; in this way it is one of the principal and capital sins from which all other sins are born. Following this way of thinking, I count pride among the deadly sins, making eight of them. The other way that pride can be considered is as a general influence on all the other sins, of which it is the original source and reason. In this way it is not counted with the others but it is more an origin, above every other vice. In the book of *Morals*,[154] St. Gregory calls it queen and mother of sins, and according to this way of thinking there are only seven deadly sins, which are called principal and capital because all the other vices proceed from them, as the head or beginning of all.

However you might think about pride, in the one way or the other, it is certain (and everyone agrees on this) that in some ways it is the root, reason, and origin of all other sins, as we will show in an orderly manner at the proper time.[155] Therefore, we should address it first and foremost.

Here begins the treatise on pride.

To better understand everything we need to know about pride, we will consider seven things. First, describing it, we will say what pride is; second, we will say from what it is born; third, we will say how many types of pride there are; fourth, we will say how all the other vices are born of pride; fifth, we will show its seriousness and how offensive it is; sixth, we will talk about the punishment for pride; seventh, we will talk about the remedy for it and its correction.

---

153 The discussion appears in *In I–IV Sententiarum* [GA].
154 The *Moralia in Job* [GA].
155 See p. 160.

First Chapter

Wherein we show what pride is.

The first thing we have to say about pride is to describe it, saying what it is. St. Augustine says in the fourteenth book of the *City of God*, *Quid est superbia, nisi perversae celsitudinis appetitus?*: What is pride if not an appetite of perverse height? St. Thomas says, by means of explanation:[156] It is called pride when someone wilfully goes above what he is. St. Isidore says in the book *On Timology*,[157] *Superbus est qui super vult videri quam est; qui enim vult supergredi quod est, superbus est*: He who wants to appear to be above what he is, is arrogant; he who wants to rise above what he is, is arrogant.

From this we understand that the vice of pride lies in disordered will, and the will is disordered when it is not according to right reason. According to St. Thomas, right reason gives order to all those things that naturally are desired by man. Then the will of each one of us, ordered by right reason, is moved to those things that are necessary and proportional to a person's condition, and then things are desired and loved virtuously and reasonably. But when appetite, will, and desire move without right reason, things are desired and loved corruptly and perversely, and all vices proceed from this. The holy Dionysius says that the evil of man or of the soul is to be without reason. This is to perversely desire status and excellence, to want it beyond right reason, i.e., more than one should and is necessary according to right reason.[158] This is perverse will, which leads to the trespassing and disdaining of God's commandments. St. Gregory describes pride in this way in the book of *Morals*, explaining, *Et liberaet eum a superbia: Contra conditiorem superbire, est praecepta eius peccando transcendere, quia quasi a se iugum dominationis excutit: cui per obedientiam subesse contempnit*: To be arrogant towards God, and trespass his commandments by sinning, and not to want to be subject to God by obedience, and to throw off the yoke of His authority. Also there follows from pride, which St. Bernard calls[159] a desire for one's own excellence, disdain and contempt towards one's neighbour, as

---

156 In the *Summa theologica* [GA].

157 The *Etymologiae*.

158 Auzzas (Passavanti, 504) locates the source of this argument by Dionysius the Areopagite in the section of the *Summa* that Passavanti is plumbing, in which Aquinas refers to him.

159 Bernard, Epistle 42.

St. Gregory demonstrates in the book of *Morals*, when explaining pride: *Si habes quid loqueris, responde michi.*

Therefore, concluding the statements of the doctors, pride is a disordered appetite or a perverse love of one's own excellence.

Second Chapter

Wherein we show the source of pride.

The second thing to say about pride is where it comes from. The sages say that it is born mainly from self-love or, which is the same thing, from someone's own will, according to which a man likes himself, and the will, taking root, contradicts God's will. St. Augustine, in the book of the *City of God*, says that the arrogant are accused of liking themselves, i.e., according to their own will. Whoever follows his own will takes from God that which is properly His and sins by pride, as did the first angel and the first man. Pride was born in that very high place of the empyrean and of that noble and high lineage of the angelic nature. Because of his haughty condition, and not finding any other creature equal to him whom he could marry, he espoused himself, though not legitimately, to his father, from whom he was born. Because this was done against God's will, the highest prince took it so badly that He chased them both from heaven, banning them from His entire realm, never to return, and He made them permanent inhabitants of the dark and painful kingdom of hell. There the mother, having conceived not legitimate sons but illegitimate daughters, on the wishes of the incestuous father moves shamelessly through the world with them in tow. They attract every man, of any condition or state, who allows himself to be drawn to their abominable adultery, some with unchaste glances, others with dishonourable appearance, some with desirous delight and others with broad promises, under the name of legitimate matrimony. From this is born again and again that adulterous generation of cruel and inappropriate sins that has already corrupted and ruined the whole world.

Pride is born in man also from the goods of nature, and the goods of fortune, and the goods of grace.

Natural goods are either in the body or in the soul, or common to both. These include health, strength, happiness, beauty, nobility, freedom, agility, awareness, having good manners, being delightful, eloquent, comely, well-complexioned, pleasant, honourable, of good appearance, and well adorned. Natural goods of the soul are noble cleverness with subtle intellect, good memory, natural disposition and attitude towards the virtues, knowledge, and the arts, wisdom, understanding, discretion, prudence, diligence, good judgment, knowing how to choose and make the best choice, having good imagination, a good capacity for understanding, good memory and retention, and being solicitous and studious. Goods of fortune are the things that are outside of us, which are not in a man's power and can be lost whether he likes it or not, like wealth, pleasures, status, privilege, fame, honour, human grace, worldly glory. The goods of grace are God's grace with charity, humility, and the other virtues, knowledge with the gift of prophecy, of tongues, of doing miracles, along with the other gifts of the Holy Spirit. Pride is often born of all these goods, because when a man feels that he has some goodness from God, from whom every gift comes, and he does not recognize it humbly, he rises up in pride, imputing that goodness to his own virtue and merit, boasting about himself, thinking of himself as revered and honoured, and in many other ways becoming arrogant, as is shown in the next chapter. St. Augustine says, in a sentence in the Rule,[160] that pride differs from other vices because other vices make us do bad things and are nourished and born of bad deeds, but pride is also born of good works and of the good and causes them to perish.

We can show this by many examples and statements in Holy Scripture and in the writings of the holy doctors, as we show in our other book, written in Latin for educated people, and as will be said again further along. For now, we have said enough for the learning of uneducated persons, so that they understand vice and sin, safeguard themselves from it, know how to protect themselves, and, having offended, confess well and carefully.

Third Chapter

Wherein we show how many types and ways of pride there are.

The third thing we want to say about pride is how many types we can divide it into, i.e., how many ways and degrees of this vice there are, and in how many ways one sins with it. According to St. Jerome,[161] there are two prides, the one good and the other evil.

---

160 The *Regula tertia vel Praeceptum* [GA].
161 In his commentary on Isaiah [GA].

The good one is when someone does not give way to the corruption of sin and holds its filthiness in disgust and abomination, as the prophet says: *Iniquitatem odio habui et abominatus sum* [Ps 118:163]: I have held sin in hatred and abomination. He flees the causes and opportunities for sin, such as bad habits, unseemly places, hanging out in the piazza, in doorways, near windows, seeing and hearing base things, dishonourable and dissolute statements and words that corrupt and vitiate honesty and good customs, playing games, touching other people's bodies, and sleights of hand. He keeps to himself in church or in his room, praying, reading, working. Since he is not social but lives cautiously, taking care to maintain and preserve his purity and honour, which is lost among people, he is held and reputed to be haughty and arrogant. Those people whose company he avoids usually say: "He does not deign to stoop so low, and he thinks he's so great that he disdains his equals," and similar words which the person should not pay attention to. Instead, he should disdain them and not become dispirited, but persevere in that holy pride, which is born of a virtuous and high-born mind, and not from one's own will, but from God's love and love of charity, and it is not one's neighbour who is held in contempt but defect and vice. St. Jerome, in the epistle he sent to that holy virgin Eustochium,[162] teaching her to preserve her virginity and flee contrary things since he had taught her to flee the practices and company of worldly and base women, so that their conduct and their discussion of worldly and carnal things would not corrupt her purity, said, *Disce in hac parte sanctam superbiam, scito te esse illis meliorem*: Learn holy pride here, and know that you are better than they.

There is another type of pride, the evil kind, and it can be considered in two ways. First, inasmuch as it has a general influence over all the vices of which it is the first principle and cause, and in this sense it is one with greed, as the apostle says, *Radix omnium malorum est cupiditas* [1 Tm 6:10]: The root of all evil is greed. This is not the place to speak of it, but in the next chapter. The other way it can be is as a special sin, distinct from the other deadly sins, and, as was said above, as a disordered love of one's own excellence. We should talk about this type of pride here. The Master of Sentences, borrowing from St. Gregory, says that there are four types of pride. The first is when someone attributes to himself some good or goodness that he has. The second type is when someone rightly believes he has received from God every good that he has, but he thinks that God gave it to him out of merit. The third is when

---

162 Epistle 22.

someone boasts of having something he does not have. The fourth type of pride is when someone desires to seem or appear uniquely to have what he has, disdaining others.

St. Paul speaks against the first type of pride, saying, *Quid habes quod non accepisti?* [1 Cr 4:7]: What do you have, man, that you have not received from God? As if to say, nothing. St. Bernard, speaking against this vice, says:[163] Who is so foolish that he believes that what he has comes from anywhere but God? At least he should not be worse than that Pharisee in the Gospel [Lk 18], who recognized that he had received what he had from God and said, *Gratias tibi ago, Domine*, etc.: I render thanks to you, Lord God. And he said what he did not have that was evil, and what good he did have, so at least he suggested that although he gave offence with another type of pride, he did not sin by not thinking that he had received what good he had from God, as those arrogant types do who do not recognize the good that they have and do not give thanks to God for it, and thus become ungrateful. This is a great vice, displeasing to both God and men; St. Jerome says it is great pride to be ungrateful.[164] These types, as St. Gregory says, who do not give thanks to God for the benefits they have received, are not worthy of receiving any more from him. Rather, they deserve to be deprived of the goods they have received. What St. Bernard says about them is true, that ingratitude is a wind that sets fire to and dries up the fountain of piety, the dew of mercy, and the river of divine grace.

Against the second type of pride, by which a man judges that he has received the goods he has on his own merit, St. Paul says, *Gratia Dei sum id quod sum* [1 Cr 15:10]: I am what I am by the grace of God. He seems to say: if I am something, or I have something good, it is by God's grace, not by my merits; otherwise, grace would not be grace. If a man were paying a labourer for his work and effort but did not thank him at all, but paid him a just debt, in like manner if God were to give us His benefices based on our merits, He would not be doing us grace but justice. This would remove God's grace, and it is a mistake to say and believe that, since grace is the origin and cause of every good.

You might reply: Therefore, does a person deserve nothing, no matter how hard he tries to live well and virtuously, since grace is independent of merit? We answer that by behaving well a person has merit by virtue of the grace God freely gives him, and not because of his deeds, which are performed without grace and which would have no value before God. So a man first has grace from God, which is not earned but

---

163 In the sermons on the Song of Songs [GA].
164 Auzzas (Passavanti, 505) traces this statement by Jerome to Aquinas in the *Summa*.

is freely given, and by acting according to that grace, because of that grace, which makes his deeds meritorious and accepted and pleasing to God, he merits greater grace, and also glory according to grace. This is what St. Paul meant when, having said, *Gratia Dei sum id quod sum*, he added: *et gratia eius in me vacua non fuit*: And His grace has not been worthless or vain in me. This suggests that he had behaved according to the grace that God had given him, which he had merited more. And he taught us about that, saying, *Hortamur vos, ne in vacuum gratiam Dei recipiatis* [2 Cr 6:1]: We urge you not to receive God's grace worthlessly. Those who are not diligent about behaving well, according to the grace received, receive God's grace worthlessly and in vain.

Here we might ask: If grace is not given by merit but is given freely, why does God give it more to one person than to another? Some reply that although God gives more grace to one than to another, nevertheless He gives each as much grace as we might deserve so we can be saved, while not creating impediments, so that we are not indisposed to receiving it or do not act according to that grace. Others say that the whole mass of human nature is sinful because of the sin of the first father, and therefore we are reasonably and justly deprived of God's grace and damned, but that God chooses some of us, at His pleasure, on whom to bestow His grace, having predestined them for eternal life, and the others He lets perish, because that is what their corrupt nature deserves. He gives grace and mercy to the former, and to the others he does not do harm but justice, even though He does not give them grace.

Still, the question remains: Why does God give grace to one and not to another, to some and not to all, since all equally, one not more than another, are sinners by virtue of the original sin of corrupt nature? Some answer that God gives grace to those whom He knows ought to receive it and can use it well, and not to the others whom He knows would not use it well, and therefore He does not give it to them. This is not a good answer, and it contains an error, because it subjects grace to a rule, making it depend on a man's merits and saying that God gives it because He knows that it ought to be used well, since only God's free will gives it, and it is itself the reason for it being well received and well used. God's will alone is the reason for grace, as God says through Scripture: *Miserebor cui voluero: et misericors ero, in quem michi complacuerit* [Ex 33:19]: I will have mercy on those whom I want, and I will be merciful to those whom I like. Jesus Christ suggested this in the Holy Gospel when speaking about the vineyard [Mt 20], where it is said that, when the owner of the vineyard gave as much to someone who had entered the vineyard to work in the evening, at vespers, as to one who had arrived on time in the morning, and someone murmured in objection, the owner said to that man: "Friend, I do you no harm, because I give you what you deserved, per our agreement. I want to give the one who came late some of what is mine, according to my wisdom, even though he has not earned it." Here we are shown that it is not merit but God's will that is the reason for grace. So, to the question about why God gives grace to one and not to the other, or more to one than to another, we answer straightaway and correctly: Because God wants to do it this way. And if we were to ask further why God wants it that way, we should again answer: Because God wants it that way; and go no farther. We cannot assign any reason to divine will if not God's will itself, of which the prophet says: *Omnia quecumque voluit fecit* [Ps 113:11]: God has done all those things that He wanted.

No one therefore should arrogantly attribute any goods that he has to his own merit, but to God's grace and mercy. As St. Paul says: *Apparuit gratia Dei Salvatoris nostri, non ex operibus iustitie, quae fecimus nos, sed secumdum suam misericordiam salvos nos fecit* [Tt 2:11]: The grace of God the saviour has appeared not by the work of justice which we have done, but He has saved us according to His mercy. Isaiah says: *Omnia opera nostra operatus es in nobis, Domine* [Is 26:12]: You have put all our works in us, Lord God. Whoever believes or says otherwise does harm to God's grace and injury to His mercy, and he makes God a cheap vendor of His grace, when He is a broad and generous donor of what He concedes and gives to us, *qui est benedictus in secula seculorum. Amen.*

The third type of pride is when someone boasts about having what he does not have. This can happen in two ways. The first is when someone thinks he has something he does not have; the second is when someone knows perfectly well that he does not have that good for which he vainly praises himself and brags about. The first way comes from great blindness, the second from great vanity. It is surely great blindness to think that you have those virtues and that goodness that you in no way have. This is not to be marvelled at if we consider what St. Gregory says,[165] that the pride of the mind blinds us and does not allow us to know the truth. This vice happens because of the disordered love of oneself, which blinds a person and keeps him from recognizing his own blindness. St. Ambrose says: Your love deceives your judgment of yourself; and therefore it is a common proverb that says, love deceives you. This blindness comes from not thinking about our condition and our defects, which, if considered well and often, would keep us humble and would not let us rise up in pride. To that end it is useful often to

---

165 In the *Moralia in Job* [GA].

look in the mirror, reading Holy Scripture, which both by doctrine and example teaches us to know ourselves, and to open our eyes and see our own misery and defect and correct it, according to what St. Gregory says.[166] Such blindness also comes from willingly listening to the praise of flatterers, whose characteristic, Seneca says,[167] is to deceive others, and to make us believe ourselves to be what we are not. This would not happen if we did not listen willingly and delightfully, because, as St. Jerome says,[168] no one speaks willingly to the mute and to the deaf listener. As Solomon says in Proverbs: *Princeps, qui libenter audit verba mendacii, omnes ministros habebit impios* [Pr 29:12]: The lord who willingly listens to the lying words of flatterers will have liars and evil men for all his ministers.

It is also a great vanity to boast of having what a person knows for sure he does not have, of whom the holy Job says: *Vir vanus erigitur in superbiam* [Jb 11:12]: The vain man rises up in pride. And the gloss says: The man who pretends to have what he does not have is called vain, and he rises up in pride, and that boasting is a type of deceitful lie.[169]

The fourth type of pride is when a person wants to appear to have, and pretends that he alone has what he has, disdaining others. This pride includes two evils, disdain of one's neighbour and showing off.

Disdain of one's neighbour is contrary to charity, according to which a man should love his neighbour as himself, but who, by disdaining him, gives offence. That Pharisee in the Gospel showed this pride when, praising himself, he said: *Non sum sicut ceteri hominum*, etc. [Lk 18:11–14]: I am not like other men, unjust and sinful; and he disdained his neighbour, saying: Nor am I like this publican. Also, such disdain is contrary to God's charity, because to disdain someone else is to judge that because of some evil or defect of his, he is worthy of being disdained. To judge someone else is contrary to God's commandment in the Holy Gospel: *Nolite iudicare et non iudicabimini* [Lk 6:37]: Do not want to judge and you will not be judged. And the apostle says: Who are you, who judges others to be servants? [Rm 14:4].

The second evil that this pride includes is showing off, and we have shown what a vain thing this is with what we said above, and with what we will say later.[170] Jesus Christ speaks against this in the Gospel, saying: *Attendite, ne iustitiam vestram faciatis coram hominibus, ut*

---

166 *Moralia in Job* [GA].
167 In *De beneficiis* [GA].
168 In his Epistles [GA].
169 Aquinas, in the *Summa* [GA].
170 See p. 153 and p. 159.

videamini ab eis [Mt 6:1]: Be careful about doing justice, i.e., just and good works, before men in order to be seen by them. Elsewhere, against those who make a show of their deeds, he said: *Amen dico vobis, receperunt mercedem suam* [Mt 6:2]: Truly I tell you that they have received their reward; as if to say, they should not expect any other reward from God for the deeds that they do in order to be seen, because being seen is their reward.

*Here we make another distinction about pride, which is
distinguished by twelve degrees.*

St. Bernard makes another distinction about pride in his book about the twelve degrees of humility,[171] and he says that there are twelve degrees of pride. The first is curiosity, which is a disordered desire to know, hear, see, and experience useless, worthless, unnecessary things. The second degree is mental lightness, which is shown in excessive and worthless words and in dissolute and unserious behaviours. The third degree is inept happiness, i.e., obscene and inappropriate happiness, which is shown in laughter and in badly organized and dishonourable acts. The fourth degree is vanity, boasting and praising oneself uselessly. The fifth degree is singularity, when a person does something that appears to be singularly beyond other acts. The sixth degree is arrogance, when a person believes himself to have greater worth and to be better than others. The seventh degree is presumption, by which a person, reputing himself to have greater worth and to know more than others, presumes to do or speak beyond what is due and to undertake things that others do not do or try to do. The eighth mode and degree is the defence of sins, by which a person, not wanting to confess his sins humbly and declare his guilt, defends and excuses them, or says that he has not done them, or if he says that he did them excuses his evil by saying: I did well. Or, even if he confesses having done bad, he says: It wasn't such a bad thing. Or, if he says that it was a very bad thing, he says: I did it for good reason and with good intention; or else: Someone else was the reason, and he made me do it. The ninth degree of pride is false confession of sins, by which, although someone confesses with his own mouth that he is a sinner, he does not do so sincerely or with a good heart, but, unable to cover up or excuse his defects, he admits them and makes them worse by exaggerating, either with words or by appearing humble, so that when others hear the impossible and incredible

---

171 The *Liber de gradibus humilitatis et superbiae* [GA].

things he says and shows about himself, what he is, or what others might think or know, is unbelievable. The tenth degree is rebellion, by which someone is disobedient to his superiors, to whom he should be subject. The eleventh degree is freedom to do evil, which a man, having put aside his shame and fear, desires to have, so that he can fulfil his desires without any impediment and do his will. The twelfth degree of pride is the practice of sin, by which a man, forgetting his fear of God and his own salvation, having surrendered completely to carnal desires, disdains God and His commandments, not using reason but following corrupt concupiscence.

These twelve degrees of pride have their opposite in the twelve degrees of humility, which St. Benedict puts in his Rule and St. Bernard in his book, and these degrees include not only the types of pride but certain corrupt things that go before and follow pride and the other vices. Therefore, they are not explained here diligently and extensively, as was done above for the types of pride, also because further along we will talk about each one of them in its place, dealing with those vices which pertain to them.[172]

Fourth Chapter

Wherein we show how all the other vices are born of pride.

Fourth, we have to say how all the other vices are born of pride, as from a bad root. As the wise Ecclesiasticus says: *Initium omnis peccati est superbia:*[173] The origin of every sin is pride. This statement can be understood in two ways. First, that it is the sin of the first man that was the cause and origin of every sin, just as St. Paul says: *Per unum hominem peccatum in hunc mundum intravit* [Rm 5:12]: Sin, that is, pride, entered this world through one man. The other way is to understand that pride is an original cause and root from which the other vices proceed and are born. If we understand pride in the first sense, it is certain that the first man's sin, which was the origin and reason for every sin, was pride, although many other sins came along as a consequence of that sin. But pride, which, as said above, is but a disordered desire for one's own excellence, was man's first sin, before which, as St. Thomas proves subtly and clearly in the *Summa*, there could be no other, assuming the

---

172 The text is incomplete and considers only pride, humility, and vainglory.
173 Ecclesiasticus 10:15. The image of the root appears in a nearby verse (10:18).

state of innocence and original justice in which man was created. After pride came disobedience and the violation of God's commandment, and then the sin of gluttony. Next, curiosity, or the disordered appetite for knowledge, which sins would not have followed if pride had not come first. We should be able to agree on our understanding of pride in the second way as the origin and root of all evil, because in some way all serious vices and sins are derived from and born of pride. And it says serious sin, because there are certain light sins, as St. Augustine says,[174] that do not proceed from pride, like certain sins that are committed out of ignorance or fragility. But among the serious sins the first is pride, as that which makes the other sins worse, because the whole weight of every sin involves the will's aversion to or turning away from God, which first and foremost comes from pride, and consequently applies to the other sins. So pride is called the greatest sin, according to the gloss on that statement in Psalms: *Ex emundabor a delicto maximo* [Ps 18:14]: Because it is the first and principal sin, from which the others are derived. St. Augustine says in a letter:[175] From pride are born heresies, schisms, rebellions, envy, anger, riots, arguments, animosities, ambition, presumption, controversies, lies; and he names many other vices which are not put here for brevity's sake, and which we will discuss later, each in its place.[176] St. Gregory says in the book of *Morals*, explaining that statement by the holy Job: *Exortationem ducum et ululatum exercitus* [Jb 39:25]: Pride is the queen of vices, etc. He adds: The root of all evil is pride, about which Scripture says, the origin of all sin is pride. Its first daughters are the seven deadly sins, which are born of the poisonous root of pride: vainglory, envy, avarice, gluttony, anger, sloth, and lust. A little further along, he says that each one of the seven deadly sins sets against us its army of vices which are born of them, and he names them one by one, and then he shows how the seven deadly sins are born of one another.

We will not explain here how that is, and how many other vices are born from each one, but we will say so in the proper place.

---

174 In *De natura et gratia*.

175 Epistle 211.

176 This remark, and the one below, anticipates the overall plan of the treatise, which was to include a discussion of all the deadly sins. Passavanti did not write beyond his discussion of pride and vainglory.

Fifth Chapter

Wherein we show the seriousness of pride and how offensive it is, and how God hates it.

The fifth thing to say about pride is its seriousness and how offensive it is.

We show the seriousness of pride, as St. Augustine says, in explaining those words of Ecclesiasticus: *Initium superbiae apostatare a Deo, quoniam ab eo, qui fecit illum, recessit cor eius* [Ec 10:14–15]: There is no greater sin than to be an apostate of God, which is what the vice of pride does. To be an apostate is precisely to leave the religion and not want to be subject to the rule that others have promised. This is what pride does, which does not want to obey the commandments of the Christian religion, nor be subject to God's will, which is the rule according to which we ought to live; indeed, it disdains God and His commandments. Therefore, pride is called the most serious vice, because whereas the other sins that cause the soul to depart from God are committed out of ignorance, or negligence, or fragility, or concupiscence, pride separates from God because it does not want to be subject to His will, and so it disdains God and His commandments, and all the other sins then follow from this disdain. Therefore, God despises it, and He says through the prophet Amos, *Detestor ego superbiam* [Am 6:8]: I hold pride in abomination and in displeasure. In the Proverbs of Solomon, He says [Pr 8:13]: I hate arrogance and pride. This should come as no surprise, because, as Boethius says, all the other vices flee from God, but only pride opposes God, resisting His will.[177] St. Jacob says: *Deus superbis resistit, humilibus autem dat gratiam* [1 Pt 5:5]: God resists the prideful, but He gives grace to the humble. God does this rightly and justly, because the prideful offend the Divine Majesty and His authority, which all things obey and are subject to, but for the prideful sinner, who does not want to be subject to God and therefore holds God's authority in hatred, and so would not want God to be the Lord. The psalmist says of the prideful: *Superbia eorum qui te oderunt, ascendit semper* [Ps 73:23]: The pride of those who hate you, the prophet says, speaking to God, always rises. St. Bernard, explaining this statement, says that man's damned pride leads him to hate God and not want God to be the Lord.

---

177 Not in fact Boethius but rather John Cassian. The claim appears in the *De institutis coenobiorum*. Passavanti's misattribution repeats that of Aquinas in the *Summa*; see Passavanti, ed. Auzzas, 173.

Pride also leads man to such foolishness that he wants to be like God, as that first proud one said: *Similis ero Altissimo*: I will be like God most high. The proud man wants to be like God because, as God is above all things and is subject to nothing, so too does the proud man want to stand over everyone and be subject to no one. Not only is it not enough for the proud man to be equal to God, but he even rises above God. So says St. Bernard, explaining what St. Paul says of the Antichrist:[178] *Qui extollitur et adversatur supra omne quod dicitur Deus*: Every proud man rises up against God and challenges Him. God, he says, wants His will to be done, and so does the proud man: this is how he wants to be equal to God. He wants to be above God, because God wants His will to be done in just and right things, and the proud man wants his will to be done also in unjust and inappropriate things and in those things that are contrary to God. We rightly say of the proud man what was said of the Antichrist: *Extollitur et adversatur*, etc.: He rises above God, and he is God's adversary and opposite.

The proud man does harm to God also by undertaking to take from Him that which God reserves especially to Himself, which He says through the prophet: *Gloriam meam alteri non dabo* [Is 42:8]: I will not give my glory to someone else. St. Paul says: *Soli Deo honor et Gloria* [1 Tm 1:17]: To God alone should we give glory and honour. The proud man does the opposite inasmuch as he wants to be honoured, and of the glory that God says He does not give to others, the proud man says: I will take it for myself. He does this by praising and glorifying himself vainly and seeking praise for it from people, which takes away the honour and glory due to God. As St. Gregory says in the book of *Morals*: the one who praises his actions and takes credit for what he seeks to do is convinced that he is denying God His glory, and it seems that this person is making war on God with His own arms, which He has given him. That happens when a person, having certain goods and graces, which God has given to him more than to many others, rises up in pride and exhibits vainglory, where he should be humble and serve God in grateful recognition of the services received. The gloss about that sentence of the holy Job thus says: *Tetendit adversus Deum erecto collo*: The proud man finds a reason to make war on God, when he should humbly take up the cause of serving him.

Because of the many offences that the proud do to God, He holds them in hatred: and as they disdain God, so too does He disdain them. One sign of that is that He often knocks them down and takes their

---

178 In the *Sermones in viglia nativitatis Domini* [GA]. The citation is from 2 Thessalonians 2:4.

status and authority away from them, also in this life, as from the use-less and undeserving, and, to their spite and shame, He turns them into a poor and lowly person. So says the wise Ecclesiasticus: *Sedes ducum superborum evertit et sedere fecit humiles pro eis* [Ec 10:17]: God has thrown the seats of the proud rulers to the ground, i.e., their status and the authority, upon which, sitting unworthily, they ruled, and He has replaced them with those who are humble and abject and of low condition.

Also, as a sign that He holds them in disdain and contempt, God often strikes them down and defeats them with base things. Sometimes this happens when a noble person of status has suffered some injurious offence and outrageous villainy, as if he were someone lowly, and dis-daining his base condition he does not attempt an honourable vendetta with his own hands but has one of his servants carry it out with a dis-gusting and abominable thing, such as a dirty rag or a full game-bag[179] or the like. Doing this to the proud, God shows how He holds them to be vile, as St. Augustine says of the sores with which God struck Pha-raoh the proud king of Egypt, who along with his people disdained His commandments.[180] God, St. Augustine says, could have humbled and plagued the proud people with lions and bears, but He wanted to do it with toads and flies and mosquitoes so that human pride might be tamed with the basest things.

And when He wants to cure and heal proud men with gentleness, He cures their sickness and their sores by medicating them with vile instruments and remedies. St. Gregory says[181] of the proud man, who lords himself over others because of some virtue or goodness that he has or appears to have, that God allows him to commit some base and scandalous sin, so that, confused and vituperated, he might be hum-bled. And St. Isidore addresses this in the book of *The Highest Good*:[182] The one ruled by pride, and is unaware of it, falls into the lust of the flesh, and God makes his sin clear, so that the confusion and infamy of his ugly sin awakens him, and, once insensitive and proud, he is now humbled. Explaining this statement in the *Summa*, St. Thomas says that to demonstrate the seriousness of the sin of pride, God allows a man to fall into other grave sins, just like the wise doctor, who in place of some serious sickness allows or causes the sick man to contract a lesser one.

---

179 The game-bag fits this category because, filled with slaughtered small animals, it would be bloody and, after repeated use, malodorous.
180 In the *In Iohannis evangelium tractatus* [GA].
181 In the *Moralia in Job* [GA].
182 The attribution to Isidore appears to come from Aquinas, *Summa* [GA].

We could give many examples of this, but to be brief, we will set down only one here.

We read in the *Life of the Holy Fathers*[183] that there was a monk who, having lived for a long time in the desert and practised great penitence and many virtues, lacked the humility he should have had along with his other great virtues. He had a high opinion of people as well as of himself, and he held himself to be superior to others. Wanting to humble his pride so that he would not perish, God allowed him to be defeated by temptation. The devil took the form and dress of a young woman, and coming one night to his cell, she began to complain very painfully of her misfortune, explaining how she had ended up in that deserted place, and that the dark night did not allow her to follow the straight path, and the great cold, which she demonstrated with continual trembling, afflicted her, and fear of savage beasts afflicted her greatly. Declaring all of her misfortunes with plangent voice and tearful sighs, she begged the holy father to save her by offering her, in God's name, some corner of his cell. Moved to pity and compassion for so much grief, the holy father at first opened the window, then asked this devil woman, or rather this woman devil, about her unfortunate condition. As she cried harder and recounted it, he finally opened the door and let her in. He asked her if she wanted to eat, and she answered no, but, as she showed signs of being very cold, the holy father relit the fire around which this devil was sitting, and sat down next to her. Sometimes yawning, sometimes stretching her arms and exposing her feet and legs to the fire, she spoke sweetly and softly of her condition, and she asked him how long he had been in that desert, and why he afflicted himself with so much penitence. Smiling a bit as she spoke, she cast a modest look at God's servant, and speaking pleasantly of this and that, as diabolical malice knew how to dress up the female tongue, little by little she moved closer to him. Touching his harsh mantle and rough cloak, and sometimes his hands and his arms, which because of his great age and long abstinence were weak and thin and cold, she moved her hands all the way to his chest, and from there to his white beard. If only you could have seen how that man, who had come to a bad place, appeared to enjoy her attentions as he awaited her next move. To make a long story short, his innate concupiscence, which had fallen asleep in his old flesh and dry bones, began to awaken, and the spark that had nearly gone out burst anew into flame, and his frigid limbs, which before had lain as if dead, began to assert themselves with outrageous

---

183 The story may come directly from the *Vitae Patrum*, or through mediation from the *Alphabetum narrationum* [GA].

pride. And so the wretch, wrought up within and completely besieged from without, seeing no way out, as if already captured and tied up, surrendered. Submitting to sin, he stretched forth his hands to embrace that fantastic figure, which suddenly disappeared, and he never saw her again. He felt confused and ashamed, as there was a great multitude of demons all around him in the cell, making fun of him and mocking him: "O you monk you, who just a little while ago were ascending to heaven, how you are fallen and ruined and basely defeated, you who wanted to do something that none of us had the heart to allow! You can never appear among the people, nor raise your eyes to heaven." Coming to his senses, the monk, ashamed and pained, cried and confessed his sin, and God forgave him. So one who had first been proud was left humbled, as the psalmist says: *Humiliatus sum usquequaque, Domine, vivifica me secundum verbum tuum* [Ps 118:107]: I am humbled on all sides: return me to life, Lord, according to your word.

Not only does God hold pride to be vile and worthy of disdain, He also has great hatred for it. As the wise Ecclesiasticus says: *Odibilis coram Deo et hominibus superbia* [Ec 10:7]: Pride is hateful to God and men. This hatred is very old, and therefore, it is not easily placated and removed, because as pride began so too did God's hatred towards it begin, as that holy woman Judith said, addressing God: *Superbi ab initio non placuerunt tibi, sed humilium et mansuetorum tibi semper placuit deprecatio* [Jd 9:16]: From the beginning of the world you did not like the proud, but the prayer of the humble and the gentle always pleased you. And although there are many reasons for this hatred, as we said, there is one special reason: the proud man is not ashamed of his sin. Indeed, and worse still, he often boasts and praises himself for it, which is something that displeases God a great deal. As St. Augustine says: nothing displeases God more than when a man holds his head high after sinning, when he should be ashamed and humble himself.[184]

Here we show what signs there are that God holds pride in hatred.

Many signs of God's hatred of pride are found in Holy Scripture. First, there are the many threats that God makes against the prideful. Jeremiah the prophet says, giving voice to God: *Ecce ego ad te, superbe, dicit Dominus exercituum: venit dies tuus, tempus visitationis: et cadet superbus et corruet, et non erit qui suscitet eum* [Jr 50:31–2]: Here is what God says to

---

184 In truth, as Auzzas points out (Passavanti, 174), St. Jerome (in the commentary on Isaiah), but possibly through the mediation of the Dominican preacher William Perrault, author of the *Summa de virtudibus et vitiis*.

you, proud one, your day will come, time of visitation, and the proud man will fall down, and no one will be there to pick him up. The holy Job, speaking of the proud man, says: *Si ascenderit in celum superbia eius et capud eius nubes tetigerit, quasi sterquilinium in fine perdetur* [Jb 20:6–7]: If pride rises to heaven and its head touches the clouds, in the end, like dirty straw, it will fall apart and be lost. Isaiah, speaking for God, said as a threat: *Ve coronae superbiae* [Is 28:1]: Woe unto the crown of pride. In many other places of Scripture God threatens it terribly, suggesting how much He hates it.

The second sign that God feels hatred towards the prideful is that He takes the assistance of His grace away from them. This is something very just and reasonable, because, as He gives grace to the humble because they refer all glory to God – saying, along with the prophet: *Non nobis, Domine, non nobis, sed nomini tuo da gloriam* [Ps 115:1]: Not to us, Lord, not to us, but give glory to your name – so too does He take grace away from the prideful because they take glory away from God and unworthily attribute it to themselves. Not only does He remove the assistance of grace, but, as St. Jacob says of them, He resists and opposes them, so that they cannot have any hope of rising to heaven, nor of having glory, once grace, by which one comes to glory, has been taken away from them. And they should have no faith at all that God will allow them to rise to a state of dignity and honour in this life, because He does it so that they will fall and suffer a greater blow, and their ruin will be greater and more serious.

The other sign of God's hatred towards the prideful is that, although He mercifully punishes other sinners, He punishes the prideful and harms them harshly with rigorous justice. As the psalmist says: *Retribuet abundanter facientibus superbiam* [Ps 30:24]: God will repay those who practise pride with torment and punishment abundantly in good measure. This is shown more openly in the book of Wisdom, where it is said: *Exiguo conceditur misericordia, potentes autem potenter tormenta patientur* [Ws 6:7]: Mercy is given to the small and humble man, but the proud powerful ones will have to suffer torments powerfully and gravely.

The other sign that God hates pride is that the first and second coming of Christ are about pride. The first coming was to heal pride with the example of his humility and the salve of his passion. As St. Augustine says:[185] Because of the great sin of pride humble God came into the world. This great sickness of the souls drew the omnipotent doctor from heaven and finally, in the form of the servant, it humbled him

---

185 In the *Enarrationes in Psalmos* [GA].

to be scorned and torn at; it led him to be nailed to the wood of the cross and sacrificed, so that through the remedy of such medicine the swelling of pride might be healed. You should feel ashamed, therefore, of your pride, for which God humbled himself. The second coming of Christ will be about pride, not to heal it but in order rightly to punish and condemn it, as the prophet Isaiah says: *Dies domini exercituum super omnem superbum et excelsum et super omnem arrogantem, et humiliabitur* [Is 2:12]: The day of God's coming to judgment will involve every proud man, haughty and arrogant, who will be humbled and defeated. Because of the great hatred and displeasure that God has against the proud, He says through the psalmist: *Non habitabit in medio domus mee, qui facit superbiam* [Ps 100:7]: The proud man will not live in my house.

Here we show how pride offends angels and men.
Pride also offends the holy angels. It is odious to them because the first angel fell from pride, and he dropped from the sky with all his followers, and the angels were made into demons. Also, because they see that pride makes a man rise up against God, and over God, which they don't like at all. And if in the demons of hell there could be the right judgment of reason, they would hate pride too, because, as St. Augustine says, the devil was made wretched because of pride.[186]

Pride offends one's neighbour in many ways. First, the prideful man offends his neighbour with his heart, by deeming him lowly and disdaining him. As the wise Ecclesiasticus says: *Sicut abominatio est superbo humilitas, ita execratio divitis pauper* [Ec 13:24]: Just as humility is an abomination to the proud man, so too is the poor man disdained by the rich man. He also offends him with words, either by boasting or by praising himself, which is a very unpleasant thing and serious to hear, as Solomon says in Proverbs: *Qui se iactat et dilatat iurgia concitat* [Pr 28:25]: He who boasts and inflates himself with words of self-praise provokes his listeners to regretful displeasure and to blame themselves, either by being argumentative or by fighting, and by obstinately defending and affirming his words, whether they are true or false, by trying to win arguments, or by saying villainous, injurious, outrageous, and excessive words, or by threats, scolding, and disrespecting others. As Solomon says in Proverbs: *Ubi fuerit superbia ibi et contumelie* [Pr 11:2]: Where there is pride, there will be outrageous and villainous words. Also, they offend others through actions, by injuring, harming, persecuting, bothering, or bullying people, because of what they own,

---

186 In *De correptione et gratia* [GA].

or their status or their fame, or by not leaving others alone or letting them live in peace. The prophet says of them: *Superbi inique agebant usquequaque* [Ps 118:51]: The prideful always did, everywhere, unfair and unjust deeds. Therefore, on behalf of all those who were injured or oppressed, the psalmist said: *Confundantur superbi, quia iniuste iniquitatem fecerunt in me* [Ps 118:78]: May the prideful be confused, because they have unjustly committed iniquity against me. Solomon says in Proverbs that proud men commit iniquity: *Arma et gladius in via superbi* [Pr 22:5]. And the wise Ecclesiasticus: *Effusio sanguinis in via superborum* [Ec 27:16]: Arms and a knife, and the spilling of blood of the prideful in the road. The prideful commit another offence against their neighbour by setting a bad example, because, although other sinners, such as adulterers and thieves and many more, hide their bad deeds, of whom the Evangelist says: *Qui male agit odit lucem* [Jn 3:20]: He who does bad hates the light, yet the prideful act in public, like those who are not ashamed of themselves, but who glory and boast about themselves. So the prophet avoided conversation with them when he said: *Superbo oculo et insatiabili corde, cum hoc non edebam* [Ps 100:5]: I did not eat, and I did not spend time with the one who had a prideful eye and a heart that was never satisfied.

Pride is therefore understandably both displeasing and odious to God and to men, and not only to the gentle and the humble as something contrary to them, but also to the prideful, because one prideful man hates another, since they are brothers in the same vice and children of the same father, to whom Christ said in the Gospel: *Vos ex patre diabolo estis* [Jn 8:44]: You are children of the devil, who is your father. So it seems that the general rule, of which the wise Ecclesiasticus speaks [Ec 13:20], fails in the prideful: every man keeps company with his like, but the proud man does not keep company with any proud man. Indeed, as Solomon says: *Inter superbos semper iurgia sunt* [Pr 13:10]: Among prideful men there are always disagreements and arguments. As St. Augustine says,[187] pride always hates peace and the company of others. And Innocent says:[188] Pride is unbearable and odious to every man; every other man of vice so loves one like him, the proud man hates the other proud man.

---

187 In his Epistle 140 [GA].

188 Innocent III, the Italian Lothar of Segni, pope from 1198 to 1216, author of *De miseria humanae conditionis*, which Passavanti is citing here [GA].

*Here we show how pride offends and harms its own subject,
that is, man, over whom it rules.*

More than all the other vices, pride harms its own subject, that is, the man over whom it rules. First, it distances him from God, who is every good, as Hugh of St. Victor says,[189] and it takes away the kingdom of heaven and sends him deep into hell. The prophet Isaiah said to that first prideful one, in the person of all the others: *Dixisti in corde tuo, in celum conscendam, etc., Verumtamen ad infernum detraheris* [Is 14:13–15]: You, proud one, said in your heart, I will be in heaven; but you will be dragged and thrown into hell. So that, as we rise to heaven through humility, so too by pride do we fall to hell, according to the order of the evangelic law, which says: *Qui se humiliat exaltabitur et qui se exaltat humiliabitur* [Lk 14:11]. Pride hurts a man also because it makes him unworthy of God's mercy and grace, of which St. Augustine says:[190] no one has greater need of God's mercy than one who is wretched; no one is as unworthy of it as the wretched prideful one, who disdains the medicine of mercy. As the wise Ecclesiasticus says, *Execratus est eos pre superbia eorum, non est misertus illis totam gentem perdens* [Ec 16:9–10]: God held them in hatred, abominating them for their pride; He did not have mercy on them, damning all their people. Pride harms somebody in another way, by taking away the light of intellect and making him dark and shadowy. Thus says the gloss on that statement in the Gospel: *Qui vident ceci fient:*[191] The prideful, who think themselves wise, become blind. And St. Gregory says in the *Morals* that pride of the mind is an impediment to the light of truth. The saviour says in the Gospel that the truth is hidden and concealed from the prudent and the wise and revealed to the little ones and the children [Mt 11:25; Lk 10:21]; where, as the gloss explains, the wise refer to the prideful and the little ones the humble. It is with this understanding that St. Gregory says in the *Morals: Viam eius intelligere noluerunt*: Humility turns on the light of understanding, pride hides it, and it leads a man to so much blindness that it causes him to fall into error and become a heretic. So what makes a person heretical is not ignorance but pride, through which he remains obstinately in stubborn error and defends it. Pride hurts a person also by disordering and breaking his moral compass, and he who should rise up to God, by rising up in pride, falls and is subject to the wretched

---

189 In the *De quinque septenis* [GA].
190 In the *De libero arbitrio* [GA].
191 John 9:39. The commentary is found in Pseudo-Aquinas, *De humanitate Domini nostril Iesu Christi* [GA].

servitude of vice. As St. Gregory says in the book of *Morals*, the vice of pride, by lifting the wretched heart above men, subjects it to vice, and a more wretched or serious servitude there cannot be. Therefore, the Holy Scripture says: *Non elevetur cor eius in superbiam* [Dt 17:20]: Let a man's heart not rise up in pride. Pride also hurts a man because it removes beauty and its lovely figure, which is made in God's image, from the soul, and it leads to the image of the devil, as St. Anselm shows in the books of *On Likenesses*.[192] The soul is transformed according to how it loves, and pride is nothing other than loving what the devil loves, so that both the figure of the devil is imprinted on the soul, and the mind turns towards and loves many malformed, filthy, and twisted images proudly and with corrupt affection. The soul, uniquely beautiful by nature and by grace, becomes all swollen, blind, and twisted; in sum, losing all its beauty, it becomes bestial, monstrous, and ugly. This happens especially when pride is born of its contrary, because, just as we say that birth is monstrous when not according to its nature, as if a woman had given birth to a bull, as the poets' fables say about that queen Pasiphae, who gave birth to the Minotaur, which was half man and half bull, or when a man or beast is born with several heads or extra limbs, or did not have them in the right place, so too is pride monstrous, which is often born of its contrary and not of its like, i.e., of the virtues and graces given by God, about which a man becomes proud. The mind becomes almost like a bull, which the wise Ecclesiasticus prohibits, when he says: *Non te extollas in cogitatione tua velud taurus, ne forte elidatur virtus tua* [Ec 6:2]: Do not rise high with pride as the bull does, so that your virtue will not be defeated and brought down to earth.

Pride does not have one head but many; because, as was said above; all the other deadly sins are born of it, and there are seven main ones, besides those that are born of them. Pride is similar to Hercules's hydra, which the poets say was a seven-headed serpent, and if you cut off one of them it grew another. So it is with pride, which, although a person sometimes conquers some of his vices, by rising up in pride he causes more to be born or added. So pride was well designed as that fierce beast that St. John speaks of in the Apocalypse [Rv 13:11], the one with seven heads and ten horns, the seven heads signifying the seven deadly sins, which proceed from pride, and the ten horns the trespass and transgression of the Ten Commandments of the Law. This is because pride is the reason and source of every sin and transgression, as the

---

192 The author of the *Liber de sancti Anselmi Similitudintibus* is in fact Eadmer, a companion of Anselm's [GA].

gloss says about those words of the psalm: *Si mei non fuerint dominati, tunc immaculatus ero* [Ps 18:14].

Pride also hurts a man by deceiving him in many ways. First of all, where it appears to raise a man up high and put him in a state of excellence and dignity, it makes him fall and drop. Indeed, to rise high is to fall, as St. Augustine says, explaining those words of the psalm: *Deiecisti eos dum allevarentur*:[193] When the prideful rose up high, you threw them to the ground. And St. Gregory says[194] that proud men, by abandoning and disdaining the glory and power of their Creator, fall upon themselves, looking for their own glory. As the holy Job said, when speaking to God: *Respice cunctos superbos et confunde eos, et contere illos in loco suo* [Jb 40:7]: Look at all the prideful ones and confuse them, and chop up the impious sinners in their place. St. Gregory explains:[195] Pride is the place of the impious, which defeats and causes those whom it raises up to fall. Solomon says in Proverbs: *Ante ruinam exaltatur cor* [Pr 16:18]: Before the fall, the heart rises up high. Pride also deceives man by making him sell his precious things as cheap and buy others' cheap things, thinking they are valuable. Man's precious things are his good works, which would be worthy of eternal mercy if he did not want worldly praise and favour for them, and pride makes him do that. St. Gregory says:[196] When a man seeks to have or desires some temporal thing for his good works, he sells cheaply that which was invaluable. The prideful man buys cheap things at a high price when, because of the wind of pride, he loses the kingdom of heaven, as St. Augustine says, adding: He who will not be swollen with the wind of pride will not die in the fires of hell.[197]

Pride also hurts a man by making him crazy and foolish. As St. Bernard says:[198] All pride is foolishness, although all foolishness is not pride. Of the foolishness of prideful men St. Paul says: *Dicentes se esse sapientes stulti facti sunt* [Rm 1:22]: By calling themselves wise and believing themselves to be so, they are made foolish. St. Augustine says of this:[199] If by calling yourself wise you become foolish, say that you are foolish and you will be wise. With these words St. Augustine wanted

---

193 Psalms 72:18. Augustine's gloss appears in the *Enarrationes in Psalmos* [GA].
194 In the *Moralia in Job* [GA].
195 In the *Moralia in Job* [GA].
196 In the *Regular Pastoralis* [GA].
197 The citation from Augustine appears to come from William Perault's *De superbia*, part of the *Summae virtutum ac vitiorum* (Passavanti, ed. Auzzas, 512).
198 Again, likely via Perault's *De superbia*, as well as one of the epistles of William of Sancto Theodorico (Passavanti, ed. Auzzas, 512).
199 In his *Sermons* [GA].

to remove the presumption from man, and his own reputation, which makes a man foolish who believes himself wise. So we read of certain holy men who, to avoid pride and protect their humility, showed themselves to be foolish while being wise.

We read in the *Life of the Holy Fathers* that there was a holy abbot, whom the lord of the province, hearing talk of his sanctity, wanted to come and see. Hearing this, the holy father dressed in sackcloth like a fool, and he put a piece of bread and some cheese in his hand, and when the lord came with a large entourage to visit him, he stood at the door of his cell and took bites of this bread and cheese, and he did not reply to anything that was said to him, nor did he stop eating: indeed, he focused on it, taking ever larger bites, which was not his habit. Seeing this, the lord disdained him, and the abbot left, preserving his wisdom, even though it seemed to be foolish humility, and he avoided foolish pride.

Is there any greater foolishness than when a man presumes, beyond his strength, to do greater deeds than his power will allow? The prophet Jeremiah's gloss puts it well: *Superbia eius et arrogantia eius plus quam fortitudo eius:*[200] Pride presumes more than strength, arrogance attributes falsely to itself that which it does not have, and both are great foolishness. Solomon puts it well in Proverbs: *Superbus et arrogans vocatur indoctus* [Pr 21:24]: The proud and arrogant man is called foolish.

And whoever wants to know more about the foolishness to which pride leads a man should read this treatise written in Latin for lettered men, where many more things are written about pride than are written here, in order not to run too long.

Sixth Chapter

Wherein we show the punishment for pride.

Sixth, we should talk about the punishment for pride. As said above, God hates this vice above all others, and therefore, where He is called merciful and pious towards other sinners, as the whole of Holy Scripture resounds with both words and deeds, only towards the prideful is He harsh and hard. He gravely punishes and condemns said vice, as we read about the first angel called Lucifer, who because of pride was chased from heaven. And Adam, the first father of human nature, was tossed from the earthly paradise because of this vice. The tower of Babel

---

200 In fact, not Jeremiah but Isaiah 16:6.

was destroyed, tongues confused and languages divided; Goliath was killed because of it, Haman hanged, Nicanor killed, Antiochus humiliated, Pharaoh drowned, Sennacherib killed by his sons, Saul defeated and killed by his enemies, Rehoboam stripped of his kingdom, Nebuchadnezzar tossed from power and relegated to the beasts.[201] Herod came to a bad end and was made a reprobate by God.[202] And we read of many other kings and princes in Holy Scripture who were defeated and judged by God because of their pride, about whom the Scripture says: *Sedes ducum superborum destruxit Deus* [Ec 10:17]: God has destroyed the thrones of the prideful princes and rulers. Elsewhere the wise Ecclesiasticus says: *Perdidit Deus memoriam superborum* [Ec 10:21]: God has lost and destroyed the memory of prideful men.

We find not only in Holy Scripture that the prideful were destroyed and judged by God, but in secular writings as well: in the histories of the Greeks and the Romans and the Chaldeans, the Syrians and Indians, and many others, whom it would take too long to tell about. The poets write about many who were struck and killed by lightning because of the vice of pride, as they tell especially of certain giants who, having risen up in pride, wanted to chase the gods from heaven. Ovid writes about one of them, named Typhoeus, in his book *Metamorphoses*, of both his pride and his punishment, recounting beautiful things in verse, which we write about extensively in our book written in Latin.[203] For now let this brief summary suffice to suggest how much God holds the sin of pride in hatred, and how gravely He punishes it, which is shown clearly in the Bible book called Numbers, where it is written: *Anima, que per superbiam aliquid commiserit, sive civis, sive peregrinus, quoniam adversus Deum rebellis fuit, peribit de populo suo* [Nb 15:30]: The soul, i.e., the man, whether citizen or foreigner, who makes a mistake out of pride, because he was a rebel against God, will perish from his people, i.e., he will be killed. Here the seriousness of the sin of pride is suggested, for although God commanded that other sins be purged with sacrifices and certain offerings, he ordered that pride be punished with death.

And that is shown by an explicit miracle that once occurred.

---

201   The stories of Adam and of the tower of Babel appear in Genesis; Goliath in 1 Samuel; Haman in the book of Esther; Nicanor in 1 Maccabees; Antiochus in 2 Maccabees; Pharaoh in Exodus; Sennacherib in 2 Kings; Saul in 1 Samuel; Rehoboam in 1 Kings; and Nebuchadnezzar in the book of Daniel.

202   Herod died a painful death in Jericho, likely in 4 BC. Flavius Josephus provides details in *Antiquities of the Jews*.

203   The myth of Typhoeus does not appear in Ovid, as Passavanti claims. Hesiod provides the first known version in the *Theogony*; others will follow. Passavanti's source for the story, and of his misattribution, remains unclear.

We read in Peter Damian[204] that there was a cleric in Burgundy who had acquired a great benefice in the church of St. Maurice, and a great dispute arose over it between him and a powerful cleric in the town. The latter, not perhaps because he was right but because he enjoyed great favour among certain barons in the area, had won the benefice and was in possession of it. One morning, when he was in church, singing that gospel where at the end Jesus Christ said, *Qui se humiliat exaltabitur* (He who humbles himself shall be exalted), he turned to his companions and said: "The other words of the Gospel may be true, but this is false; because if I had humbled myself before my adversary, I would not get to have this benefice with so much wealth." When he said these words, there suddenly came a great clap of thunder, and a lightning bolt entered his mouth which had spoken this abominable blasphemy, and it killed him right there, his tongue and throat all burned and turned to coal.

The holy Job, considering the grave offence of the prideful, said to God, *Disperge superbos in furore tuo*; and further along: *Respice cunctos superbos et confunde eos* [Jb 40:6–7]: Look at all the arrogant men and confuse them, and disperse them in your furore, so that they never find one another.

Seventh Chapter

Wherein we show how pride can be corrected, and how difficult it is.

The seventh thing to talk about now is how difficult pride is to correct. There are several reasons.

First of all, because pride is not easily recognized. No matter how prideful a man is, he doesn't think of himself that way. Therefore, he does not try to take care of it, like a sickness that someone does not recognize and does not think he has and does not try to get a doctor's advice and other remedies to cure it. St. Augustine says[205] that no one is more incurable than someone who thinks he is healthy. Seneca says that it is hard therefore to reach the salvation of cleanliness, because we do not recognize that we are sick.[206] Since pride, as St. Gregory says,[207] is a blindness

---

204 The *De variis miraculosis narrationibus* but likely via the *Alphabetum narrationum* [GA].
205 In the *Enarrationes in Psalmos* [GA].
206 In the *Epistulae Morales ad Lucilium*, 50 [GA].
207 In the *Moralia in Job* [GA].

of the mind, and as St. Augustine says,[208] the face of my swollen mind did not let me see, it follows that pride cannot easily be cured.

The second reason why pride can only be cured with difficulty is that it renders a man insensitive. Seneca says: In those illnesses in which a man is afflicted and carried away by passion, the man who does not feel it is so much worse off.[209] St. Bernard says[210] that the stupid and unfeeling limb is farther away from salvation. St. Gregory shows the insensitivity that pride makes when explaining the gospel of the conversion of the Magdalene, where it says that the prideful Pharisee, who judged the humbled Magdalene, lost his feeling and therefore, not sensing his illness, was farther away from salvation.[211]

The other reason why pride is hard to cure is that, although the prideful man sometimes recognizes the sickness of his pride, he is ashamed to confess it and to show it to the doctor, when confession is the reason and source of salvation, as that wise Boethius says:[212] If you expect the doctor to do his job, you must show him the wound. And Seneca says[213] that confessing vices is the source of salvation.

Another reason why pride is hard to correct is that the remedy is painful and the medicine becomes toxic. The more goodness and wisdom a man has, the more does rise up in pride, as the gloss about those words that Christ spoke to the Pharisees shows: *Si ceci essetis, non haberetis peccatum* [Jn 9:41]. And St. Gregory says[214] that the celestial doctor does not look with his pitying eye on those who are sick and get worse with medicine, with which they should get better.

Here we show how there are three ways to correct pride.

Although, as has been shown, it is difficult to cure the vice of pride, still it is not impossible. In the *Summa* St. Thomas teaches three things by which the vice of pride is cured and healed.

The first thing is consideration of one's own fragility, of which the wise Ecclesiasticus says: *Quid superbis, terra et cinis?* [Ec 10:9]: Why do you rise up in pride, you who are earth and ashes? If we think about it, the wise man cannot better demonstrate man's baseness in coming

---

208 In Book 7 of the *Confessions* [GA].
209 *Epistulae Morales*, 53 [GA].
210 In *De Consideratione* [GA].
211 The discussion appears in the *Homiliae in evangelia* [GA].
212 In the *Consolation of Philosophy* [GA].
213 *Epistulae Morales*, 53 [GA].
214 *Homiliae in evangelium* [GA].

into this world than by being born, living in it, and departing through death. A man comes into this world conceived and generated, and it is not necessary to say how ugly and base the seminal material is, both the father's and the mother's, from which a man is generated, because it is obvious. St. Bernard, in his meditations,[215] and Innocent, in the book *On the Vileness of Human Misery*,[216] clearly show it. The holy Job, speaking to God, said it: *Memento, queso, quod sicut lutum fecisti me, et in pulverem reduces me* [Jb 10:9]: I beg you, remember you made me as mud is made, and in the end, you will unmake me and make dust of me. Elsewhere he said: *Comparatus sum luto et assimilates sum faville et cineri* [Jb 30:19]: I am like mud (as far as my conception and birth are concerned), and the spark of fire (as far as life) and to ashes (with regard to death). The fact that a man is lowly and wretched in life is shown by his vanity, about which the psalmist says: *Universa vanitas omnis homo vivens* [Ps 38:6]: Everyone who lives in this world is full of vanity, and there is nothing solid or stable about him. St. James, considering such vanity, said in his epistle: *Que est vita nostra? Vapor esta ad modicum parens* [Jm 4:14]: What is our life? And he replies: It is a wisp of smoke, which lasts little and quickly disappears. What a misery it is that life is so brief that a man can barely realize that he has lived by the time he dies. As Seneca says,[217] a man dies before he has begun to live, wherein by living he means virtuous living. The holy Job was aware of the brevity of a man's life when he said: *Homo natus de muliere, brevi vivens tempore repletus multis miseriis* [Jb 14:1–2]: A man is born of a woman, living for a brief time, full of many miseries. And he continues: *Et fugit velut umbra, et nunquam in eodem statu permanent*: And he flees like a shadow and never stands still. The prophet David says: *Adhuc pusillum, et non erit peccator, et queres locum eius et non invenies* [Ps 36:10]: Before long a man will no longer be a sinner, and you will look for his place and not find it.

Not only is a man base and wretched in this world as far as his body and his bodily life are concerned, but also with regard to his soul, which as soon as it is created in the body contracts the stain of original sin, which leads to all the miseries of body and soul, such as effort, pain and sadness, fear, hunger and thirst, illness, old age with its defects, ignorance, wrath and concupiscence, the sins and errors that dirty the soul, corrupt the mind, stain the conscience, and dishonour one's fame. As the prophet said, full of regret: *Ecce enim in iniquitatibus conceptus sum, et in peccatis concepit me mater mea* [Ps 50:7]: Here I am, conceived by my

---

215 Pseudo-Bernard, *Meditationes piissimae de cognition humanae conditionis* [GA].
216 Innocent III, *De miseria humane conditionis* [GA].
217 *Epistulae Morales*, 23 [GA].

mother in sin. Acknowledging those sins that he had then committed, he prayed that he would be forgiven for them, so he said: *Amplius lava me, Domine, ab iniquitate mea et a peccato meo munda me; quoniam iniquitatem meam ego cognosco, et peccatum meum contra me est semper. Tibi soli peccavi et malum coram te feci* [Ps 50:4–6]: Not only do I need to be cleansed of original sin, with which my mother conceived me, but even more to be washed of my iniquities and cleansed of my sin, and therefore, Lord, do it, because I know my iniquities, and my sin is always before me; I have sinned only against you, and done evil before you. And it is a great misery, among others, that a man has in this life when he does not realize his miseries; and in order to make him aware of them, he tells him in the Apocalypse: *Tu dicis: quia dives sum, et nullius egeo, et nescis quia miser es, et miserabilis, pauper, cecus et nudas* [Rv 3:17]: You say that I am rich and lack for nothing, and you don't see that you are wretched, poor, blind, and naked.

With regard to leaving this world by dying, how miserable and corrupt we are, how much suffering the sick have in their pains, in their punishments, in not being able to find rest, with their anxiety, torments, anguish, bitterness. Martyred with irons and fire, in the end they die in pain, with fear, and with doubts about their soul ending up in a good place. The wretched flesh goes into the ground to be a meal for stinking vermin, not to mention those who die a bad death, and whose flesh is devoured by wolves, by dogs, by fish, and by rapacious birds. But even while he lives, how lowly is he? Scripture says that his life is more corrupt than mud; indeed, it is a sack of shit and filth. The prophet Micah said [Mh 6:14]: At your centre is the reason for your humility. And the wise Ecclesiasticus spoke of this wretchedness and said: *Cum mortuus fuerit homo, hereditabit serpentes et bestias et vermes* [Ec 10:13]: When a man dies, his inheritance will be serpents and beasts and vermin.

The second thing St. Thomas says is useful for healing pride is considering the excellence of His Majesty, whose knowledge sees all things, whose providence governs and rules all things, whose justice punishes and corrects all things, whose power defeats and overcomes all things. How therefore will someone be so daring as to rise up against God with pride, and will not instead be subject to His will and serve Him with fear and reverence? The holy Job said to the prideful man: *Quit tumet contra Deum spiritus tuus?* [Jb 15:13]: Why does your spirit swell with pride against God? And elsewhere: *Quis restitit ei et pacem habuit?* [Jb 9:4]: Who is it, who has challenged God and has peace? As if to say, no one is left whose head is not broken, because he who throws a stone against God, it comes back at his head. St. Peter put it well: *Humiliamini sub potenti manu Dei* [1 Pt 5:6]: Humble yourselves under God's powerful hand.

O mortals, consider your baseness and the condition of your wretched and ineffable life, and live humbly, putting aside your haughty attitude and dulling your outrageous pride, which is subject to the will of omnipotent God!

The third thing that St. Thomas says makes us abandon our pride is by considering the imperfection and vanity of those things about which others rise up in pride, which are the goods of nature, of either the body or the soul. Bodily things are beauty, strength, health, lightness, nobility, and liberty. Natural goods of the soul are acuity, memory, wisdom, art, and knowledge. A man rises up in pride also about the goods of fortune, like things outside of him, beyond his power, such as wealth, dignity, status, honour, power, glory, fame: things he can lose, whether he wants to or not. Also, the goods of grace, like the virtues, make a man proud, and he misuses them. All these things are most imperfect in this life, and one should not rise up in pride because of them, and because they offer little stability they should not be judged great things, of which the prophet Isaiah says: *Omnis caro fenum, et omnis gloria eius quasi flos feni* [Is 40:6]: All flesh is like hay, and all glory is like the hay flower. St. Gregory explains:[218] The power of the men of the world and the glory of the flesh directly resemble the hay and the flower; because when it stands up, it falls, and when it is more beautiful, then it disappears and shrinks.

Tully[219] speaks of Alcibiades who, after acquiring great glory and much wealth, came into great misery, and he says that it seemed like two contrary fortunes were distinguishing themselves: the one gave him great nobility and measureless beauty, valour, much glory, the fame of great praise, the love of the citizens, grace among people, most abundant wealth, subtle acuity, eloquence, the favour of the people; the other followed in turn, giving him poverty and hatred of the fatherland; he was driven from office, condemned and sent into exile, and finally died a bad death. We could say this about many others, of whom we read both in Holy Scripture and in the worldly histories that their glory and prosperity lasted little and ended in great misery. It often happens this way, and for all that there are still many who become proud about such defective and imperfect things and deem them to be great things, judging that they are the highest and most perfect good and locating their final beatitude in them, as that wise Boethius demonstrates in his

---

218 In the *Moralia in Job* [GA].

219 Auzzas (Passavanti, 515) believes this is an erroneous attribution to Cicero derived from the *Alphabetum narrationum*; the true source is Valerius Maximus, *Factorum et dictorum memorabilium*.

book *The Consolation of Philosophy*. As the prophet David said: *Beatum dixerunt populum, cui hec sunt* [Ps 143:15]: There are many who say that the one who has these worldly things is blessed. But it is not so, he says: indeed, blessed is he who has God as his lord.

Each of the aforementioned things fills men with pride, and how imperfect, unstable, vain, and defective they are is shown clearly in many places of Holy Scripture by doctrine and example, and Boethius, in his book, and Seneca, in his epistles and tragedies, show it in a clear and orderly manner. Anyone who wants to know more, either to lift his spirit from worldly things and not prize them, or in order to know how to speak well about them, should read the books of said wise men, or this book of ours written in Latin in the treatise on pride, where we write about it extensively; and we will talk about it later on in the treatise about vainglory.

Another thing that helps to correct pride is the tribulation or adversity that God sends to people, like poverty, infirmity, lowering of status, shame, infamy, temptation, and the like, which take away their reasons for pride.

Severus writes[220] that there was a holy man who took care of all those possessed by the devil, not only by being present but also, when absent, by sending his hair shirt or some writing in his own hand, with which the possessed were touched, and he healed them. As the fame of his virtue spread, bedevilled persons of different states and conditions came to him from distant lands. Seeing that he could exercise so many virtues and enjoy such good fame, he started to think he was worthy of honour, and that he deserved the grace he had because of his goodness. So pride, which is often born of good, touched his mind, and the devil, pursued by him, inflamed him so strongly that he who took care of others and freed them from the power of the devil, was in turn embattled and defeated by the devil. Feeling overwhelmed by the vice of pestilential pride, he turned to God, devoutly praying to Him to remedy his evil and free him from said vice. Since the vice of pride had come into him as he chased demons from human bodies, he asked God to give the devil power over his body, so that his soul would be saved. This was granted, and the demon entered him, and he remained so fiercely possessed for five months that he had to be tied up and put in irons, so that he would not hurt himself or anyone else. After five months his body was freed of the devil, and his mind of pride.

---

220 The fourth-century Christian author Sulpicius Severus, known for his *Chronicle*.
   Here Passavanti cites the *Dialogues*, likely through the *Alphabetum narrationum* [GA].

As St. Augustine says,[221] God lets us fall into some obvious and evident sin because of pride, so that we will be dishonoured and confused and not dare to appear among the people, and will dislike those who, by liking themselves in the wrong way, first became prideful. St. Augustine explains the words of the psalmist in this way: *Imple facies eorum ignominia, et querent nomen tuum, Domine* [Ps 82:17]: Speaking of prideful men, the prophet tells God to fill their faces with shame and confusion, and then those who first magnified their own name will seek your name, magnifying and honouring it. Of these people the prophet says: *Vocaverunt nomina sua in terris suis* [Ps 48:12]: Prideful men focus on being known in their own lands. And what God does, by humbling prideful sinners, according to what the prophet David says: *Humilians autem peccatores usque ad terram* [Ps 146:6]: God humbles the sinners all the way to the earth – He does it all mercifully, castigating and correcting the sinners, so that they will not perish. The holy King David, who in his great prosperity was full of pride, and whom God humbled with great adversity and by letting him fall into adultery and homicide, recognized this and said: *Bonum mihi, quia humiliasti me, ut discam iustificationes tuas* [Ps 118:71]: It was a good and useful thing for me that you, my Lord, humbled me, so that I might learn your reasons, that is, how you set men right in obeying your commandments, or how you are just in all your operations. Elsewhere he said: *Priusquam humilarer ego deliqui, propterea eloquium tuum custodivi* [Ps 118:67]: Before I was humbled, I erred by sinning, then I obeyed your commandment, which first I had violated.

There is another very effective remedy against insolent pride: the example of the humility of Jesus Christ, about whom St. Paul says: *Humiliavit semet ipsum factus obbediens usque ad mortem* [Ph 2:8]: Jesus Christ humbled himself, making himself obedient all the way to death. St. Augustine explains this statement: In order for the source of all evil to be cured, the son of God descended and humbled himself.[222]

How is it, therefore, that you become prideful, o man, since God humbles Himself for you? If you are ashamed of following the humble man, you should not be ashamed of following the humble God. And St. Gregory says:[223] given that the only son of God took the shape of our sickness, humbling himself so that he might teach man not to be prideful, how great is the virtue of humility, by which, teaching it alone, the God of measureless greatness and infinite majesty shrank all the

---

221 In the *City of God* [GA].
222 In *In Iohannis evangelium tractatus* [GA].
223 In the *Moralia in Job* [GA].

way to His passion and death on the cross? As pride is an instrument of the devil for our perdition, so too was God's humility an efficacious remedy for our salvation. The highest teacher, Christ, taught this virtue of humility in his school, saying: *Discite a me, quia mitis sum et humilis corde* [Mt 11:29]: Learn from me, because I am gentle and humble of heart. St. Augustine explains this statement:[224] the true teacher did not say, learn from me how to create heaven and earth or how to resuscitate the dead; rather, he said that man should learn his humility. Without this, as St. Gregory says,[225] when someone gathers together all the other virtues save for humility, it is as if he were bringing dust to the wind. His blessed mother, the Virgin Mary, learned this most excellent virtue from Christ. Indeed, before she saw Jesus Christ incarnated and humbled, the virtue of perfect humility was infused in her most excellently by the Holy Spirit when, as the angel Gabriel told her that she was full of grace and blessed by God over all other women, and said she was chosen to be the mother of the son of God, humbling herself she said: *Ecce ancilla Domini:*[226] Here is God's servant, may it be done to me according to your word. Later, in the presence of St. Elizabeth, she added a stanza about this humility in that joyful song she made, full of the Holy Spirit, thanking God and prophesying, which says: *Quia respexit humilitatem ancille sue: ecce enim ex hoc beatam me dicent omnes generationes*: Since God looked at his servant's humility, all the generations of peoples will say to me that I am blessed. The Baptist followed this highest virtue of humility, and he was of such perfection that Christ said of him: *Inter natos mulierum non surrexit maior* [Mt 11:11]: Among all the sons born of women none rose higher than he, so that because of his holiness many believed that he was Christ, but humbling himself he said that he was not Christ, and that he was not worthy of unfastening his garter. As Holy Scripture and the legends show, the holy apostles who came after them followed their examples, which should very much move us to true humility. As St. Gregory says,[227] if holy men, by virtue of their humility, are reputed to be small and held to be lowly when they do wonderful things, what will those men say to defend those who, having done nothing good or virtuous, rising up in pride, think of themselves or want to be reputed to be great?

Since virtues are medicines for vices, which are sicknesses of the soul, the one being contrary to the other, and necessarily, according to the

---

224 In his *Sermons* [GA].
225 In the *Homiliae in evangelia* [GA].
226 The story appears in Luke 1.
227 In the *Homiliae in evangelia* [GA].

rule of medicine, sicknesses are cured by their opposites, in this treatise, in which we intend to correct and heal vices, we must perforce write about virtues, as of medicinal remedies. Therefore, having finished the treatise about each deadly sin, next we will write about the contrary virtue, so that the opposite, put next to the other, will be better understood by comparison, and so that the medicine, being brought near to the illness, might more efficaciously work its effect.

Here we present the treatise on humility.

Having therefore completed the treatise on pride, we should next speak about humility as its opposite and medicinal remedy. Writing briefly, we will say five things. First, we will say what humility is, describing it; second, we will say how many degrees of humility there are; third, we will show praise for its utility; fourth, we will say what those things are that cause and lead us to humility; fifth, we will show what the signs of true humility are, and how many there are.

First Chapter

Wherein we show what humility is.

First of all, we should describe and say what humility is. St. Ambrose says in the book *On Duties:*[228] *Humilitas est si nil quis sibi arroget et inferiorem se extimet*: Humility is when a man attributes nothing to himself with arrogance, and judges himself to be lesser and lower than others. Or, as St. Augustine says in the homily on the Gospel of St. John: *Humilitas vera est extimare se nihil esse*: True humility is to judge oneself to be nothing. And St. Bernard in the book *The Steps of Humility and Pride*[229] says: *Humilitas est virtus qua homo verissima sui cognitione sibi ipsi vilescit*: Humility is a virtue by which a man, with most true knowledge of himself, abases himself. Or, as he says in his epistles: *Humilitas est contemptus proprie excellentie*: Humility is a disdain for one's own excellence. These two descriptions appear sufficiently to include what humility is, in an intellectual sense. It is self-knowledge, as the first one says, and, with regard to its effect, it is disdain for one's own excellence, as the second one says. It is quite contrary to pride, which, as we said

---

228 The *De officiis ministrorum*, dated to between 377 and 391.
229 *De gradibus humilitatis et superbiae.*

above, is but a disordered appetite that drives the soul to some excellence or greatness, more than is appropriate according to right reason. Humility, on the contrary, tempers and restrains a man's spirit, so that it does not rise and extend to those things that are above it. Knowledge of one's own defects, by which some are thought to be base and unworthy of any excellence, is necessary for that purpose.

The difference between true and false humility is that a false and fake humility is seen only on the outside, like the pretend humility of the hypocrites, of whom the wise Ecclesiasticus says: *Est qui nequiter se humliat, interiora autem eius plena sunt dolo* [Ec 19:23]: He is someone who humbles himself neither directly nor truly, and what is inside is full of deceit. This means that humility shown only on the outside is not true humility, for it must be mainly in the heart; because true virtue is not in external acts but in mental choice, which is inside, as the wise philosophers and doctors say. So that the gloss of those words of the Gospel says:[230] *Discite a me, quia mitis sum et humilis corde*; true humility is that of the heart, so external humility should proceed like a branch from a root. And St. Jerome in an epistle says: flee from false humility, and follow what Christ taught, which is true.

Many follow the shadow and appearance of this virtue; few follow the truth. Words and sophisticated acts should cease, wherein oftentimes pride is hidden, and let us hold true humility in the heart, to which external semblances may respond.

Second Chapter

Wherein we show how many degrees of humility there are.

The second thing we should say about humility is how many ways or degrees it has. According to the gloss on those words in the Gospel that Christ said to St. John the Baptist,[231] *Sic decet nos implere omnem iustitiam, idest omnem humilitatem*, perfect humility has three degrees. The first is to subject oneself to one's superior, and not to put oneself above one's equal. The second is to subject oneself to one's equal, and not to put oneself above one's inferior. The third degree is to subject oneself to one's inferior. First-degree humility is called sufficient, because such humility is enough for salvation; the second is abundant humility, which is more than is necessary; the third humility is called superabundant, because it cannot be greater. This is what Christ had when he

---

230 Matthew Perault, *De humilitate*, in his *Summa* [GA].
231 Passavanti is referencing a gloss on Matthew 3:14 [GA].

subjected himself to baptism by St. John: he was submitting himself to his inferior, which is perfect humility.

Humility is also distinguished in four degrees, which are: *Spernere mundum, spernere nullum, spernere sese, spernere se sperni*: disdain the world, not disdain anyone, disdain oneself, disdain to be disdained.[232]

In *The Rule*, St. Benedict posits twelve degrees of humility, opposite the twelve degrees of pride, of which we spoke above.

The first degree is to always show humility with one's heart and one's body, keeping one's eyes to the ground. It is the opposite of the first degree of pride, which is called curiosity, by which a man goes looking about everywhere, with his head held high, in a disorderly way. The second degree is to speak few words, and those should be reasonable and not with a loud voice. It is opposite to the second degree of pride, which is called mental lightness, when someone speaks too much with proud words. The third degree of humility is not being too quick to laugh, and it is opposite to the third degree of pride, which is called obscene happiness. The fourth degree is to remain silent until you are asked; it is opposite to the fourth degree of pride, impulsiveness, which is when someone speaks too much, bragging about himself. The fifth degree is following the common rule of the monastery. It is opposite to the fifth degree of pride, singularity, which is when someone wants to seem better than others by doing something that someone else does not do. The sixth degree of humility is believing and stating aloud that you are lower than all others. It is the opposite of the sixth degree of pride, arrogance, by which someone promotes himself above others. The seventh degree is confessing and believing oneself to be useless and unworthy of everything; it is opposite to the seventh degree of pride, presumption, by which someone believes himself to be sufficient and worthy of greater things. The eighth degree of humility is to confess sins, and it is opposite to the eighth degree of pride, which is defending sins. The ninth degree is to embrace patience in harsh and hard things. It is opposite to the ninth degree of pride, which is confessing sin insincerely and not simply but with malice, in order to avoid due punishment. The tenth degree of humility is obedience, and it is opposite to the tenth degree of pride, rebellion, by which someone is rebellious and disobedient towards his superiors. The eleventh degree of humility is when a person does not take pleasure in doing one's will, and it is opposite to the eleventh degree of pride, freedom, which is when someone wants to be able to do everything he wants to do. The twelfth

---

232 Perault, *De humilitate* [GA].

degree of humility is fear of God, and it is opposite to the twelfth degree of pride, which is the habit of sin, by which a person disdains God and His commandments.

That these twelve degrees sufficiently include every humility that there should be in inner disposition and intellection, and also in external acts and appearances, St. Thomas subtly demonstrates and proves in his *Summa*. In our treatise written in Latin we write about it at length, making certain distinctions between the degrees of humility given by St. Anselm and by Cassian in his *Conferences*, which we won't put here in order to be brief and because they boil down to the above-stated twelve degrees of St. Benedict, if we consider them carefully.

Third Chapter

Wherein we commend humility and its great utility.

The third thing to say about humility is to commend it and its great utility. St. John Chrysostom says: No virtue can equal humility; it is the head of every virtue, the mother of knowledge, the foundation of the entire spiritual edifice, without which the other virtues perish, having nothing to lean on. St. Jerome says there is nothing that makes us so pleasing to God and to people alike than when we are great by merit of a holy life and small through humility.[233] This agrees with the statement of the wise Ecclesiasticus, who says: *Quanto magnus es, humilia te in omnibus et coram Deo invenies gratiam* [Ec 3:20]: No matter how great and superior you are, humble yourself all the more, and you will find grace before God. St. Bernard explains:[234] although it is good for everyone to be humble, still, the greater a person is, and the greater his dignity, so does the virtue of humility better reside in him and shine more clearly, like a gem in a ring.

In the next part we will write about how useful this excellent virtue is for a man whom it adorns.

First, through humility a man merits divine grace. St. Jacob says: *Humilibus autem dat gratiam* [Jm 4:6]: God gives His grace to the humble. St. Bernard explains these words,[235] saying that grace does not enter the heart of one who is confident of his merits and rests on his own laurels, because he is full of self-regard and therefore grace finds no place there. Just as someone who wants to fill a vessel with water from

---

233 In his *Epistles* [GA].
234 In *De consideration* [GA].
235 In the *Sermones in adnuntiatione dominica* [GA].

a river or fountain tilts it, so too should one who wants to draw in divine grace not remain erect with pride, but rather bend with humility. Water descends from mountains to low valleys, and the waters gathering there in abundance make a river and copious fountains; so too does the abundance of grace descend to the valleys of humility. As St. Augustine says:[236] The more humbly did Mary sit, the more grace did she receive. The reason is that when grace is given to a person, it makes all the other virtues grow, and it makes humility grow, and the person becomes ever more capacious to receive more grace. As well, the more grace humility receives from God, the more it empties itself, or the mind wherein it resides, deeming itself nothing. The truly humble person does not hold himself to be humble, and so by making himself unworthy of every other thing and of himself, he becomes that glorious nobody in which God is found, and without which no virtue finds its basis. Jesus Christ – who annihilated himself for us, as the apostle says, *Exinanivit semetipsum* [Ph 2:7], taught about this nobody when he said in the Gospel: *Cum feceritis omnia que praecepta sunt vobis, dicite: servi inutiles sumus* [Lk 17:10]: When you have done all those things that you are ordered to do, say: we are useless servants. As the wise Ecclesiasticus said: *Humiliare Deo et expecta manum eius* [Ec 13:9]: Humble yourself before God and await His help.

Second, humility introduces wisdom to a man's mind and gives him knowledge of truth. As Solomon says in Proverbs: *Ubi humilitas, ibi sapientia* [Pr 11:2]: Where there is humility, there is wisdom. St. Augustine speaks about that when explaining the Gospel of St. John: Humility opens understanding to know the truth, and pride closes it. Christ spoke of this to his father in the Gospel: *Abscondisti hec a sapientibus et prudentibus et revelasti ea parvulis* [Mt 11:25]: You have hidden those things – i.e., the truth of divine things of which he was speaking – from the wise men – i.e., from those who hold themselves to be wise, which is pride – and you have revealed them to the small – i.e., to the humble, according to the gloss. As the philosopher Didimus said to the proud Alexander: God would be ready to give you wisdom, if you had somewhere to receive it; in other words, if he were as humble as he is full of pride, suggesting that wisdom accompanies humility and not pride.[237] And the astrologer Ptolemy said: among wise men the wisest is the humblest.

We read in the *Life of the Holy Fathers* that a friar, wanting God to reveal to him a certain passage of Scripture that he did not understand,

---

236 In his *Sermons* [GA].
237 Passavanti likely borrowed this anecdote from Perrault's *De humilitate* [GA].

set about to fast and pray. Having fasted for seven weeks, and not having received the grace that he asked for, he thought about going to one of the friars who lived in the desert and asking him his question. Along the way, God's angel appeared before him and said to him: "Your seven weeks of fasting have not brought you closer to God, and have not been useful to you in your quest. Now, because you have humbled yourself in going to ask your brother, I am sent by God to teach you what you wanted to know"; and he answered the question clearly for him. Thanking God and knowing the virtue of humility, he returned to his cell doubly instructed, and he understood the Scripture, which says that God reveals His secrets to the humble.

The third use of humility is that it frees a man from the temptations and ties of the world, as the prophet David said: *Humiliatus sum, et liberavit me* [Ps 114:6]: I humbled myself, and I was freed.

We read in the *Life of the Holy Fathers* that St. Anthony was once praying, and he saw the whole world tied up in knots, and tearfully he said: "Now who can escape so many knots and not be caught up in one of them?" And he heard a voice that answered him and said: "Humility alone."

This is what it seems the psalmist meant when he said: *In via hac qua ambulabam absconderunt lequeum michi*, continuing, *Intende ad deprecationem meam, quia humiliatus sum nimis* [Ps 141:4, 7]: In the street where I was walking, the prophet says, they have hidden the knot from me in order to capture me and tie me up; but I have humbled myself. Therefore, understand my prayer, my Lord, and free me.

Fourth, humility vanquishes the devil and never allows itself to be defeated by him. St. Gregory talks about how humility defeats the devil, in the homily[238] where he says that each deed we do with humility is an arrow and lance thrown at the devil, in order to wound him and defeat him.

As we read in the *Life of the Holy Fathers*, the devil once said to St. Macarius: "Why do you defeat me? Because if you fast, I never eat; if you see, I never sleep; if you tire yourself out with good works, I never rest." And he answered the question himself: "Only your humility defeats me, which I do not have, nor can I."

And the gloss[239] on the epistle of St. Paul says that humility wins: Be humble and not presumptuous, and you will be able to win. This appears to be what St. John said in his epistle: *Fortes estis, et vicistis malignum* [1 Jn 2:14]: You who are humble, be strong, and you will

---

238 In the *Moralia in Job* [GA].
239 Peter Lombard's gloss on Romans [GA].

defeat the malign one, i.e., the devil. St. Augustine says that humility never lets itself be defeated: only he who is presumptuous is defeated, only he who out of humility is not presumptuous wins. This is correct, because God fights for humility; humility attributes the glory of victory to God, saying: *Non nobis, Domine, non nobis, sed nomini tuo da gloriam*: Not to us, Lord, but to your name it gives glory. It leaves the battle to Him, giving Him the glory of victory. As well, a man defeats himself through humility, which is the most difficult victory there is, through which we defeat every other thing and cannot be defeated by any other thing. And humility cannot be defeated because its wounds strengthen it, and infirmity reinforces it, poverty enriches it, it results from harm and is brought back from death.

Fifth, humility fulfils a person's requests and prayers, as the prophet David says: *Respexit in orationem humilium et non sprevit preces eorum* [Ps 101:18]: God has looked at the prayers of the humble and has not disdained their requests. That is correct, because humility pleases Him so much that everything it desires pleases Him. As that holy woman Judith said: *Humilium et mansuetorum semper tibi placuit deprecatio* [Jd 9:16]: The request of the humble and the gentle always pleased you. And because the eye is drawn to love and pleasure, God with the eye of His mercy always sees the humble (so says the psalmist): *Humilia respicit in celo et in terra* [Ps 112:6]; and Leah said in the Scripture: *Vidit Dominus humilitatem meam* [Gn 29:32]: God has seen my humility. Therefore, He delivers us from the evil of guilt and from the evil of punishment. The prophet said of the evil of guilt: *Humiliatus sum, et liberavit me* [Ps 114:6]: I humbled myself, and God has delivered me.[240] God said to the prophet about the evil of punishment: you have seen King Ahab humbled before me, I have pardoned him, and I will not in his time bring to his house the evils that I said I would.[241] Elsewhere Scripture says of certain sinners: *Quia humiliati sunt, aversa est ab eis ira Dei*:[242] Because they are humbled, the wrath of God has turned away from them. God does not feel wrath towards humility, and this is why a humble person deems himself base. As the prophet, humbled, said: *Ego autem sum vermis et non homo*:[243] I am vermin, not a man. Elsewhere he

---

240 Passavanti's translation here differs from the one he gives a few paragraphs above, suggesting that he is translating freely as he goes along.

241 The words are directed at the prophet Elijah in 1 Kings 21.

242 The sentence, which Passavanti borrows from 2 Chronicles 12:12, appears in the singular, not the plural, and refers to the humility of King Rehoboam.

243 Psalms 22:6. Passavanti is performing some sleight of hand here, suggesting that David's words in the psalm are a direct reply to the words of 2 Chronicles 12.

calls himself a flea and a dead dog. It would not be an honour to God to claim to be such a base thing as a flea or a dead dog, because God is magnanimous. Therefore, He takes revenge on the boastful, haughty, proud ones and pardons the humble subjects, as that poet Virgil said of the Romans: *Parcere subiectis et debellare superbos*,[244] those who were subject to the prideful and defeated them are pardoned. We say this of the lion, who lacerates and kills the ferocious animals who challenge him, while those who humble themselves he lets go safe. God does the same thing, revoking sentences given, as we read in Holy Scripture about that King Hezekiah, and of the king and the city of Nineveh, and of King Ahab, and of many others.[245] About whom the psalmist says: *Cor contritum et humiliatum, Deus, non despicies* [Ps 50:19]: God, do not disdain the contrite and humbled heart.

The sixth useful thing about humility is that it exalts and honours a man in this life, and then he deserves honour and the exaltation of glory in the next, as the Lord says in the Gospel: he who humbles himself will be exalted. St. Peter said: humble yourself beneath God's powerful hand, so that He will exalt you. That God also honours and exalts the humble in this life is shown by many examples in divine Scripture, as we read about that King Saul, to whom God said: *Cum parvulus esses in oculis tuis, capud in Isdrael factus es* [1 Sm 15:17]: When you were small in your eyes you were made leader and king. St. Gregory explains:[246] When you were small before yourself, you were great before me, because the humble one is all the more precious before God, the lowlier he is before himself. God made the humble David king of his people; likewise Moses, most humble, God made prince and duke of his people; so too Gideon and many others.[247] As the holy Job said, speaking to God: *Ponis humiles in sublimi* [Jb 5:11]: You elevate the humble.

And how God exalted and lifted up the humble, who stay low, was shown once by a beautiful miracle.

It is no wonder that God honours the humble, because they honour Him, as the wise Ecclesiasticus says: *Magna potentia Dei solius, et ab humilibus honoratur* [Ec 3:21]: Great is the power of the one God, and He is honoured by the humbled. As God said through Scripture: *Qui honorificavit me, glorificabo eum* [1 Sm 2:30]: He who honours me, I shall

---

244 *Aeneid* 6.853.

245 The narrative of Hezekiah appears in 2 Chronicles 32 and Isaiah 38; Nineveh in the book of Jonah; Ahab in 1 Kings 21.

246 In the *Moralia in Job* [GA].

247 For David consult 1 Samuel; for Moses the book of Exodus; for Gideon the book of Judges.

glorify. The holy Job says that humility merits finally to have glory and the kingdom of heaven: *Qui humilitatus ferit erit in Gloria* [Jb 22:29]: He who will be humbled will be in glory. Christ showed this in the Gospel when he said: *Nolite timere, pusillus grex, qui complacuit Patri meo dare vobis regnum* [Lk 12:32]: Do not fear, little (i.e., humble) people, because it has pleased my Father to give you the kingdom. This is what he meant when he said: *Sinite parvulos venire ad me, talium est enim regnum celorum* [Mt 19:14]: Let the little ones come to me, because the kingdom of heaven is theirs. Elsewhere he said: *Nisi efficiamini ut parvuli, non intrabitis in regnum celorum* [Mt 18:3]: If you do not make yourself small, you will not enter the kingdom of heaven. As Solomon said in Proverbs: *Humilem spiritu suscipiet Gloria* [Pr 29:23]: He who is humble in spirit will receive glory.

Fourth Chapter

Wherein we show the reasons that lead one to have humility.

The fourth thing to say about humility is what things cause and induce us to have humility.

The first thing is the consideration of one's own defects, of which St. Gregory says:[248] Holy men, in order to safeguard the virtue of humility in themselves, keep their defects and infirmities in their mind's eye, so that by considering them they might remain humble, and their spirit, no matter how good they are, does not rise up in pride.

Man has the capacity and reason to be humble in both body and soul. In the body, if he considers his origins, the state of his present life, and its ending in death. St. Bernard spoke of this, saying:[249] Look at where you come from, and be ashamed of where you are, and cry over it; look at where you are going, and tremble in fear. We spoke above about these three things, in the treatise on pride, where we showed what the remedies for pride are. Regarding the soul, we have the capacity for humility because, if a man is in mortal sin, he is worse than a pig or a dog, who are due just one death, that of the body; and he is due two, bodily and eternal. Also, man has the wretchedness of guilt and punishment, and the pig and the dog, who are without guilt, have the wretchedness of punishment.

If a man wonders about being in deadly sin, even this uncertainty is great wretchedness, as Solomon says: *Sunt justi atque sapientes, et opera*

---

248 In the *Homiliae in evangelia* [GA].
249 In the *Sermones de diversis* [GA].

eorum in manu Dei, et tamen nescit homo utrum amore vel odio dignus sit, sed omnia in futurum reservantur incerta:[250] There are some just and wise men, and their deeds are in God's hands, and nevertheless a man does not know whether he is worthy of love or hatred, but all things are kept uncertain. St. Gregory explains:[251] All things are uncertain, so that we might hold one thing certain, i.e., humility.

Let's assume that a man is sure that he is not in a state of deadly sin. If he considers the everyday risk of falling, either out of negligence or ignorance, because of concupiscence and the temptations of the devil, the world, and the flesh, so that wherever he turns he finds slippery paths and traps, he has reason to be humble and fearful. Despite all these things, our pride is neither dulled nor humbled, as St. Bernard says:[252] O wonderful vanity! O great foolishness of our heart! Whose pride cannot overcome the capacity for such humility, so that even earth and ashes do not rise!

The second thing that leads us to humility is time spent with humble people, because, as Scripture says, he who frequents and talks to the prideful draws pride from them; so too does he who frequents the humble person learn humility from him. As St. Jerome says, just as one who trains his mind on deeds of the proud man has an inducement to pride by his bad example, so too does the act of considering the good deeds of the humble person lend the caution of humility.

The third reason for humility is getting used to lowly duties and enduring injuries, attacks, vituperation, slander, shame, spite, and not responding or taking revenge, but judging oneself to be deserving of that and worse. As St. Bernard says:[253] Humiliation is the path to humility, as patience to peace and study to knowledge; therefore, if you desire the virtue of humility, do not flee the path of humiliation.

The fourth thing that leads us to humility is the memory of death, about which God said to the first father of human nature, Adam: *Pulvis es, et in pulverem reverteris* [Gn 3:19]: You are dust, and to dust you shall return. The Holy Church reminds us about this on the first day of Lent, when it puts ashes on our head and says to each of us, remember that you are dust, and to dust you shall return.

A man should think of himself as ashes even while alive, because it is certain that before long he will return to ashes. And the things that are

---

250 Ecclesiastes 9:1–2. Passavanti relies here on the commonplace that Solomon had
     authored the book.
251 In the Homilies on Ezekiel [GA].
252 In the *Sermones de diversis* [GA].
253 In his Epistles [GA].

certain about the time to come must be taken as if they were present. As St. Paul says: *Corpus mortuum propter peccatum* [Rm 8:10]: The body is dead because of sin, i.e., destined and given to the need of death. Therefore, St. Gregory said:[254] He who believes he shall surely die is held already to be almost dead. That holy patriarch Abraham was thinking of himself in this way when he said to God: *Loquar ad Dominum, cum sim pulvis et cinis* [Gn 18:27]: Although I am dust and ashes, still I shall dare to speak to my Lord.

Someone who dresses up in silk and scarlet does not think of himself as dust and ashes. Who would make such clothes into ash bags if they were not already crazy? Someone who puts himself in a state of elevation and dignity does not think of himself as dust and ashes, because ashes put on high are carried away and scattered by the wind. Although they do not think so, yet they are, as the psalmist says: *Non sic impii, non sic, sed tamquam pulvis, quem proicit ventus a facie terre* [Ps 1:4]: Prideful sinners do not think of themselves in that way, and yet they are like the dust that the wind chases from the face of the earth.

A man must be humble not only because he is ashes and dust, but also because he is something even more base, dung and vermin. Scripture says: *Gloria eius stercus et vermis* [1 Mc 2:62]: Man's glory is dung and vermin. And the wise Ecclesiasticus says: *Vindicta carnis impii ignis et vermis* [Ec 7:19]: The revenge of the sinner's flesh is fire and vermin.

Man on high, when your thoughts turn to vanity, think about the baseness of burial! Go, you haughty and unrestrained young man, when you have fun with your friends and wander intemperately with your companions, chasing your desires, and think about the graves full of ugliness and stinking filth. Go, you elegant made-up lady, when you delight in being watched and enjoy being praised and judged as beautiful, look at the vermin-infested and putrefied flesh in the ditches of the cemeteries! Go, graceful young lady, focused on looking good, cleaning yourself up, adorning yourself to win the title and reputation of beauty or to be loved by lovers, and see yourself in the graves, full of abominable putrefaction! Let's all go see if ever there was the vermin-infested coat of a rotting dog or the carcass of an ass skinned and tossed into the ditches, or if ever someone smelled the annoying stench of a corrupt corpse as displeasing and abominable and of such horror as are the bodies of men and women that have been underground for some time, before they are completely consumed. Not to mention the ugly things that are born of this putrefied flesh, because they draw annoying

---

254 In the *Moralia in Job* [GA].

vermin and are generated from the whole body. From certain of a man's members, the wise experts say, there is born a serpentine scorpion, poisonous and black, and from those of the woman, a poisoned toad, bothersome and fat. It seems that the wise Ecclesiasticus was talking about this when he said: *Cum mortuus fuerit homo, hereditabit serpentes et bestias et vermes* [Ec 10:13]: When a man dies, his legacy will be serpents, and beasts, and vermin.

How therefore, as St. Jerome says, will a man become prideful, when he possesses so much baseness? And although the memory of death is bitter, as the wise Ecclesiasticus says: *O mors, quam amara est memoria tua?* [Ec 41:1] (O death, how bitter is the memory of you), still a man must want to endure this bitterness, considering the fruit that comes from it; because by such a memory the humbled and fearful soul forbids sinning. The wise Ecclesiasticus says: *In omnibus operibus tuis, memorate novissima tua, et in etternum non peccabis* [Ec 7:40]: In all your deeds, remember your purpose, and you will never sin. As St. Jerome says in one of his epistles, it was the judgment of the philosopher Plato that the entire life of wise men should be spent thinking about death. That other philosopher said that that was the highest philosophy. By such a memory a man disdains himself and all the things of this world. Thus does St. Jerome say:[255] He who always thinks about having to die easily disdains everything, and especially because of the memory of death he tempers himself and disdains the vain happiness of temporal and carnal things. As Solomon said: *Si annis multis vixerit homo et in hiis omnibus letus fuerit, meminisse debet tenebrosi temporis et dierum multorum, qui, cum venerint, vanitatis arguentur preterita* [Ec 11:8]: For a man to live happily for many years, he must remember the dark time of death, and the many days that will come to pass, and he will see how what has been and passed is vanity. Therefore, the wise Ecclesiasticus said: *In die bonorum ne immemor sis malorum* [Ec 11:27]: In good times and prosperity, do not forget evil and adversity.

The fifth thing that leads us to humility is the example of Jesus Christ and his saints. St. Augustine says of Christ's humility:[256] Take the path of Christ's humility if you want to come to the glory of his eternity; if you want to have his height, first assume the baseness of his humility. Jesus Christ showed this, so that we might follow his example – as he said: *Exemplus enim dedi vobis* [Jn 13:15] – by being born to a humble mother, a humble home, a humble bed, humble clothes, and by living,

---

255 In his Epistles [GA].
256 In his *Sermons* [GA].

circumcised like a sinner, bought and sold like a servant, questioning his teachers like a disciple, and being subject to Mary and Joseph. As someone lesser, without precisely being poor, he wanted his humble company of fishermen to be baptized by the man and tempted by the devil, and to pay tribute or passage, endure villainy, offence, infamy, reproof, without defence. Preaching and doing miracles, he fled glory and honour, and when he was to be made king, he left, and he scolded his disciples for their ambition. He embraced children, offering them as an example of humility and subjugation. He rode an ass when he came to the place of the passion. He washed his disciples' feet and ate dinner with them at a big table, eating out of a bowl and serving as a minister, and then he gave them communion. When dying, he endured being betrayed, accused, seized and bound, interrogated, beaten, scorned, judged, yelled at, and sent to the place of justice with the cross of derision on his neck. He did not disdain the basest death on the cross, which he climbed naked, thirsty, whipped, wounded, in the place of public justice, between the thieves like an evildoer. After his death, he wanted to be buried underground, and he wanted to descend to hell for the salvation and liberation to those who were imprisoned.

St. Paul spoke of this most profound humility that Jesus Christ showed by being born, living, and dying when he said: *Exinanivit semet ipsum formam servi accipiens, et habitu inventus ut homo humiliavit semet ipsum formam servi accipiens, et habitu invetus ut homo, humiliavit semet ipsum factus obbediens usque ad mortem, mortem autem crucis* [Ph 2:7–8]: Jesus Christ, being God, vanished and nullified himself, taking the form of a servant and the clothing of a man, that is, the flesh of human nature; he humbled himself, making himself obedient all the way to his death on the cross. The apostle, having demonstrated Christ's humility, added the glory and exaltation that he deserved for his humility, whereupon he said: *Propter quod et Deus exaltavit illum et dedit illi nomen, quod est super omne nomen, ut in nomine Iesu omne genu flectatur celestium, terrestrium, et infernorum, et omnis lingua confiteatur quia Dominus noster Iesus Christus in gloria est Dei Patris* [Ph 2:9–11]: Because of which God exalted him, and gave him a name that is above every name, so that in the name of Jesus everyone in heaven and on earth and in hell will kneel, and every tongue will confess that our Lord Jesus is in the glory of the Father. This means that whoever follows Christ in his humility will follow him in having the exaltation and glory of his divinity.

He who wants to know the humility of the saints should read about it in their legends, where a man can reflect himself, and know his pride, and by their example take the form of true humility.

Fifth Chapter

Wherein we show what the signs of true humility are.

The fifth thing left to be said concerns the signs of true humility. The first sign that a person is humble is if he loves humble people and willingly spends time with them. As the wise Ecclesiasticus says, *Omne animal diligit sibi simile* [Ec 13:19]: every animal loves what is like it. The second sign is the love of one's own baseness, i.e., that a man holds himself to be lowly, and loves to be deemed lowly. As St. Bernard says:[257] The truly humble man wants to be reputed to be base and does not want to be judged as humble, nor praised for his humility, so that, just as he does not see himself as humble but as base, so too does he want to be judged base by others, and not as humble. It so happens, as St. Gregory says, that the more a man sees himself as base, the more precious he is in God's eyes. Therefore, that holy King David said [2 Sm 6:22]: I will make myself lowlier and be humble in my eyes. The third sign of true humility is that a man seeks the advice of others about his own affairs and accepts it. As the prideful man trusts his own wisdom more than the advice of others (about which St. Gregory says, if he did not think himself better than others, he would not put the advice of others last in his deliberation), so too does the humble man trust the advice of others more than his own opinion. The fourth sign is when someone flees honours and high offices and willingly takes low offices.

We read in the *Life of the Holy Fathers* that a holy father, adorned with many virtues, prayed to God to show him what the perfection of the soul consisted of. When another holy father asked about it, the first one answered by revelation, and asked him whether he was prepared to do everything he said, and he answered yes. "Go then," he said to him, "and feed the pigs," and so he did, and people said that he was crazy, and they made fun of him. But he retained the virtue of humility, and he enjoyed the scorn from without and the low office. After a certain time the holy fathers, having recognized his perfect humility, recalled him to his monastery.

The fifth sign of true humility is if someone is quickly obedient, without delay or excusing the delayed obedience. As disobedience comes from pride, so too is quick obedience born of true humility. As a sign of this, the apostle, speaking of Christ's obedience, put humility first, saying: He humbled himself, having made himself obedient until death.

---

257 In the *Sermones super Cantica Canticorum* [GA].

The sixth sign of humility is enduring injuries and attacks and villainous acts and words, not only with patience but with happiness. As St. Jerome says:[258] patience in the face of injuries shows that a man is humble. And St. Gregory:[259] the villainy done to others proves what a man is within.

He writes that there was a holy man by the name of Constance, who, although he was very unattractive and small, had great virtue and holiness before God. As his reputation for holiness grew among the people, many came from different countries to see him and to ask for the goodness of his prayers. Among them there once came a peasant, rough and uncultured to the eye. He asked for him and was shown to where he was lighting the lamps and resupplying the oil. When this man saw this ugly little person, his humble clothing, his lowly duty, he could not believe he was the one about whom he had heard such great things. Even as it was affirmed to him that he was the one, he said: "I thought he was a great and attractive man, about whom so many wonderful things were said. Has this man nothing of a man of goodness about him?" Hearing this, the servant of God left the lamps and ran and embraced this man and kissed him, saying: "You have judged the truth about me: you have recognized me, you alone have opened your eyes to my deeds." Offering himself to him, he thanked him greatly.

This man, St. Gregory says, was of such humility that he felt greater love for the man who disdained him! Like those who are proud of their honours, so too do the humble find happiness in disdain and dishonour, and they are happy to see themselves as base and scorned by others, as they are to themselves.

But that is enough about humility.

Here begins the treatise on vainglory.

Having spoken of the vice of pride, which St. Gregory says is the mother and poisonous root from which other vices proceed and are born, we come now to vainglory, which St. Gregory says is pride's firstborn daughter, which it so resembles that oftentimes, as almost indiscernible, they are mistaken for one another. One should not marvel at such a similarity, because she is the daughter to whom her mother gave all the power of her poison, and a general disposition to her nature, and

---

258 In the *Treatise on Psalms* [GA].
259 In his Dialogues [GA].

the father used all his power to endow her with the formal figure of his malice. Teachers and doctors, speaking and writing of both mother and daughter, often mistake the one for the other, speaking of the mother instead of the daughter and the daughter instead of the mother, even though there is a formal difference and real distinction between them. Therefore, as we did for pride, we will write a special treatise on vainglory, about which we will say some things.

First Chapter

Wherein we show what vainglory is.

The first thing that we should say about vainglory is what it is. This name, vainglory, includes two things: the one is glory, and the other is vain. In order to know what vainglory is, it is necessary to know what glory is, and then we will see which glory is vain, and so we will know what vainglory is.

It is first necessary to know what glory is. St. Augustine says: *Gloria est frequens fama cum laude:*[260] Glory is a fame and an ongoing recognition that perseveres with praise; or, as he says elsewhere: *Gloria est iudicium hominum de aliquo bene oppinantium:*[261] Glory is a judgment of men, who esteem others well. St. Ambrose says: *Gloria est clara cum laude notitia:*[262] Glory is a clear recognition with praise. And Cicero says that glory is *frequens de aliquo fama cum laude,*[263] as was explained above; and elsewhere he says:[264] *Gloria est quedam solida res, et expressa, non adumbrata:* Glory is a solid and explicit thing, not nuanced. Through all these statements, which say the same thing, we understand, along with St. Thomas, that glory means something clear, the clear thing means a beauty and a manifestation, and therefore, this noun, glory, is important precisely as a declaration of something that by popular opinion is or seems beautiful, or good, or noteworthy, whatever it is, corporeal or spiritual, as long as it is honourable or worthy of praise. Therefore, glory is a manifest and clear awareness that people have of something

---

260 *In Iohannis evangelium tractatus* [GA].

261 In the *City of God* [GA].

262 Passavanti may be borrowing from an attribution to Ambrose in Aquinas's *Summa* [GA].

263 In *De inventione* but also reported in the *Summa*, which may have been Passavanti's source [GA]. See also p. 179.

264 In the *Tusculan Disputations* [GA].

that is excellent or good in someone else, that is worthy of praise or honour, according to the judgment and opinion of the people.

The appetite for this glory can be without vice and without sin. This happens when a person wants to demonstrate some good, or in fact shows it, with right reason and to good purpose, such as doing it so that God would have praise and glory for it, as Jesus Christ said in the Gospel: *Sic luceat lux vestra coram hominibus, ut videant opera vestra bona et glorificent Patrem vestrum, qui in celis est* [Mt 5:16]: May the light of your goodness be so manifest and in such a way before men that they see your good works, and glory in your father God, who is in heaven. Also, when someone does it to set a good example for others, so that others might become better, as St. Paul showed us when he said: *Providentes bona non solum coram Deo, sed etiam coram omnibut hominibus* [Rm 12:17]: Endeavour to do and show good works not only before God, but also before all men, setting a good example. Likewise, when a person does it in order to persevere in goodness and become better, such as when certain people, hearing their good works praised and approved by others, become better for it – as the wise man said, that virtue that is praised grows – and they persevere in the good. The wise Ecclesiasticus teaches us this understanding when he says: *Curam habe de bono nomine* [Ec 41:15]: Look after your good name. And Cicero says[265] that men burn to do good for the sake of glory. By whichever of these three things a man desires glory, showing his good works, or any goodness or virtue that he might have, it is not a sin or a vice but virtue and mercy, because it is done for love of God and one's neighbour.

The appetite and desire for glory can be a sin when it is desired for none of the reasons stated above, but vainly, and then it is called the vice of vainglory. As St. Thomas says,[266] to desire any base thing is a vice and a sin, according to what the psalmist says: *Ut quit diligitis vanitatem et quaeritis mendacium?* [Ps 4:2]: Why do you love vanity and try to hear and say the lie? It may be called vainglory in three ways. First, with regard to the thing about which someone tries to gain glory, which is a base, fragile thing, unworthy of glory, or when someone tries to gain glory for something he does not have. Of this vanity the prophet Jeremiah says: *Vana sunt opera eorum, et risu digna* [Jr 51:18]: Their deeds are base and deserving of laughter; that is, others should make fun of them. The second way is on the part of him or those from which others want glory, i.e., from men, whose judgment is uncertain and false most of the time, and therefore lowly. Of this the psalmist says: *Universa*

---

265 In the *Tusculan Disputations* [GA].
266 In the *Summa* [GA].

vanitas omnis homo vivens [Ps 38:6]; and elsewhere: *Dominus scit cogitationes hominum, quoniam vane sunt* [Ps 93:11]: Every living man is all vanity, and God knows well that men's thoughts are base. The third way is called vainglory with regard to someone who desires glory but does not order his appetite to the due objective, i.e., God's honour, and his and his neighbour's salvation. Of this vanity the prophet Jeremiah says: *Ambulaverunt post vanitatem, et vani facti sunt* [Jr 2:5]: Men pursued vanity, and they are made vain.

Reasonably, therefore, vainglory is what somebody desires to have of something vain, from something vain, or through something vain. A vain thing, as Hugh of St. Victor says, is something that does not last through the day that one has it, does not take fruit of what it does, and never arrives at the end to which it is directed. As Solomon said, considering the vanity of these created things: *Vanitas vanitatum, et omnia vanitas* [Ec 1:2]: Vanity of vanities, all is vanity. The other reading has *vanitantium*, that is, of men who boast about themselves, suggesting that vanities are those things of which men glory in vain, vain are the men who desire vainglory, or from whom someone else desires glory. Vain is the end to which such glory leads, as St. Peter says: *Omnis gloria eius tamquam flos feni* [1 Pt 1:24]: All of man's glory, however you take it, is worthless, like the hayflower. Chrysostom put it well: Such glory is not real, and it is not glory, but unworthy of glory. So the ancients called it vainglory, that is, a worthless thing, because the thing that is worthless is called vain.

Second Chapter

Wherein we show the difference between vainglory and pride, and when vainglory is a deadly sin.

The second thing to say about vainglory is what difference there is between it and pride, and when it is a deadly sin. Because of the great similarity between these two vices, the one is often mistaken for the other by Scripture and by the wise doctors. Nevertheless, if we consider them carefully, we see a great difference and inequality between them; each is a vice unto itself, distinct from the other, which seems clear if we recall what was said above.

It was said above that pride, properly speaking, is a love or disordered appetite that pushes the soul towards some greater excellence or superiority than is appropriate according to right reason. Vainglory, according to what we can gather from what was said above, is an appetite for human praise or reputation in the judgment and opinion of the people, by which some excellence, virtue, or goodness is manifested and shown, not being rightly directed to the proper end but for vain pleasure. Pride is therefore one thing and vainglory another, and vainglory adds to and stands over pride, because whereas pride desires some excellence or greatness, vainglory is not content just to have, but wants to show it and make a show of it in order to acquire praise, name, and honour and fame among people. Sometimes a vainglorious man wants to be praised, honoured, and revered in order to be noticed by people, and so that some excellence and goodness of his is made manifest for honour and reverence to be shown to him, and praise and fame given him. Sometimes praise and honour are the reason for vainglory; sometimes they are the effect and end to which a man tends out of vainglory.

With regard to vainglory as a deadly sin, it should be noted that, as St. Thomas says in the *Summa*, a sin is deadly when it is contrary to the love of God and of one's neighbour. Properly understood, vainglory would not be contrary to love of one's neighbour were it not already consequently or indirectly so. Somebody might do harm to or attack his neighbour, oppressing him or defaming him or otherwise attacking him, in order to acquire glory, honour, praise, or fame. This would indeed be contrary to love of one's neighbour, and it would be a deadly sin or cause for deadly sin. Vainglory can be contrary to love and charity towards God in two ways. First, according to what a person glories in, so that if you were to glory in something false that is contrary to divine reverence, just as the prophet Ezekiel says about that king: *Elevatum est cor tuum, et dixisti: Deus ego sum* [Ez 28:2]: Your heart is raised up high, and you said: I am God. Likewise, St. Paul says [1 Cr 4:7]: Why do you glory in yourself, o man, for the goods that you have received from God, as if you had not received them from Him? Or when someone puts some temporal or corporeal or spiritual good ahead of God, which God prohibits through the prophet Jeremiah, saying: *Non glorietur sapiens in sapientia sua nec fortis in fortitudine sua nec dives in divitiis suis, set in hoc glorietur qui gloriatur scire et nosse me* [Jr 9:23–4]: The wise man should not glory in his wisdom or knowledge, nor the strong man in his strength, nor the rich man in his wealth, but he who glories, let him glory in knowing me. Or when someone else puts the witness of men before that of God, which Christ discussed in the Gospel: *Qui dilexerunt magis gloriam hominum quam Dei* [Jn 12:43]: They have loved the glory of men more than that of God. This can be understood in two ways: either they have loved having glory from men more than from God, or they have loved more to glorify men than to glorify God.

The second way that vainglory can oppose God's love is when a person engages in vainglory and his intention refers to and aims at the same glory to which virtuous works are directed, but once he has it he will not quit doing those things that are against God, and stops doing those things that God commands; in this way it is a deadly sin. As St. Augustine says:[267] this vice, i.e., vainglory, is the enemy of true faith if there is greater desire for glory and human praise in the heart than fear or love of God. As Christ said in the Gospel to certain vainglorious people: *Quomodo potestis credere, gloriam ab invicem expectantes, et gloriam que a solo Deo est, non quaerentes?* [Jn 5:44]: How can you believe and have true faith while awaiting one to receive glory from another, and not looking for the glory that is only from God?

But if the love of human glory, even if vain, is not contrary to charity, neither with regard to what others glory about, nor with regard to the intention of he who glories, as was explained, then it is not a deadly sin but a venial one. As St. John Chrysostom says,[268] while other vices find their place in the devil's servants, vainglory finds its place in Christ's servants, and this makes sense when it is understood as a venial sin.

Third Chapter

Wherein we show how people are inclined to the vice of vainglory, and how easily and in how many ways one does oneself harm.

The third thing to say about vainglory is how people are inclined to and desirous of this vice, and how easily and in how many ways we harm ourselves and sin. The wise Valerius Maximus says[269] that no humility is so great that it is not touched by the sweetness of this glory. He tells of that wise Themistocles who, while going to the theatre where they were recounting in song and in praise the virtuous works of strength, knowledge, and art, and being asked which singer or song he liked the best, replied: "The one that will best praise my art." St. Augustine, in the *City of God*, reciting the great deeds of the Romans, says that the love of glory and human praise led to all those wonderful things being done, by desiring which the Romans both wanted to live and did not worry about dying. He gives many examples of that throughout the fifth book, and among other things he tells of that Brutus who killed his sons out of love for the fatherland and out of a desire for human

---

267 In the *City of God* [GA].
268 This attribution to John Chrysostom likely derives from Aquinas's *Summa* [GA].
269 In the *Memorable Deeds and Sayings* [GA].

glory, about which Virgil said: *Vincet amor patrie laudumque immensa cupido*, etc.[270]

This desire, and the desire for glory, are so great that men look for it on crooked paths, and through its opposite. Valerius also says that there are many who, while wanting to acquire glory, have disdained it in both word and deed and, being praised and cited for their disdain, have acquired glory by disdaining it. People endeavour to have glory not only through good works and virtue, but also through evil and malevolent works. Valerius tells of that Pausanias[271] who, when he asked someone how to be instantly recognized and known, was told that that would happen if he were to kill a glorious man of high status. So he went and killed King Philip, Alexander's father, and because of this the whole world spoke of him, and someone who at first was obscure and unknown was written about in chronicles and histories. He tells a similar story of a person who, in order to gain notoriety, set fire to the rich and magnificent temple of the goddess Diana in Ephesus, and who, when captured and put to the rope, confessed that he had done it in order to be recognized and famous, because he did not have any other quality by which to make a name for himself. The mind of those who glory in evil is truly perverse; and Seneca says:[272] There are those who glory in their vices. As the prophet David said: *Quid gloriaris in militia, qui potens es iniquitate?* [Ps 51:3]: Why do you glory in malice, you who are powerful in iniquity? Meaning: it is not something to receive glory and praise for, but rather blame and infamy. As that holy lady Esther said: *Tu nosti, quo oderim gloriam iniquorum* [Es 14:15]: You know, Lord, I always hated the glory of iniquitous men. And the psalmist, to whom the glory of sinners seemed evil, said: *Usquequo peccatores, Domine, usquequo peccatores gloriabuntur?* [Ps 93:3]: For how long, Lord God, for how long will the sinners glory in themselves?

Fourth Chapter

*Wherein we show what reasons and inducements there
are to the vice of vainglory.*

The fourth thing we should say about vainglory is what reasons and inducements there are to it. In *Policraticus*[273] it is written: You can hardly

---

270 *Aeneid* 6.823.
271 Pausanias of Orestis, bodyguard to Philip II of Macedon and his eventual assassin.
272 In the Epistles to Lucilium [GA].
273 John of Salisbury's *Policraticus*, a work of political theory, written in the second half of the twelfth century.

find anybody who does not have an appetite for vainglory and does not desire to be praised by men. We get there through different paths, some by virtue or by the image or appearance of virtue, others through the good work of fortune, and some seek them with the gods of nature. From these three parts we take the substance and reason for all human praise and glory, i.e., the soul, the body, and the external things of fortune.

There are certain natural goods in the soul and some that are acquired, either by an infusion of grace or by exercise and continuous study. The natural goods of the soul are a clear intellect with subtle wit, reason, free will, hard and fast memory, and other intellectual powers that are also in the soul, and other sensory powers, common to the soul and the body. The goods acquired by the soul are the theological and divine virtues, intellectual and moral virtues, wisdom, and the sciences and arts. The goods of the body are health, strength, beauty, nobility, freedom, happiness, being alert and quick, strong and well behaved, comely, honourable and well adorned, being high-spirited, courageous and quick with good judgment, studious, solicitous and agile, being a good conversationalist with affable pleasantness, courteous, lovable, delightful and robust, having graceful speech, being eloquent and quick-witted, having a soft and sweet and sonorous voice, a composed look and walk, and in general good style. And although many of these conditions come from the virtue of the soul, they are attributed to the body, because they are shown through external actions. The goods of fortune are external things that are neither in us nor in our power, so they can be lost and every day are lost against our will: wealth, prosperity, status, honour, dignity, power, pleasure, fame, grace, people's favour, authority, having many friends, having a large following, honourable possessions, a large family, a graceful and honourable wife, lovable, beautiful, of noble lineage and clear fame, many and good children, beautiful palaces with comfortable living spaces, wide gardens with cultivated farms. There are those who glory in having beautiful and costly books and precious clothing, beautiful images and lovely paintings, frequent dinner parties, and setting a table with rich tableware and many dishes, having arms and horses and well-equipped servants, undertaking great projects and supplying them well, and having glorious victories over enemies, and then having peace.

Through all these things and many more, which it would take too long to list, the men of the world go about looking for glory and fame, as Holy Scripture speaks of in various places. In the book of Judith, it is written of King Arphaxad: *Gloriabatur quasi potens in potentia sua, et in Gloria quadrigarum suarum* [Jd 1:4]: He gloried in his power and his horses and his armoured vehicles. In that same book it is said: *Gloriantur in sagiptis et lanceis* [Jd 9:9]: Certain people gloried in their arrows and lances. And the psalmist says of the glory that some seek through wealth: *In multitudine divitiarum gloriantur* [Ps 48:7]. The wise Ecclesiasticus says of the glory that some have through their friends: *In medio amicorum gloriabitur* [Ec 30:3]. Of the glory that some have in their lineage and their nobility of blood, Isaiah says: *Gloriabuntur in antiquitate* [Is 23:7]; and Hosea: *Gloria eorum a partu et vulva* [Hs 9:11]. Of those who glory in beauty and the external appearance of things, St. Paul says: *Ad eos, qui in facie gloriantur* [2 Cr 5:12]. And of those who glory in any virtue of theirs, that holy woman Judith says: *Et de sua virtute gloriantes humilias* [Jd 6:15]. The book of Judges discusses the glory that some have in victories: *Nec tradetur Madian in manibus eius, ne glorietur* [Jg 7:2]. Of the glory of images and pictures the prophet says: *Qui gloriantur in simulacris suis* [Ps 96:7]; and Jeremiah: *Terra sculptilium est et in portentis gloriatur* [Jr 50:38]. Of a graceful wife Solomon says: *Mulier gratiosa inveniet gloriam* [Pr 11:16]. Of that glory that others want to have for a beautiful voice and song we could refer to the prophet Isaiah: *Gloria vocis suae in letitia* [Is 30:30]; and to the psalmist: *Cantabo, et psallam in gloria mea* [Ps 107:2]. Of the luxuries in which others glory, we could offer those words of Isaiah: *Delitiis affluatis ab omnimoda gloria eius* [Is 66:11]. And Jeremiah writes of the excellence of authority: *Solium gloriae altitudinis tue* [Jr 17:12]. Of the glory of house and family, the prophet Haggai says: *Magna erit Gloria domus istius* [Hg 2:10]. Of horses and victory in battle, Zachariah says: *Portabit gloriam et sedebit equum glorie sue in bello* [Zc 6:12]. Of the glory of being agile, quick and brave, and the like, we read in the book of the Maccabees, where it is written: *Iuvenes induebant gloriam* [1 Mc 14:9]. In that same book it is said of the grace and favour of the people, and of fame: *Dilatavit gloriam populo suo* [1 Mc 3:3]. We also read there of the glory of honour and status and awards: *Cum summa gloria exaltabitur* [2 Mc 5:20]. Of the glory of precious clothing, we could understand the holy Job: *Esto gloriosus et speciosis induere vestibus* [Jb 40:5]. And Christ in the Gospel: *Salomon in omni gloria sua non coopertus est sicut unum ex istis* [Mt 6:29]. And that wise Boethius, in the book *The Consolation of Philosophy*, shows how men seek to have glory and a name for themselves through many of the above-mentioned things, and having spoken of wealth and power and honours, and of the luxuries in which many place their beatitude and their happiness, he adds: *Aut quibus optimum quiddam claritas videtur, hii et belli vel pacis artibus gloriosum nomen propagare festinant*: There are certain people who, judging the brightness of glory to be a most excellent thing, try to make a glorious name for themselves with the art of war and peace. Then he says: *Velut nobilitas favorque popularis, que videntur quandam claritatem et gloriam comparare*: Like nobility and the favour of the people, by which it appears that one glows with glory. He says the same about many other things regarding the body and fortune; like health, strength, beauty, one's wife, one's children, friends, and many other things.

Now that we have seen what those things are for which others engage in vainglory, it follows to say how others should not glory vainly about these things.

Fifth Chapter

Wherein we show how people should not glory in the things said above.

The fifth thing to say about vainglory is how others should not glory in the things mentioned above, which are an inducement to vainglory. We will first speak generally about all things, and then about many of them, addressing each in its particulars.

A person should not glory in the goods of the soul, which God extends and gives us freely and not out of merit, like the graces and the virtues, for which one should refer praise and glory to the giver, and not to the one who receives them. St. Paul shows this in those words said above, to which we might add: *Quid habes quod non accepisti? et si accepisti, quid gloriaris quasi non acceperis?* [1 Cr 4:7]: What do you have that you have not received? And if you have received it, why do you glory in it as if you had not received it, indeed, as if you got it on your own? St. Bernard says of these words:[274] If the honour and glory go to God alone, then how is it that you want glory for the victory when you were not in the battle? You are shameless if you want glory without victory, and if you want to claim victory for yourself without the battle. He goes on: If you have the holiness of life, remember that it is the Holy Spirit that gives life and sanctifies; if you have the grace of expressing healthy doctrine, do not forget what the truth says: it is not you who speak, but the Holy Spirit; if you do miracles, it is by divine virtue. He speaks of many other things that God makes use of in us and through us, because we alone cannot and do not know how to make use of the good, indeed, we ruin it. He concludes: if you attribute glory or the favour of praise to yourself for whatever good you might have, not referring it to God, you

---

274 In the sermons on the Song of Songs [GA].

are certainly a robber and a thief. Therefore, we want to attribute glory and praise to the giver of every good. Hence St. Paul: *Soli Deo honor et Gloria* [1 Tm 1:17]: Honour and glory to God alone. The prophet Isaiah said as much metaphorically: *Nunquid gloriatur securis adversus eum qui secat in ea* [Is 10:15]: Is the axe glorified instead of the one who uses it? Meaning: no, because all the glory of good effort belongs to the master who artfully wields the axe. So man is the instrument with which God accomplishes all the good that is done, and therefore all the glory goes to the principal master. St. Paul put it well: *Exclusa enim est gloriatio tua* [Rm 3:27]: Your glory is excluded.

People should not glory in the soul's natural goods, like intellect, memory, free will, and others, both because they do not acquire them on their own and because they are common to all, the good and the bad, and because they can be used to good and bad purpose. As St. Bernard said:[275] If a man has subtle wit, a clear intellect, a strong memory, he cannot glory in them, because they are instruments of both vice and virtue.

A man should not glory in the goods of the soul acquired through exercise and study, like the sciences, the arts, and the moral virtues, for the reasons stated above about natural goods, and for many others that we will state further on. As St. Bernard says:[276] God is the Lord of the sciences, all the treasures of knowledge and wisdom are in Him, from that living fountain flows what comes to men, from there comes the hard work of the heart, the rectitude of good will, clear wit, beautiful speech, and all other goods. You will be a faithful servant if the great glory of your Lord, which, although it does not come from you, passes through you, you will not let anything stick to your hands but will say faithfully: glory goes not to us, Lord, but to your name.

How will a man dare to glory in the goods of the body, like health, beauty, strength, and others, since, as Boethius says,[277] they are so easily lost that a three-day fever uses up and ruins all the goods of the body? As well, most times the goods of the body are enemies and contrary to virtue and the soul.

It is a foolish thing to glory in the goods of fortune which are outside of you, like wealth, and honours, and worldly prosperity, since they are not your goods. The proof is they can be lost and taken from you, whether you like it or not. Seneca puts it well:[278] No one can properly

---

275 In his sermons [GA].
276 In the sermons on the Song of Songs [GA].
277 In the *Consolation of Philosophy* [GA].
278 In the Epistles to Lucillium [GA].

glory except in what is his. And St. Augustine says[279] that the goods of fortune are not ours: nothing is ours, because it can be taken from us against our will; what you cannot hold on to belongs to someone else. And Seneca in one of his epistles *Ad Lucilium* shows extensively how external goods are not ours, and how they do not make a man great or worthy of glory; indeed, he calls them lies and untruths of fortune.

The prophet Jeremiah says in a few short words that a man should not glory of all the above-mentioned goods in this world: *Non glorietur sapiens in sapientia sua nec fortis in fortitudine sua nec dives in divitiis suis* [Jr 9:23]: The wise man should not glory in his knowledge regarding the goods of the soul, nor the strong man in his strength regarding the goods of the body, nor the rich man in his wealth regarding the external goods of fortune.

Having said how a man should not vainly glory in any good in general, we come now to speak in particular about some goods with which people commonly offend and sin.

Among the other goods of the soul there is knowledge, which is a man's great good and perfection when he uses it well in God's honour for the benefit of one's neighbour and for his own edification. But if you use it badly and vainly, which happens in particular when you seek recognition and fame for his knowledge and to be judged wiser and praised by others, it becomes a great evil and a great danger because you use the good badly, and it turns the medicine into poison. As St. Isidore says in the book of *The Highest Good*, there are many who use their knowledge not for God's glory but to praise themselves, and they rise up in pride, sinning when they should make amends for their sins. We could understand those words of Jeremiah the prophet as being about these types: *Stultus factus est omnis homo a scientia* [Jr 10:14]: Every man who does not put his knowledge to good use becomes foolish, when he should have been wise.

There are three types of knowledge: divine knowledge, human knowledge, and diabolical knowledge.

Divine knowledge can be understood in two ways: either as the knowledge by which God does all things, which is sometimes called wisdom, or prescience, or predestination, and sometimes arrangement or providence; this knowledge is eternal. It is not many different things but one wisdom, which is nothing other than the divine essence, for which we have different names with respect to the things created, which He creates, governs, orders, provides, and sets up. We need not

---

279 In his Epistles [GA].

address this here, because these things are too profound and subtle for laymen and could not be explained well in our vernacular, and they would require too much writing, which I want to avoid if I can.

The other way we can understand divine knowledge is as that knowledge by which a man knows divine things. This can happen in three ways: first, by infusion or revelation, as Solomon and many prophets had, and as the apostles and many other saints had, who, without human doctrine and the exercise of study, learned and understood the highest things of God and the hidden mysteries and profound sacraments of Scripture. They had this knowledge mostly because they had received the Holy Spirit, of which Scripture says: *Spiritus Domini replevit orbem terrarium, et hoc quod continet omnia scientiam habet vocis* [Ws 1:7]. So knowledge is one of the gifts of the Holy Spirit, although the Holy Gospel says that Christ opened understanding and explained Scripture to them. The second way is by doctrine heard from doctors and teachers. The third way by study, exercising one's natural talent by reading and meditating.

There are those who have, and have had, the knowledge of divine things and of Holy Scripture, through either one, or two, or all three of these ways. In the first way, we acquire this divine knowledge through God's grace and through prayer; in the second, through humility and subjugation; in the third way, through solicitude and exercise. To acquire this knowledge the holy prophet prayed and said: *Bonitatem et disciplinam et scientiam doce me* [Ps 118:66]. And that other saint said: *Da mihi, Domine, sedium tuarum assistricem sapientiam* [Ws 9:4]. In order to acquire this sovereign knowledge of Holy Scripture, St. Paul heard the doctrine of that doctor of law Gamaliel; St. Jerome resigned his office and refused the hat, and he went to Constantinople to hear that great Greek doctor Gregory the Nazarene; St. Augustine wanted to hear from St. Ambrose, and he asked intently about the doctrine of the Holy Scriptures from St. Jerome; and St. Thomas Aquinas went to Cologne and to Paris to hear the doctrine of that great theologian and highest philosopher, Friar Albert the Great of the Friars Preachers. There are many more who, with great diligence and much humility, by hearing the doctrine of others, became highest doctors. There are many others who, with great study and much effort, undertook to acquire this divine knowledge. Leaving others aside for brevity's sake, we read of St. Dominic, patriarch of the Preachers, who abstained from wine for ten years in order to learn this divine knowledge through study and much diligence, so that later, in the apostolic life, through preaching he might convert the world to the path of truth from the error of the darkness of sin. And we read of St. Peter the Martyr with the witness of the

Holy Church who, because of the great diligence that he had, spent his nights studying Holy Scripture, with very little sleep.

Every Christian must have this knowledge of Holy Scripture, each according to his status and condition. The prelate and rector of souls should know it in one way, and the teacher, the doctor, and the preacher in another. They have to enter the deep sea of Scripture and be able to understand the hidden mysteries in order to explain them and teach them to others, being prepared to explain, as the apostle says, the tenets of faith and of Scripture to whoever asks about them. Laymen and unlettered people should know it in another way; it is enough for them to have general knowledge of the commandments of the law, the articles of faith, the sacraments of the Church, sin, the ecclesiastical orders, the doctrine of the Holy Gospel, enough for their salvation, and as much as they hear from their rectors and preachers of Scripture and faith. They should not go into too much detail or wade too far into the sea of Scripture, which not everyone can or should want to cross, because one can slip there and oftentimes drown in it, like an incautious and curious and lowly hunter. But everyone should know, and endeavour to know, as much as is required for his job and his status. Rectors, teachers, doctors, and preachers should know Scripture very well, as they have to teach it to others, and they should endeavour to study and learn it before they become officers of doctrine; otherwise they surely get there unprepared. As God said through the prophet Hosea: *Quia scientiam repulisti, repellam te, ne sacerdotio fungaris mihi* [Hs 4:6]: Since you have not sought after knowledge, I will chase you away, so that you will not have the office of my priesthood, which involves ruling and teaching others, and which you cannot execute well without knowledge. But there are some who are so ambitious and desirous of being teachers and teaching others that they do not first learn what they should teach, and because they are in such a hurry, not wanting to be disciples of truth, they become teachers of error. As St. Jerome says, no one should presume to call himself a teacher of any lowly art if he does not first learn it, but everyone, no matter how insufficient, should become a teacher of Holy Scripture and of the governance of the souls, which is the greatest art there is. To succeed as a teacher and preacher requires not only knowledge but also a good life. St. Gregory says that someone who wants to teach others well should first study living well, because good works confirm and approve good speech and the bad life ruins every good word, because the man who disdains his own life will find that his doctrine will be disdained and not valued. So it is not without great presumption to want to speak well and act badly, or to want to say a lot and do little. God scolds such a speaker through the psalmist when he says: *Peccatori autem dixit Deus: quare tu ennaras iustitias meas?* etc. [Ps 49:16]: God said to the sinner (who speaks and does not do what he says well): Why do you tell of my justice and teach my law with your mouth, but not obey it by acting well, and hold it in contempt and toss it behind your back?

To have good doctrine but not a good life is a great shame to the speaker, and God very much dislikes it; and it does great harm to the Church, which abhors such a doctrine. Those who speak well and live badly almost always carry a light in their hand, which shows their bad deeds to their audience, so that they themselves make their shame evident, as Christ says in the Gospel: let the light of your doctrine show and manifest your good works. He also reads the letters of his condemnation, contradicts himself, and gets confused in his words. As Prosper[280] says, to speak well and live badly is nothing other than to damn oneself with one's own voice. And St. Jerome says:[281] Your words should not confuse your life and it should not happen that, as you are preaching, your listeners say: Why don't you do what you say? Heed the reproof of the common proverb: Physician, heal thyself, and first remove the beam from your own eye, then you can take the mote out of the eyes of others. Let the preacher's hand therefore accord with his tongue. Those who do not bring their hands to their mouth will get their fill late, and they will stay hungry while sating others, and those words of Scripture will be a reproof to them: *Vox quidem, vox Iacob est, set manus, manus sunt Esau* [Gn 27:22]. The Holy Gospel shows how much God abhors this, when Jesus Christ condemned the fig tree, where he found leaves but no fruit, and it dried up. Here we understand the fruit to mean good works, and the leaves, words. He said of those Pharisees, who were masters of the law: Remember to do what they tell you to, but do not follow their actions, because they talk the talk but do not walk the walk. This doctrine hurts the listeners when there are no good works; since it is not efficacious it does not produce the result for which it is intended, because the one who does not burn does not start a fire. Therefore, St. Gregory: It is better, for the purpose of doing good, for your audience to have an awareness of fervent love than knowledge of subtle sermons, and the softness of the sweet tongue is worthless if not dressed with the flavour of the holy life; and those who have fervently sought to love God know how to speak sweetly of Him. Otherwise,

---

280 Prosper of Aquitaine, a disciple of Augustine and author, among other works, of commentaries on the Psalms.
281 In his Epistles [GA].

when preachers speak the truth only with the sound of their voice, they are not believed, and they easily fall into the vice of vainglory, because, being empty and lacking the fruit of good actions, they vainly direct their intention towards pleasing people and being praised and judged wise and holy. St. Paul spoke of these people when he said: We are not like some who spoil God's word [2 Cr 2:17]. Wherein he notes that wisdom, according to Scripture, is the wife of the just man, from whom he wants to grow legitimate fruit with the seed of God's word. So, just as someone is called an adulterer when, abandoning his own wife, in whom he should want to harvest fruit by inseminating her, he inseminates another, not in order to produce legitimate fruit but for pleasure and delight, the preacher of the word of God is an adulterer when he preaches not with wisdom and to produce spiritual fruit, but for the pleasure of praise and vainglory, because he spreads his seed uselessly. He is a very serious adulterer, because he commits adultery with the very wife of God. For just as God gives wisdom to a man to be his spouse, as if she were His legitimate and firstborn daughter, as Scripture says, so too does he want to keep her for himself, and he does not want anyone else to touch her or even look at her while he is alive in this life. This is the most beautiful and lovely glory that He speaks of through the prophet: *Gloriam meam alteri non dabo* [Is 42:8]: My glory, my wife, I shall not give to others. As St. Paul, God's faithful chamberlain and guardian of his Lord's wife, said: To God alone the glory. It is quite permissible to speak of her, and to write sonnets and ballads of love out of love for her, as the psalmist says: *In templo eius omnes dicent gloriam* [Ps 28:9]: and elsewhere: *Gloriam regni tui dicent* [Ps 144:11]; and he said also: I will sing and play music for love of glory, and he did it in the morning, saying: *Exurge gloria mea, exurge psalterium et cithara, exurgam diluculo* [Ps 56:9]. God wants every man to live with her in love, and to languish for her and be consumed with and die for her, but not to approach her or stare at her, but rather to admire her and leave her alone. To whoever looks at her in this way in this life, He will be very generous in the next, giving him everything he wants and for perpetual enjoyment, which the Scripture gives sure hope of when it says: *Gratiam et gloriam dabit Dominus* [Ps 83:12]: God will glorify in the next life those to whom He gives the collateral of grace in this one. But this will not happen to someone who wants to touch her here, and the seed would be lost, thrown away in vain, and he will be judged by God for his great and shameless daring, as a shameless adulterer.

We could say many things about this celestial wife of God, so that others would fall in love with her and want to see her dance, but I realize that I am writing too much, and no song is so beautiful that it cannot be shortened. Returning therefore to our topic, it is a clear sign that teachers and preachers are adulterous lovers of vainglory when, while preaching and teaching, they leave aside the things that are useful and necessary for the salvation of their audience and say subtle and unusual things and base philosophies, using mystical and figurative words, versifying and trying to mix in rhetorical flourishes, which might delight the ears but not go to the heart. These things not only are not fruitful and useful to the listeners but often provoke uncertainty and lead to dangerous and false errors, as has been shown in both old days and new. So the vices and sins we wanted to cut with the knife of God's word, that must be wounded with the arrow of preaching and burned with the fire of loving and fervent speech, are left intact and untreated, tumorous and abscessed, in their hearts, thanks to the bad treatment given by the doctor who does not love souls and is himself greedy and vain. These so-called preachers, indeed foolish minstrels and romancers, to whom listeners run as if to the storytellers of knights who strike great blows, even with the bow of the viola, these are unhappy and disloyal dispensers of their Lord's treasury, i.e., of the knowledge of Scripture, which God entrusts to them so that they might redeem souls with Christ's precious blood, and instead they trade it for the wind and smoke of vainglory. It seems the time has come, indeed it did come (were it not so!), as St. Paul predicted when, as he writes to Timothy [2 Tm 4:3–4], the impeccable doctrine of Holy Scripture and of the true faith will not endure, but people follow their appetites in looking for teachers and preachers who will scratch the itch on their ears, i.e., who will tell them what they want to hear for their pleasure and not their benefit, and they will turn away from the truth and lend an ear to fables. There are few today, indeed very few, who speak and want to hear the truth! Anyone who has any feeling or awareness or zeal about souls should very much suffer and cry about this! What's worse, not only does no one want to hear the truth, but it is held in contempt, along with those who speak it, proving the truth of the words of the poet Terence: *Veritas odium parit*: The truth gives birth to hatred.[282]

[II][283]

Not only do teachers and preachers, who teach and instruct others, have to study to have knowledge of Holy Scripture, but others as well, each according to his condition. Without it we cannot come to salvation, because it teaches us what we should believe, it shows us what

---

282 *Andromache*, but a widespread proverb [GA].
283 The numbering of these sections follows the original text.

we should hope for, it teaches us how we should love and behave. It is necessary for every man, no matter his status. Therefore, we should diligently read and study. Scripture itself leads us there when it says: Blessed is the one whom you teach and instruct about your law [Ps 93:12]; and elsewhere it says: Blessed is the one who has found wisdom [Pr 3:13]. In the Gospel, Jesus Christ commends and praises it, preaching it and citing it against the Jews, interpreting it and explaining it to his disciples, revealing its meaning to them so that they might understand, and scolding the Sadducees who did not know it, saying: You err, because you do not know Scripture and God's commandments.

There are three things to know in order to find this necessary knowledge: first, the place where it is found; second, how it is found; and next, why a man should find it.

First, we should look for divine knowledge in the holy writings of the prophets and in the Holy Gospel, and in the writings of the apostles, where the truth is revealed and inspired by the Holy Spirit, as St. Peter says: *Spiritu Sancto inspirati locuti sunt sancti Dei homines* [2 Pt 1:21]: The holy men of God spoke and wrote inspired by the Holy Spirit. We should read the books of the holy doctors, approved by the Church, who explain Scripture perfectly. We should not go looking in the worthless books of the worldly philosophers and poets who, although they said many beautiful things, discussing vices and virtues, heaven and the stars, and the customs of peoples, nevertheless, in telling many worthless stories and untrue fables, spoke rather to delight the ear than to correct vices, not by inspiration of the Holy Spirit but by the ingenuity of natural spirit. Although there are wise and learned men who know how to tell true from false and good from evil, who can sometimes read these stories and fables, it is not certain that idiots and the unlearned can read them. Nor should lettered men spend much time with them, because for the most part they are wasting their time or doing it out of vanity. It is particularly forbidden to clerics and religious men, who should read the Holy Gospel, and the epistles of St. Paul, and the Psalter and other Scripture, which are read and sung in the Holy Church. And yet many of them study the comedies of Terence, and Juvenal, and Ovid, and romances and love poetry, which is wholly forbidden.

St. Jerome recounts that, when he was young, even though he was a faithful Christian, he greatly enjoyed reading the books of Cicero, for his beautiful rhetorical speech, and the books of the philosopher Plato, for his high and mystical style. He did not take so much pleasure in the books of the prophets and other Holy Scripture, because the style seemed unpolished and heavy to him. Now, it so happened that he became seriously ill, so much so that, as the doctors offered no hope, his funeral was prepared. As people gathered around him, waiting for him to pass, suddenly his spirit was brought before God's judgment, where he says that there was so much light of glory and clarity around the chair where the highest judge sat that his eyes could not bear it. Because of his trembling and fear of the judge's presence, and because of the power of that unbearable light, he lay down on the ground in front of the judicial seat. When the judge asked about his condition, he answered that he was a Christian. "You are lying to us," said the judge, "you are not a Christian; indeed, you are a Ciceronian; for wherever your treasure is, your heart is there." He was silent, not knowing how to answer. Then the judge ordered that he be harshly beaten, whereupon he cried out in a loud voice, "Have mercy, my Lord, have mercy on me." Many of those present begged the judge to forgive his ignorance and youth. And he, crying over his error, and because of the pain of the harsh beatings, began to swear that he would never again own or read schoolbooks or worldly books. Having said these words, he left and returned to his body, and he came to before those who believed he had died. St. Jerome says that he found himself completely awash in tears, and as sure proof that it had not been a dream but a true vision, all around his shoulders there were bruises and marks from the beatings he had received. Punished in this way and obligated by his oath, he never again read such books, but he put all his study into the books of Holy Scripture, which he, as the Holy Church approves and holds, translated, interpreted, explained, and commented on better and more faithfully and accurately than any other Greek or Latin doctor.

We can read certain books of Scripture and of the doctors, which have been rendered in the vernacular, but with caution, because there are many false and corrupt ones, both because of defects in the writers, who are not commonly good at understanding, and because of defects in the translators, who do not understand the powerful passages of Holy Scripture and the subtle and obscure statements of the saints. They do not explain them according to an intimate and spiritual understanding, but rather carry into the vernacular only the superficial, literal layer, following the Latin. Because they do not have a spiritual understanding, and because our vernacular lacks for words, they often explain them clumsily and inelegantly, and many times they truly do not explain them at all. This is such a great danger that a person could easily fall into error: not to mention that they debase the Scripture, with its high Latin sentences that are both exquisite and proper, adorned with beautiful rhetorical colourings and a light style. Sometimes they cut it down with disjointed speech, as with the French and Provençal, and sometimes make it opaque with obscure language, like that of the

Germans, the Hungarians, and the English. Sometimes they make it harsh, with a plebeian and rustic vernacular, as with Lombard. Some divide it up by cutting it down with ambiguous and dubious words, like the Neapolitans and members of that kingdom. Some rusticate it with a hard and rough accent, like the Romans. Others rough it up with rustic, alpine speech from the Maremma, and some, like the Tuscans, who are not as bad as the others, mishandle it, muddying and darkening it too much. Among them the Florentines, with their shortened and ill-mannered words, stretch it out and make it tedious with their Florentine speech, obfuscating it and mixing in *occi* and *poscia, aguale, vievocata, pur dianzi, mai pur sì, ben reggiate, ch'avrete delle bonti se non mi ramognate.* So every man becomes an explainer, so that, in order to render it well in the vernacular, the author would have to be proficient not only in Latin, but he would also have to know theology and have an expert understanding of Holy Scripture, and be a rhetorician, and well versed in vulgar speech, and have a feeling for God and a spirit of holy devotion. Otherwise many mistakes would be made, and they have already been made. And they should be forbidden from ever translating again, and what they have done should be corrected by someone who knows how to do it well.

The second thing that someone who wants to learn the divine science of Scripture must understand is how to learn. According to the holy doctors, we must seek and learn in three ways: humbly, innocently, fervently.

First, someone who wants to acquire this divine knowledge must do so by studying humbly, in two ways. The first way is to try to get it from God; the other way is when a man humbles himself and submits to some master, who teaches it to him.

The first way is to ask God for it. You must do this by praying with humility. As Scripture says, the prayer of one who humbles himself passes through the clouds. God looks at the prayers of the humble and does not disdain them, especially when they ask for wisdom, which comes from God, as Scripture says: *Omnis sapientia a Domino Deo est* [Ec 1:1]. St. James says: He who needs wisdom, let him ask God for it, because He gives it abundantly [Jm 1:5].

The other way of acquiring divine knowledge is by submitting humbly to a teacher, so that he will teach it to you, either by reading or by preaching. As St. Jerome says, although some were taught by God alone, like Moses and Solomon and certain others, we should not, however, make a general rule about that which is the privilege of a few. Indeed, it would be greatly presumptuous not to want to learn from someone else, and to expect to have a revelation from God, because it could happen that, not wanting to be a disciple of truth, one would become a master of error. This happens to some presumptuous people, who want to be teachers rather than good disciples and are ashamed of asking or learning from others what they do not know.

The example given above,[284] of the eremite who fasted and prayed for God to disclose a certain understanding of Scripture to him, would apply here. He deserved to have understanding when he decided to go away and ask humbly of a companion of his. Then the angel appeared to him and taught him everything he wanted to know.

We see that God very much likes such humility, because, having beaten and struck down St. Paul, He sent him on to Ananias, telling him to hear what he had to do. St. Paul received the revelation of the doctrine of the Holy Gospel, which he had to preach, from God, when he was taken up into the third heaven. From there he went on to Jerusalem, to St. Peter and St. James, to talk and confer with them about everything that had happened, so that they might study and approve the revealed doctrine. He did not want to trust himself so as not to make a mistake. St. Jerome tells in the prologue to the Bible how, with many arguments and examples of saints and wise philosophers, he induced his friend Paul to find a teacher from whom he could hear the doctrine of Holy Scripture. Elsewhere, St. Jerome says of himself that, after he became a great doctor both of the seven liberal arts and of three languages, Hebrew, Greek, and Latin, having been sufficiently taught and educated in Rome, and fully schooled in divine Scripture in Constantinople by Gregory the Nazarene, he went to Bethlehem, where he submitted to and became the disciple of a Jew in order to learn the Hebrew language well, which he believed was necessary in order to translate Holy Scripture. For many years there, as an old teacher and a new disciple, studying with great effort, he became a sovereign scholar of Hebrew.

We must, therefore, for the aforesaid reasons, understand and find the truth of divine Scripture, and be grateful, recognizing the benefit of the doctrine of the teachers and preachers, who are doctors and spiritual fathers of the soul. In truth, if we consider the great effort they make in studying, surveying, and thinking in the service of people; and the great danger and risk to which they are subject as teachers and scholars of doctrine, which is very risky and cause of the ruin of many; and the great service they do by teaching us doctrine, not for us to find earthly and temporal things, which quickly pass and vanish, but

---

284 See p. 187.

eternal life and beatitude and God's glory, which is the highest good without end, then we will never be able to thank them enough. God ordained that they should be provided with some leftovers and first fruits and offerings, and that they be held in great reverence, because they are called the eyes of the Holy Church. As the eyes are held dear and studied intently by the other bodily members, so too are the doctors and the preachers by the people; and as blindness is a scandal for the entire body, so too is the ignorance of the prelates and the doctors a scandal and danger for the entire body of the Holy Church. Christ said to them in the Gospel: You are blind, and the leader of the blind: and if the blind leads the blind, they both fall into the ditch [Mt 15:14]. The leader has the worst of such a fall, suffering two blows, whereas those who are led suffer only one. The ignorant and blind prelate and preacher will be judged, and he will carry a double punishment, both for his own sins and for those of the people and their subjects who, out of ignorance, could not counsel and correct their defects and bring light to their blindness. Therefore, they should study both for themselves and for others, because as God says through Malachi the prophet: *Labia sacerdotum custodiunt scientiam, et legem requirent ex ore eius* [Ml 2:7]: The lips of the priest safeguard knowledge, and they require the law from his own mouth. Therefore, he must know the law in order to conform to it. As a prelate and preacher with knowledge of the law communicates it usefully and fruitfully by preaching, advising, correcting, and teaching, so too are the people obligated to assist him in all his needs. A person should not wait to be asked but, recognizing the need, should help according to his ability; nor should he pretend not to know how, or deny what is asked of him by his doctor or preacher, either directly or through somebody else, for this is a grave sin. As St. Paul said: Let he who is taught the word of God share his every good with him who teaches him [Gl 6:6], because, as he said elsewhere, speaking of himself and of the other preachers, if we sow spiritual things, which are very precious, it is no big deal if we reap material things, which have little value [1 Cr 9:11]. Jesus Christ said in the Gospel to his disciples in the person of preachers: When you arrive somewhere, you will eat and drink what you find there; because the worker is worthy of his mercy [Lk 10:7]. Therefore, preachers may take and receive, as they require, from usurers and evil men and the like, which other people may not do.

The second way to seek and study divine knowledge is innocently, that is, by living in a holy and just way without mortal sin. Scripture says: *In malevolam animam non introibit sapientia, nec habitabit in corpore subdito peccatis* [Ws 1:4]: Wisdom will not enter the malevolent soul, which is stained and bad-willed, and it will not live in a body subject to sin. Thus, as one holy father put it, the soiled soul cannot receive the gift of spiritual knowledge.[285] Although there are many men who are both highly learned and evil sinners, it is one thing to know how to argue, dispute, and question with subtle arguments, thinking about Scripture, because any great sinner with ingenuity and a naturally good memory can acquire that learning through study. But it is something else again to enter into the intimate marrow and hidden sacraments with spiritual understanding and a feeling for Scripture, which only the holy and spiritual man can do. St. Augustine says:[286] He who believes that he has found the truth, and still lives badly, errs. And the wise Ecclesiasticus [Ec 1:33]: My son, who desires to find knowledge, pay attention to justice, i.e., live justly, and God will give it to you. Otherwise, someone who does not live justly, although he has much knowledge, cannot have the truth of divine knowledge. St. Paul says of those men: *Semper discentes et numquam ad scientiam veritatis pervenientes* [2 Tm 3:7]: There are those who always learn and never get to know the truth.

The third way of seeking divine knowledge is fervently and with perseverance, i.e., with the desire to find it, and with all your heart. Since you will not find it quickly (because God sometimes makes the desire grow), you must neither disdain nor abandon study and the diligent search. Divine knowledge teaches us about that, saying: Blessed is he who keeps watch continuously at my gate; for he will find me [Pr 8:34–5]. The wise Ecclesiasticus teaches this way of looking for divine knowledge, when he says: If you will seek wisdom as a man seeks treasure, suddenly it will let itself be found by you.[287] Therefore, Jesus Christ said in the Gospel: *Petite, et accipietis: querite et invenietis, pulsate et aperietur vobis* [Mt 7:7]: Ask humbly for knowledge, as the first way, and you shall receive it; as the second, seek it innocently and in a holy way, and you will find it; knock fervently and with perseverance, as the third way, and the understanding of divine knowledge will be opened to you.

The third thing that someone who wants to acquire divine knowledge fruitfully should note is his purpose in seeking it, and he should direct all of his attention at it. That purpose is eternal life, of which St. Paul says: *Finem vero vitam aeternam* [Rm 6:22]: The end is eternal life. Holy Scripture teaches how to acquire it, because it teaches a man to know

---

285 John Cassian [GA].

286 In *De agone christiano* [GA].

287 More likely Proverbs 2:3–5 than Ecclesiasticus; see Passavanti, ed. Auzzas, 174–5. Passavanti appears to be misremembering his source.

himself and be humble, to know God and to love Him and obey His commandments, to know the baseness of earthly and material things and their instability, to know the excellence of spiritual and celestial and eternal things and their nobility, and it teaches us to love and desire the latter and to disdain and reject the former. This way we arrive at the final purpose of eternal life. Therefore, the doctrine of the Scriptures is given by God in a general and common way, so that all peoples, no matter their status and condition, can find fruitful instruction and useful food for their needs. St. Gregory says[288] that Scripture is a deep and shallow river, which the elephant swims in and the lamb crosses. This means that a great, wise, and very learned man will not find the bottom, and the simple unlearned man will find fruitful instruction; in other words, both will find their place. Briefly put, the benefit and fruit of Holy Scripture is so great that nobody can be confident of his feelings or inspirations unless he agrees with it, according to St. Anthony. Although sometimes it is not understood, we must nevertheless hold it in great reverence, thinking that it is all holy and true, because it is from God. By doing so we draw forth spiritual fruit, either by understanding it or not. There are indeed many (if only there were few, as it should be) who study and learn Scripture with corrupt intent, which they direct to an evil end. Of these St. Bernard says:[289] There are some who study and learn in order to know, not organizing their knowledge to any other end, and this is curiosity; and there are others who want to know in order to be known, i.e., in order to be recognized and deemed wise, and this is vanity; there are certain others who study and learn to gain their knowledge, and this is cupidity; and there are others who study to know in order to perform well, both for themselves and for others, and this is charity, which should move our intention to acquire divine knowledge, because, as the apostle says: *Scientia inflat, caritas hedificat* [1 Cr 8:1]: Knowledge in any way swells you up, making a person vicious and proud and vain, but with charity he builds and fruitfully teaches himself and others.

[III]

The second type of knowledge is human knowledge, which can be understood in three ways: either as the knowledge through which human things are known, or as that which is found by human ingenuity, or as that knowledge through which men know what they

---

288 In the *Moralia in Job* [GA].
289 In the *Sententiae* [GA].

know. However you understand it, it is certainly very defective, for as that philosopher Themistius[290] said, what men know is the minimal part of what they do not know. Our knowledge is mixed with so many errors that it is rather a case of not knowing than of knowing. As Socrates, according St. Jerome, said:[291] *Hoc unum scio, quot nescio*: I know one thing, which is that I do not know. Lactantius said about that:[292] Socrates said that he knew nothing, except that he did not know. Nevertheless, human ingenuity, depending on the strength of the light of natural intellect, has been used to find many subtle things, giving them a certain order and rule, according to which men should speak and act and think, and the various sciences and arts are named according to the variety of things to which they lend themselves. Principal among them are the seven liberal arts, i.e., grammar, logic, rhetoric, arithmetic, geometry, music, and astrology, about which, and about those who discovered them, we could say many beautiful and delightful things. However, there are still many more useful things to say, according to our plan. So, in order not to leave the beneficial for the entertaining, and so that this book does not run too long, we will say nothing of this human knowledge except that, given how defective and small and full of many obscurities it is, you should not be vainglorious about it. Listen to what Solomon said: *Qui addit scientiam addit et dolorem* [Ec 1:18]: He who increases knowledge increases his pain and suffering, because the more someone knows, the more is required of him, and he has a greater burden to bear, and he knows more things that give him affliction and pain.

[IV]

The third type of knowledge is diabolical knowledge. The name refers to two things: either the knowledge that the devil has, or the knowledge by which a man knows or seeks to know what the devil knows, or what comes from the devil.

The first diabolical knowledge is the one through which the devil knows what he knows. This knowledge is very great, because although the devil, when he sinned and fell from the sky, lost grace and glory, he did not lose his knowledge of nature, which God the Creator put in the angelic nature. Just as the devil did not lose anything of his natural

---

290 The fourth-century philosopher, nicknamed Euphrates ("eloquent"), was active in Constantinople. Many of his speeches survive, as do commentaries on Aristotle.

291 In his Epistles [GA].

292 In the *Divine Institutes* [GA].

and essential substance, so too did he not lose his knowledge of nature, by which he most excellently knows and understands all the sciences and arts, having a clear understanding, both general and specific, of all natural and spiritual and corporeal things more than any godly man, either by natural ingenuity or by the exercise of study. He knows and understands about God, to the extent that natural understanding can comprehend without the light of grace. He knows the various substances, i.e., the angels and their substances, their natural properties, their orders and duties, and how far their virtue and natural power extends. He knows and understands the locations, spheres, and circles of the stars and planets, their heights and sizes, their differences and properties, their courses, equations, conjunctions, and judgments, and their influences, virtues, divine inspiration, and varieties. He knows and understands the nature and substance of the soul, its cognitive and sensory and appetitive powers, both those that are independent of the body and those that are common with the feelings of the body. The devil also knows about the nature and properties of the elements, the composition of bodies, the natures and species of fish, birds, and beasts. He knows the species of trees, the nature, quality, and virtues of herbs, of precious stones, the qualities of gold and silver and other metals. In brief, the devil understands and knows only too well everything that can be known, either naturally or through the exercise of study by any human intellect. The doctors, considering his very great knowledge, ask whether he knows the thoughts of the heart or what will happen, and regarding the thoughts of the heart they say thoughts can be known in two ways. The first is through some external effect, and in this way our thoughts are known not only by the devil but often by someone else, according to the subtlety of people's judgment, either by natural disposition or by knowledge or by experience of hidden things. So a man will become aware of an inner thought or feeling not only by external operations but also by a sign, a look, a change in the face, just as expert doctors will recognize, through the pulse or some other sign, the disposition of the thoughts and passions and feelings of the spirit, like love, fear, sadness, and many others. Thoughts can also be known through the intellect, and in the feelings that are in the will or the heart, which is saying enough. In this sense, no creature besides man can know them except for God, to whom the will and heart of man are directly subject and manifest, as St. Augustine proves in the book *De divinatione demonum*, and St. Thomas in the *Summa*. Therefore, God said through Jeremiah the prophet: *Pravum est cor hominis et inscrutabile, et quis cognoscet illud? Ego Dominus scrutans corda* [Jr 17:9–10]: A man's heart is deep and perverse and impenetrable; who therefore can know it? And he continues: I, who am the Lord, search the heart. And the prophet David: *Scrutans corda et renes Deus* [Ps 7:10].

The devil cannot therefore know the thoughts and desires of the heart unless they are somehow out in the open, through either act, or a sign, or an external appearance. He knows everything men say, and what they do and try to get in any place at any time in any way. Further, he knows what men imagine in their fantasies, and what they dream; because the imagination and the dream are not shut up inside by the intellect or the will but are corporeal sentiments, even if they are inside with respect to outward sentiments.

Regarding things that have not happened but are going to, the doctors say that they can be known in two ways. First is to know the causes, and in this way the things that are going to happen, and when they necessarily follow and happen, are known by a certain knowledge: such as that the sun will rise tomorrow, and that the sun goes dark when the moon gets in its way, and so forth for everything else that necessarily happens. But when things are not predictable out of necessity, even if they do happen most of the time, then they are not known for sure but by conjecture or awareness, just as the doctor, who knows by the science of medicine the reasons for health and applies them to heal the sick, knows and predicts when the sick man will get well. But when things follow from their causes very rarely, even if sometimes, then they cannot be known, because they happen by chance and by fortune and indirectly, so that one cannot have knowledge of those things.

This one way of knowing what is going to happen by its cause is manifest and clear to the devil even more than to man, since the devil knows the causes more perfectly. He is just like the doctor who, knowing the reasons for health more subtly and more certainly, judges and predicts the condition of the sick man, and his future health. However, the devil does not have foreknowledge of things that happen by chance. If on occasion he should predict something, this would not be because he had foreknowledge but because he guessed right, which could happen to anybody. However, there are those who take the devil's side and say that he knows the casual and specific things that are going to happen, and that in fact he predicts them. We reply that they do not speak the truth and are liars, like the one whom they favour; because as Christ says of him, he is a liar and the father of lies.

Regarding their statement that in fact the devil can predict future things, both those that happen by chance and others, I say this can happen in three ways. The first is by chance, because, by saying many things, as is required of him, or as he usually does presumptuously, he might say something that is true, even though he does not know for sure. The other way is by revelation, because God and the holy angels sometimes reveal things to the demons which are otherwise hidden from them, according to the order of divine providence and His justice, which uses not only the good angels but also the evil spirits to carry out His will. The other way can be by human ignorance, when men believe certain things are causal and contingent when they are not. Men do not know the reasons that the devil necessarily knows, as there are many effects that come from the stars or from other hidden movements of nature, which men do not know, or few know, and the devil surely does. So they are not casual and contingent to him as they are to ignorant men, who want to attribute greater knowledge to the devil than he has, and on the other hand want to take from him what he has. So he tells them what he does not know, and he does not tell them what he does know, and in the end, having deceived them about both what he knows and what he does not know, he will steal their souls and destine them to eternal punishment, which he does know about. And they will feel it when they get there, since they do not want to know before they go.

The other way by which future things are known is in and of themselves. Only God, who sees all the things that have happened, both present and future, no matter their condition, necessary or contingent, knows them in this way. He knows them eternally, for all time and all things that are done in time, and He sees them in the present as well. As St. Paul says, all things are uncovered and open to God's eyes [Hb 4:13]. And elsewhere: *Vocat ea que non sunt, tanquam ea que sunt* [Rm 4:17]: God calls and knows the things that are not, just like those that are. Isaiah the prophet showed that what is going to happen is known only by God in this way, and not by any other creature, when he said: *Adnuntiate que ventura sunt in futurum, et sciemus, quod dii estis vos* [Is 41:23]: Tell us what is going to happen, and we will know for sure that you are gods.

It follows from the devil's great knowledge and great knowing that he has great strength and much power, because, as the doctors say, the whole nature of material things is subject to the good and the bad angel, naturally to be able to move it here and there. No body, or city, or castle, or mountain, is so large that the devil cannot move it at will; and so too for everything else, whether large or small. Therefore, since he knows every science and every art, he connects things to one another, and they all obey him in their local movement: and he makes awesome things happen and appear to happen.

I am not saying that the devil can perform true miracles, but rather awesome things. By true miracles I mean precisely things done above and beyond the order of all nature, like raising the dead, or creating something out of nothing, or restoring sight to a blind man, and so forth; and only God can perform such miracles. I call awesome things certain unusual things that men cannot do, so that, when they do happen, they marvel at them, because they do not know the why or how of them. The devil can do many such things, like making serpents appear all at once, not by creating them out of nothing but by taking them from that forest where they were and putting them elsewhere; or creating a storm in the sea and in the air; or healing a sick man, not all at once and without medicine, which would be a true miracle, but with appropriate medicines, which he knows better than any other doctor in the world; or by curing a sickness that he made happen, which he can do, by removing its causes, and then the person would return to health, and so it would seem that the devil had healed him.

For all his knowledge and power, of which Scripture speaks, and which is unlike anything else on earth, the devil still cannot change a person's will, over which, and over all of one's cognition, to be clear, he has no control or power whatsoever. He cannot put a thought or desire in the heart of somebody who does not want it, and he cannot enter or operate in the heart or the mind if someone does not wilfully consent to open the door to him. Considering his malice, or his obstinate will to evil, and the odious envy he feels for man, if he could enter wherever he wanted no one would resist him, and he would take away our free will, and no one would have authority over his own operations, and neither merit nor sin could be imputed to man.

Although he cannot work directly in the mind, the devil can do a great deal of evil indirectly. If not inside the door of the inner feelings, he can at least get past the front gates of the outer feelings, and he can change, alter, inform, and shape them all day long. All of our senses, inside and out, are subject to his knowledge and power. He provokes and incites the cognitive part, i.e., will and reason, which are moved in lowly men, who are not used to governing and controlling them though the exercise of virtue. Unbridled, they surrender to the sensory appetite, which, moved by the devil – either out of wrath, or concupiscence, or happiness, or sadness, or fear, or love, or because of an overwhelming humoral intemperateness, or an exuberant movement of the spirits, or a disordered heating of the members – attracts the will, strongly provoking it. Unassisted by reason, it is so occupied and clouded by the passions of the sensory appetite that it does not use judgment to discern what the will should reasonably want. In this way, the devil can provoke a man's will by tempting and inciting it, but he cannot necessarily direct it. We understand this from Scripture, where it says: *Cum diabolus jam misisset in cor, ut traderet eum Iudas*, etc. [Jn 13:2]; and in any other place where it might speak of that.

The devil can therefore alter our perceptions, in our sleep, when we dream, and when we are awake, making us think we are seeing figures, impressions, appearances; delightful, terrible, and disturbing things; true things or things that seem to be true. Regarding both himself and others, he can make someone think that they are what they are not, and that they are not what they are. This happens to the delirious and the insensate, and to those who, because of some love passion or fear or other serious occurrence, with their imaginative capacity perturbed, lose their memory and their awareness. We read in the chronicles that at the time of Pope Leo, in the lands of Rome, there were two lady inn-keepers who, by giving men some enchanted cheese, turned them into donkeys. In the *Life of the Holy Fathers*, we read that a young girl who had become a horse was brought by her relatives before one of the holy fathers. The books of the poets are all full of such transformations, as Ovid's book of *Metamorphoses* shows, and that of the Platonic Apuleius of the *Golden Ass*. All these things, as St. Augustine proves in the *City of God*, were truthful, but only seemed to be so, as the devil was play-ing games and creating fascination, in other words, making something appear in the imagination and the eyes of those who saw it by using ingenuity and visual tricks. So, the holy father said to the relatives of that young girl who had been brought to him as a horse that he saw a young girl and not a horse. Having prayed to God to remove that deceit from their eyes, once that brute figure of the horse that the devil had put there left their eyes, they got their daughter back in her proper form, which was not in itself changed but just seemed so.

Therefore, although he can make them seem so, the devil cannot substantially change one thing into another, transforming or recreating them, as this is the proper and unique virtue of God.

You might ask: since the devil, according to what was said above, knows how to do so much, why does he not use his knowledge and power for more evil than he does, since he always has evil will? We answer that the devil does plenty of evil, much more than people know, to both souls and bodies. Nevertheless, he does not do as much harm as he would like, because God and the holy angels rein him in and don't allow him to do all the evil that he might.

[V]

The other diabolical knowledge is the one by which men desire to know or do certain things that the devil can do, and they want to acquire this knowledge and ability from the devil. Since the devil always desires men's perdition, he has found certain ways to lead them there in the end. Besides vice and sins, which are common to all people, he has introduced another path to perdition which many desire and pursue with great delight, not thinking about the great danger and ultimate damnation to which it leads them. This is a certain science and art that the devil has taught and revealed since the beginning of the world, and especially after the flood, to some evildoers, so they would know certain occult things and be able to do certain things that men cannot do. These include Zoroaster and Hermes Trismegistus,[293] and many others whose writings and books have taught this accursed art to many. It is called by the general name of magical art, although it has many types, means, and observances, and rites that give it special names. Everything said and done though this art is illicit and prohibited and forbidden by God and by the Church.

It is illicit because it involves making an explicit or tacit pact with demons. It is explicit when, by invocation or oath, or through any sacrifice of blood or something else, the demon is called to answer, to show, to do something hidden or difficult, and in answering or doing that little demon often claims he was forced by invocation or oath, either by sacrifice or promises made, which is not true. Anything said about him being closed in an ampule or a ring or a mirror, or any other place or material thing, is entirely false, because the devil cannot be compelled by something lesser than himself, like a man or any other corporeal creature. However, deceiver and liar that he is, he claims otherwise, and men believe him and do what he, when thus imprisoned, asks, since he shows and does what is asked of him, pretending to be trapped and compelled. He acts like a card sharp who pretends to lose in order to win, and to have lost in order to get back. A tacit pact is when that art is used in certain times, ways, figures, signs, with secret words, under which, either by pact or agreement among those to whom this art was first revealed, the impudent devil involves himself in useless and false things, so that people get used to believing him and trusting in him. He says and teaches some true things so that the false ones will be believed, and in this way, he can deceive people and put them into error. Men use this diabolical art to become diviners, evildoers, enchanters, and ministers of the devil, and many go to perdition. In many places in Scripture God forbids us to turn to them, to seek to know anything about them, and to trust in them. In the book of Leviticus it is written: *Non declinetis*

---

293 Zoroaster was thought to have invented magic. Hermeticism, which the Middle Ages attributed to Hermes Trismegistus, addressed such topics as alchemy, magic, and astrology.

ad magos, neque ab ariolis aliquid sciscitemini [Lv 19:31], and *Non auguri-abimini neque observabitis sopnia* [Lv 19:26]: You shall not go to evildoing magi, and you shall not seek to know anything from the diviner, and you shall not be diviners, and you shall not obey dreams. In Deuteronomy it is said: *Non inveniatur in te, qui ariolos sciscitetur et observet sopnia, atque auguria, ne sis maleficus neque incantator neque pythones consulas nec divinos nec queras a mortuis veritatem* [Dt 18:10]: May you not find among yourselves, my people, someone who asks anything of diviners, or who obeys dreams or other auguries, and is an evildoer or enchanter, and do not try to learn the truth from the dead.

The grave punishments that He has enacted show how much this sin displeases God. We read in the book of Kings [2 Kg 1] that, when King Ahaziah of Israel sent to Ekron to find out what would become of him, because he was sick, God got angry at him for what he had done and spoke to him through Elijah the prophet: Because of what you have done, you will never leave the bed in which you lie, but you shall be carried off when dead. And so it happened. And we read of King Saul in the book of Chronicles [1 Ch 10] that, among the other sins for which he was punished by God and defeated and killed by his enemies, he had asked a sorceress what would happen in the battle with the Philistines.

Divine law forbids such a sin under grave punishment, as it says in Leviticus: *Anima, que declinaverit ad magos et ariolos, ponam faciem meam contra eam ad interficiendum eam* [Lv 20:6]: Any person who turns to magic and diviners, I shall put my face against him to kill him. Elsewhere: Either a man or a woman, if they have a prophetic spirit or are a diviner, let them be killed, let them be stoned, and let their blood be upon them [Lv 20:27]. According to human, civil, and Church law, these diviners and enchanters are infamous, and should not be received to testify or to take communion; indeed, they should be excommunicated. As St. Augustine says: This vanity, indeed, iniquity of magical art, introduced into the world through the work of malign spirits, should be far from the faithful Christian. Whoever uses it, or asks those who do it, or gives help, counsel, or favour, or receives it in his house or goes to the practitioners' house or sends for or allows them to act or speak, it is as if he had renounced the Christian faith and baptism and is worse than a pagan. Therefore, St. Paul, prohibiting this accursed art, said: *Nolo vos esse socios demoniorum* [1 Cr 10:20]: I do not want you to be companions of demons.

Those who use this art, discovered and taught by demons with express or tacit agreements made with demons, become companions of demons, with whom, as companions in guilt, they will be companions in the eternal punishment of hell and the punishing fire.

This magical art, and superstitious and diabolical science, is used in many ways and to many effects, and so it takes many names. When it is used to learn certain things that are hidden or should happen, it is called divinatory art. Those who use it in such a way are called diviners, almost "full of God" as St. Isidore says,[294] because they show people that they are full of that knowledge which is God's alone, that of knowing the future. To want to know those things, apart from those that can be foreseen and known through natural reasons, as astrologers detect the natural impressions of the sky, and learned doctors the paroxysms and the critical days[295] of corporeal infirmities, is a most serious sin. Those who presume to know or foresee those things that only God knows, if they did not already know them through divine revelation, usurp and take away what is God's alone. This was our first parents' first sin, and we can see how displeasing it was to God by the harsh judgment and very serious sentence with which they and all their descendants were punished, so that none of the sons of Adam ever dared to commit such folly. Nevertheless, we repeatedly find those who, despite such punishment, insanely repeat the sin. Not only do they fail by wanting to know what they should not, but also, much more seriously, by turning to the one to whom they should not turn, i.e., the devil, either by explicitly invoking him or by covertly using his art in different ways, to which, even if not called, he responds as if he were. As St. Thomas says in the *Summa*, every act of divination, whether explicit or tacit, uses the counsel and the help of the devil, who shows men certain things they do not know, and he knows them by the means stated above, predicting them, when explicitly invoked, in many ways. Sometimes, by assuming shapes or using voices that can be heard, he shows and tells men what they want to know; this type of divination is called prestidigitation. Sometimes he shows a man what he wants to know in a dream; this is called divination by dreams. Other times, by the appearance and speech of the dead, and this type is called necromancy. Sometimes he shows them through living men, like through the possessed, entering into some people and sharing what he knows through their speech; this is called divination through prophecy. Sometimes the devil reveals certain hidden things though figures and signs that appear in inanimate bodies, which, if they appear in some earthly body, like iron, glass, polished stone, mirror, or fingernail, is called geomancy; if in water,

---

294 In the *Etymologies* [GA].

295 Paroxysms are the days during an illness when symptoms worsen; critical days are the most serious phase of the illness (see Passavanti, ed. Auzzas, 437n).

hydromancy; if in air, aeromancy, if they appear in fire it is called pyromancy; if in the innards of animals, which are offered to demons, it is called haruspicy.

There is another means of divination, done without explicitly invoking the devil, which can happen in two ways. The first is when people want to know the future through the arrangement of certain other things, such as by considering the location and movement of the stars, which is called divination by astronomy; or by the movement or voice of birds or other animals, or through men's sneezes, and this is properly called augury; or by consideration of the movement of the eyes or ears of animals. If such a consideration centres on the words of men, which, although spoken with another intention, the diviner uses for his own purposes, this would be called omen. If sometimes, in order to know occult things, someone were to consider certain arrangements of shapes in bodies that are visible to the eyes, this would be another type of divination; and if some were to study the lineaments, i.e., the lines and creases of the hands, it would be called chiromancy; and if one were to consider certain figures that appear on the shoulders of some animals that are sacrificed to the gods, as the pagans do, it would be called spatulamancy.

The other means of divination, without explicitly invoking the devil, is when certain things are thought to happen through purposeful actions aimed at knowing some occult things, like drawing points, or lines, or figures, which belongs to geomancy; or by studying shapes made of molten, boiling lead tossed into cold water; or by making risky investments, or rolling dice, or suddenly opening a book and thinking about what first comes to hand, or similar things which involve taking chances.

In all these things, there is a general source of sin, but not the same specific cause, because it is a more serious sin to invoke the devil explicitly than to do certain other things for which he gets involved when not called. It is much more serious to make some sacrifice or show of devotion to him, which is what he wants above all, since he retains the pose of his first arrogance. This was shown in the third temptation of Christ, when he said to him: *Hec omnia tibi dabo, si cadens adoraveris me* [Mt 4:9]: All these things – which he had shown, i.e., the glory of the world – I will give to you if, throwing yourself on the ground, you will adore me. Also, he endeavours to make a person fall for that because it is the greatest sin there is, i.e., idolatry.

[VI]

This magical art is sometimes used in order to do, or have, or acquire something with the demon's help, which a person could not do or have by himself, such as wealth or treasure, either in one's own caves and mines, or in tombs or other hidden places that the devil knows about. However, he does not have the capacity to direct them or give them to whomever he wants, but only when and to whom God allows, like finding missing or lost things, which the devil knows about, and especially those things that he causes other people to lose by theft.

Evil effects are also produced, and those who practise this art are called maleficent, and the art is called evildoing. This happens when, with the devil's favour, such an art causes a bewitched person, man or woman, to lose their memory, fall in love with someone else, and be horrified by their company. It can look like their house is on fire and is collapsing: they will lose their appetite, be consumed, unable to sleep or rest, have terrible and fearsome dreams, dark and unpleasant visions and fantasies. Their flesh will appear to be full of thorns and needles, their heart stabbed, their members collapsing and weak, that they are forgetful and blinded by the light, and senseless; they will find no rest by either day or night, and their conduct and words will resemble that of a frenzied and feverish person. This art can transport a person from one place to another, suddenly making and bringing back embassies and news from a faraway land. To do these things, evildoers sometimes explicitly invoke and appeal to demons, who appear in some of the ways stated above, seemingly compelled by such appeals, although they are not, as was said above. They use incantations, giving people enchanted foods and beverages, they make images in wax and lead and other materials, they tie big knots, and they make written promises in the name of demons and with signs and shapes and characters discovered and taught by the demons, which contain the agreements between the demons and those who use said signs to some effect, according to the aforementioned art.

Some of these evildoers boast that they can change minds and transform one thing into another, such as turning a man or a woman into a beast or a bird, and create new things, as the poets write in their fables. To this false claim we reply that they know perfectly well that they are lying through their teeth, and that they have no more power than their master, i.e., the devil, whose power, we said above, does not extend so far, although he can make some things appear to be something other than what they are.

They falsely boast about another thing, namely, that at their request their master imparts knowledge to any idiot, while observing certain rules of the art, and they have written a book about it which is called *The General Art*. St. Thomas[296] proves that, like other magical

____

296 In the *Summa* [GA].

and diabolical books, it is forbidden and banned because it contains characters and figures of tacit agreements with the devil, with whom no agreement or convention, or company, or any friendship at all is ever allowed; indeed, we are commanded by God to hold him to be a faithless enemy. As St. Paul says: *Nolite locum dare diabolo* [Ep 4:27]: Do not make any room for the devil. And St. Peter: *Cui resistite fortes in fide* [1 Pt 5:9]: Your adversary the devil looks everywhere, like a rapacious lion, as if he might devour someone, and you must oppose him by remaining strong in faith. St. Thomas proves that there is no efficacy at all in the general art, because the devil's power does not extend to illuminating a man's intellect, because it would necessarily mean that a man would seem different than his usual and natural way. Although the devil could teach with the sound of his voice as a man would do, or perhaps even better, depending on how subtly and better a man might know it, still, he could not suddenly inform a person's intellect with any habitual knowledge, since he cannot illuminate him. It would take time and order in the learning, and even more depending on how stupid and ill-disposed to learning the student might be.

What vanity and false iniquity there is in these evildoers! Their evildoing, with whatever help the malign one can lend, is not enough for them; they also try to show his power, and theirs, when neither they nor he have any! It is a sign of their great evil and foolishness, and that of those who have faith in him. Their great evil is to trust or befriend the enemy and adversary of omnipotent God, who has power over them both. He has forbidden them, under pain of eternal death, to have any familiarity or company with him. Those of Christian faith know that he is the ancient serpent, the archenemy of all human nature, and that all his efforts are aimed at leading men to that same damnation and misery in which he finds himself. It is no secret that all the practitioners of this art typically come to a bad end and a bad death, as many stories and chronicles tell. The devil does not save them from it, but rather he leads them to it: not just to mortal death but, even worse, to the death of the soul. Theirs is a great foolishness, because they know for sure, and they show it by practising the art, that he is an unfaithful liar and deceiver, and that he promises more than he can deliver. Since he is proud, he never admits that he does not know how to do what is asked of him or that he cannot do it. Instead, he always answers that it'll be done. Then, not knowing how, or not being able to provide, he falls short of his promise, and he never confesses that he didn't know how to or could not in the first place. Instead, he blames the evildoers, saying: You did not understand me, or you did not perform well; you failed in following such-and-such instruction. As well, being envious, he does not teach what he does know, and he does not do what he can. A liar and a deceiver, he will say one thing instead of another, and he will say many half-words and double words, which can have different meanings because of misunderstanding, like *Reginam interficere bonum est timere nolite, etc.*, and: *Vinces non perdes, etc.*, and similar ambiguous and dubious things. Being presumptuous, he thinks he knows how to do what he does not. The holy angels, by God's pleasure, often remove things from the notice of demons and from their power, so that they cannot do whatever they want, and so that they are confused and ashamed of their undertakings and the promises they make.

Nevertheless, certain men, who ignore or forget about their own salvation, risking their own souls, follow after them, seeking their friendship, asking for their advice and help, indeed, harassing them about it. One time the devil said to a holy man: "People often blame me quite wrongly for the many bad things they do; so-and-so says: 'The devil tempted me, he made me commit such-and-such a sin, the devil appeared before me, and I would not have sought him out, nor will I take any blame at all.' Men and women often tempt me and bother and beg me, involving me in their affairs, and I don't argue with them, because, when I let them go ahead and do it, they do so much evil that they take the opportunity away from me."

Although this magical art is very effective, according to God's hidden judgment which permits many sins, nevertheless, by letting evildoers operate according to the rule of the demonic arts, we can sometimes see in certain persons, men and women of low condition, what they do not. In truth there are few who know how to practise this art, but, either by hearing about it or on their own, they learn about certain enchantments, imprecations, writings, briefs, and attachments with certain practices that look like those of the magical arts and yet have nothing to do with them. But because the people who perform them, and those in whose name and stead they are done, believe and trust in them, thinking that they are doing what evildoers do with the devil's help and advice, they have some efficacy. This is because the devil, who willingly favours every bad operation, helps them out, taking command and control over such persons, who are evildoers by intention, if not in deed, and think they are practising the devil's magical art. Without a doubt they sin mortally, and they assist the devil by finding another art that the devil has not found, which he then adopts and validates, trusting in it. As St. Augustine says,[297] speaking of these enchantments and doings, they

---

297 In *On Christian Doctrine* [GA].

should not be believed because they might be true, but they become true because they are believed.

There are others, both men and women, who do not know the magical art, or how to invoke or implore demons, and are not diviners, nor do they think they are, who know for sure that they are not, and nevertheless, either for gain or because of some other vanity of theirs, claim to be enchanters and diviners. With their gadgets and their way of making people's heads spin, they easily deceive many simpletons, who are ready to follow such things. Some say they can see the dead and speak with them, and that at night they meet up with witches. Others say they know how to cure eye sickness and dental pain, migraines, sore throats, and body aches through enchantment, and they make little amulets that will keep the wearer from having pain in his flanks or bodily sickness, nor will he die in water or fire or be hurt by his enemies, and he will have all the protections people want; and therefore they easily believe them. These types are deceivers and blowhards, and by sinning mortally, they are made to repay all their gains. Whoever trusts in them sins gravely and suffers harm for what he gave them.

Nor should people let themselves be deceived by true evildoers, or by those who call themselves diviners and enchanters and are not, who say that masses and prayers are said, alms given, fasts done, because they do it all maliciously and in order to be more trusted, and so that they can secretly pour out the poison of their evil.

Although we hear of certain persons who, neither speaking the truth nor believing they speak it, for gain or some other deceit say they see the dead and that they move about in groups, nevertheless we find, among the devil's other illusions, that he pretends to make the dead appear. These are not the true spirits of dead men and women, because he cannot do that, but he assumes the shape and appearance of the dead person, and he lies and says he is that person. We read in Holy Scripture[298] about that seer who, when asked by King Saul, made Samuel appear, who predicted the outcome of the battle with the Philistines. He was neither Samuel nor his spirit, as the saints explain, but the devil bearing his likeness, claiming to be Samuel. Taking the shape of living men and women, and horses and pack animals, demons troop around at night in certain neighbourhoods, where the people who see them believe that they are those persons whose likeness they bear; in some places this is called a brigade. The demons do that in order to spread error and sow scandal, and to defame those persons whose appearance

---

298 This is a tale repeated in Aquinas's *Summa* that does not in fact appear in
    Scripture [GA].

they take, showing that they can do dishonourable things as part of the brigade. There are even those people, especially women, who claim to go about at night with this brigade, and they list many men and women in their company. They say the leaders of the group are Herodias, who had St. John the Baptist killed, and Diana, the ancient Greek goddess. Whatever the case may be, one should think about how this is possible. There is no doubt that the devil can lead both men and women, in groups small and large, from one place to another as he wishes, through his own natural power, as long as divine virtue does not stop him, but we find that he rarely does so. The other, more likely, way was already discussed above,[299] making it appear to others that he or somebody else is what he is not, and that he does what he does not do. He does that either when you are awake or asleep, altering the mind and creating the impression, through images, of what he wants someone to appear to be or say or do. This way, while you are in bed, it will seem that you are going about doing wonderful things; and then you will recount them, believing that he really did them. This commonly happens to evildoers, or to people who have been turned into evildoers – i.e., that some evil of magical art is done to them or through them – or to persons who believe in such things.

Some things do not involve the invocation of the demons or figures, or the practice of magical art, but still are not permitted, because they are either false or do not have any efficacy, or because the way in which they are done is suspect. Words spoken or written down, either in a small amulet or any other type of container, have no efficacy whatsoever – even words of Holy Scripture, or the Gospel of St. John, or *Dirupisti vincula mea* [Ps 115:16], or *Iesus autem transiens per medium illorum ibat* [Lk 4:30], or any other statement – for preventing either drowning or falling into the hands of demons, or for winning a legal dispute or any other enterprise, or for not dying without confession, or for not dying a sudden death, or for surviving childbirth, or for avoiding any infirmity. Indeed, it is a sin to use them for any of these purposes, or for any other temporal or material purpose, because they were written and inspired by the Holy Spirit either for instruction and learning or for prayer, and for nothing else. If Scripture had been revealed by God or ordained for such a use, the Holy Spirit would have revealed it to the apostles and the Holy Church, as it did with the sacramental words. This did not happen, and therefore a living man may not direct or appropriate them to such a use as carrying them in writing on one's

---

299 See p. 227.

person or saying them or having them said for any material or temporal purpose. It would be even worse when some unknown words or figures or signs were mixed in or inserted, which according to the saints contained tacit pacts with the demons.

Let the words of the Holy Scripture be carried in the mind and not around the neck, in the heart and not in the purse.

The same holds true for the money first offered at the cross on Good Friday, and for the grasses that are cultivated and maintained when one sings the Gospel, or the passion, and the like.

If God's words have no virtue or efficacy for such a purpose, even less so do the words of a man or woman that are said in enchantments and to summon serpents or other beasts, or for illness or any other infirmity. The name of God and of our Lord Jesus Christ, the help of the Virgin Mary and the other saints, devoutly and purely, without any self-mortification or vain superstition, must be invoked in every necessity, bodily and spiritual. This goes as well for fasting, silence, masses, remission of sins, the procedures followed under certain rules of time and number, thinking that otherwise they would not be valid, as is said about the twelve Mondays of St. Catherine, the Friday of St. Nicholas, the masses of St. Gregory, the Wednesday of St. Lawrence, the silence of the 10,000 martyrs, and the like.[300] This is not to say, however, that masses and fasting and prayers and other good things are not good things to do, but rather that those rules of time and number and certain ways are neither permitted nor good. In their vanity and cupidity, mortals want to attach a law to divine justice by which deeds or words, or goings or offerings, draw certain souls out of purgatory within a certain time. To believe or say this is great presumption and a dangerous mistake.

The rules regarding time which certain people follow – i.e., on what day, at what hour, or at what point someone may do something new, like entering a new house for the first time in order to live in it, or putting on new clothes, or bringing home one's wife, or opening a business or spending time with someone, boarding a ship, taking office, shaving for the first time, looking for a good tip on the first day of the month, the first day of the new year, the first day of the week, which might

---

300 The traditions Passavanti references are difficult to specify today. I have found no information regarding the Mondays of St. Catherine (of Alexandria) or of Friday celebrations involving St. Nicholas. The reference to masses of St. Gregory may involve the report that he witnessed an apparition of Jesus while officiating at a Good Friday mass. The Wednesday of St. Lawrence is likely Ash Wednesday. The reference to the 10,000 martyrs probably relies on the medieval legend according to which Roman soldiers converted to Christianity and subsequently were martyred on Mount Ararat.

mean that some hour on one day is better than another, indeed, that one is good and the other bad, and so forth – are useless and not without great sin. This is especially true about observing certain days that some call Egyptian,[301] in which you should not undertake anything that you want to turn out well, because these are evil and unlucky days, and there are some in each month of the year. St. Paul speaks out against these practitioners: *Dies observatis, menses, tempora, et annos. Timeo ne sine causa laboraverim in vobis* [Gl 4:10]: You follow the days, the months, the times, and the years, and because of that I fear I have wasted my time with you.

We should not therefore think that it is bad to follow the times and the signs from heaven for certain natural things for which both time and heaven are a reason, as Solomon says: *Omnia tempus habent* [El 3:1]: All things in their time. Doctors when giving medicines, sailors when navigating, farmers when working the land can, indeed should, follow and keep in mind the time and the signs of the stars and the planets of the sky. The same holds true for certain activities of animals, who move according to the instinct of the sky, and it is seen and proven by human experience that they understand something should happen, not that they are the cause of it. For example, when dolphins approach ships while swimming upon the waters of the sea, it means a storm is approaching. When a cat cleans itself with its claws, women say that it is a sign of rain, and when the cock crows more than usual, it signals a change in the weather. Observing and remembering these things is not a sin, but anyone who might want to predict, because the rooster crows, or the dog barks, or the crow or the night owl sing on the roof, or any other bird or animal moves, that a sick man will get well, or die, or a person should live to a certain age – like that old lady who said she would live five more years because she had heard the cuckoo sing five times on the first of May, because she did not want to confess, and so died without confessing – this would be a grave sin and an illicit and forbidden practice.

That same goes for certain superstitions, which should not be followed or considered, such as if, when walking out the door in the morning, you were to sneeze even once, which some empty-headed believers say means that you should go back inside, or if you were wearing a sock or shirt inside out, you might think that the whole day will go wrong; and if your left foot were to go in front of the right, or you were to stumble or fall, that you should not go any farther. All

---

301 According to medieval superstition, there were two unlucky or "Egyptian" days per month, so-called because they marked a date on which a disaster befell the ancient Egyptians.

such things, for which there is no natural reason or cause, must not be followed or believed. They are false and worthless opinions, and they are the remnants of paganism, or introduced by the false doctrine of demons.

With regard to the drawing of lots, the saints say that in certain cases it is not permitted. Indeed, it is forbidden by the *Decretum*, as it would be for someone who wanted to know any hidden thing by chance, or what might happen, through the taking of chances, or the arrangement of the stars, or the operation of demons; this is called divinatory chance. Also, whoever might want to know, by chance, what he should do or say, wondering what is better, like choosing some church prelate, or receiving some spiritual benefit, is not today permitted, although it was practised under the old law; this is called consultatory chance. There is yet another way of taking a chance called divisional chance. This is allowed, for example, if certain persons have to distribute certain things held in common and could not agree on how to divvy them up through sharing. They can then draw lots, leaving luck to decide which part should come to each of them. This type of chance may also be used in lay offices to determine who goes first, as is done with city officials who are elected for several years, and their names, written on slips of paper, are put in a bag or a small box, and then at certain times their names are drawn, and according to how they are drawn, they take office.

[VII]

It is necessary to say some things here about dreams, which many believe in, and many make mistakes about, as Solomon says [Ec 34:1–8]. As we find in various places in Scripture and in the people of God, dreams are studied and interpreted, and one means of prophecy of God's prophets was by revelation and visions shown in dreams, as the holy Job says: *Per sopnium, in visione nocturna, quando irruit sopor super homines, et dormiunt in lectulo, tunc aperit (scil. Deus) aures virorum e eruntiens eos instruit disciplina* [Jb 33:15–16]. He says that God teaches men in dreams by visions at night, when they sleep in their beds. Elsewhere, in the book of Numbers, God says: If there is a prophet among you, I will appear to him in a vision through a dream [Nb 12:6]. The angel appeared several times to Joseph, wife of St. Mary, both in a dream and in a vision, and to the Magi also, so that they would not return to Herod, as the Holy Gospel recounts about the one and the other.[302] So

---

302 These episodes appear in the Gospel of Matthew.

too, in other Eastern nations that pay attention to dreams, like the Chaldeans, the Arabs, the Persians, and the Indians. Joseph interpreted Pharaoh's dream [Gn 41], and Daniel Nebuchadnezzar's [Dn 2]. Therefore, it is not wholly to be rejected that you can pay attention to a dream, and learn some truth through an imaginary apparition or by a vision and revelation made by a dream, notwithstanding what God commands in Deuteronomy: *Non inveniatur in te qui observet sompnia* [Dt 18:10]: Let there not be found among you, my people, those who obey dreams. So it is necessary to consider why dreams happen, and how far the imaginative power of dreams extends. Once we have made that determination, we will understand which dreams should or can be obeyed as true, having some reasonable efficacy, and which should be shunned as false and worthless.

Summarizing the science and theory of dreams, about which some wise philosophers have written great books and said many things, we should know that dreams either are the reason why something is or is not done, or they are signs and effects of something done or that is still to be done or to happen.

Dreams can only be the reason why something is done or not done in one sense, and this is when a person, remembering that he dreamed something pleasant or unpleasant, amusing or fearsome, is moved to do or to avoid what he had dreamed with delight or fear. For example, if somebody dreams, when it was very hot, that he took a bath with great pleasure, and then, remembering the pleasant dream, goes to take a bath, we could say that that dream was the reason why the dreamer took a bath. If someone were to dream that he had been attacked by his enemies and fled from them in great fear, and then, remembering the fearful dream, did not leave his house, we could say that that dream was the reason why the dreamer stayed home and did not go out. We could say the same about everything that, when dreamed with pleasure or with pain and fear, makes one do or avoid any pleasant or fearful thing.

Dreams can be effects and signs in many ways, just as there are many reasons for dreams, which we must consider in detail, so that we have a true understanding of what we are looking for.

There can be one of two sources for dreams, from either within or without. The inner reasons are two as well, because what causes someone to dream comes either from the soul or the body. From the soul is when, because of some thought, or image, or intimate feeling that one might have, while awake and aware, his fantasy and imaginative power are moved and form some image and resemblance according to that thought and feeling, which the soul then contemplates and sees once the body is asleep and the external feelings are bound up and closed. Therefore, various and different dreams occur more or less according to passions and feelings, and more or less according to whether someone is more or less feeling and passionate. For those who are not learned and understand them more broadly than philosophers do, the passions and feelings of the soul are love, hatred, hope and fear, happiness and sadness, wrath and concupiscence. Each one of these causes dreams to happen that conform and correspond to that feeling. Love, which makes someone who loves think fixedly about the beloved person and desire that person affectionately, can make someone dream either in one way or another, according to whether the imagination is moved and takes the form of the beloved object with the imprint of burning love.

The same thing happens with every feeling, each in its own way. I won't detail each one here, in order not to run on too long, because the material is multiplying in my hands.

Every person who dreams should think about whether his dream corresponds to whatever he is feeling, to what most urges him on. If so, he should not expect something else to happen, because the dream is not the reason why some other effect should follow, but it is the effect of the person's feeling. To follow such a dream, i.e., to consider its source, is not in and of itself bad, because it is the effect of natural reason. True, it is difficult to make sense of such dreams, and especially to understand that a single person has various and contrary feelings that will stimulate the imagination in contrary ways, and which, when combined, will lead to confused dreams that cannot be understood clearly. Therefore, we should not chase after dreams. As wise Cato said, *Ne cures sopnia*: Don't worry about dreams, because the human mind, whatever it desires and hopes for while awake, also sees when dreaming.

The second reason, having to do with a body part inside someone, is the disposition and quality of the person and of the bodily humours, which, because of their contrarieties, will jump about, and the one, by defeating and overcoming the other, draws the habit of the body to its quality, which in sleep moves the fantasy, in which is formed some resemblance and figure according to that same disposition. When that humour known as phlegm, which is cold and wet like water, overwhelms the body, the dreams correspond to that quality, so that a person dreams that it is raining, or that he is taking a bath, or that he is falling into water, and similar wet and cold things. When anger, which is hot and dry like fire, is superabundant, it makes one dream of fire, dryness, heat, thirst, wrath, arguments, riots, battle, and the like. When the blood, which is hot and wet like air and a sweet humour, surpasses the other humours, the dreams are happy and gay, involving laughter and fun, love, music, and clean air, and some dream of flying. When that humour which is called melancholy, which is cold and dry like the earth, is greater than the others, then we dream of fearful and sad, dark and shadowy things, of falling, of being captured and tied up, and similar terrible things. And when the humours are intemperate and mixed together, they make for heavy, bothersome, and fearsome dreams, and then it is a sign that someone is sick or disposed to sickness. Therefore, the ancient doctors used to ask the sick man about his dreams, as about other incidents and signs by which one knows the attitude and disposition of the body within; and this is still done in some places. Dreams like these can be attended to, and the reasons why they might come about can be considered without sin; they are natural and do not imply that something else should follow from the dreams.

The other reason for dreams comes from without. This happens in two ways: the one is bodily, the other is spiritual.

The bodily reason can take several forms. First, by the impression of celestial bodies, i.e., of planets and stars, which, according to their sites and aspects, conjunctions and movements, have influence, or make impressions on the brains of man and other animals, and make them dream of things that conform with and correspond to their disposition; and the sages have seen that, among other animals, the horse and the dog dream.

Dreams vary according to the weather and its influences, so that winter makes for some dreams, spring for others, and summer still others, and we dream otherwise in autumn: and the soft and clear air makes for some dreams, and heavy and foggy air for others. Dreams also vary according to the variety of the winds, and the new and full moon, when it rises and sets, and as it alters the bodily humours, also makes for changes in dreams.

Eating and drinking, both in quantity and quality, are an external reason for dreams. Just as excess, by the many vapours and fumes that leave the stomach and go to the brain, makes a person dream a lot (and it could be too much, and not allow you to dream or discern the dream), so too does lack, i.e., hunger and thirst, allow one to dream little, or perhaps all one's sleep is a dream of fainting or eating or drinking. The quality of food or drink creates variety in dreaming, because foods that are light and thin make the dream light and clear; those that are thick and heavy make the dream about heavy, dense, and fearsome things. As the sages say, leeks, onions, and garlic, and every raw citrus fruit, fava beans and every legume cause terrible and bothersome dreams, and must and every heavy and dense drink likewise make dreams heavy and dark. Among the other things that make dreams evil and dark is the intemperate and disordered use of lust, because it troubles and weakens the brain, and the virtue of sight and imagination is clouded.

Also from without, the arts, duties, labours, and every job and enterprise which are continuously done with effort and care are reasons for dreams, so that the farmer dreams of the plough and oxen and the hoe; the smith, the workshop, the anvil, the hammer; the doctor, sick people, elixirs, and medicines; the lawyer, disputes, arguments, and issues; the soldier, arms and horses, war, battles, double pay, and good money; the priest, the altar, the mass, the divine office, and the tithe; the woman who is a good housewife dreams of linen and good weaving, the cloth structured and woven well.

We see in a dream what others often see and hear with great pleasure or displeasure, either persons or other things, whatever they may be. Among the other external things that influence dreams, there is a person's sleep position. When one sleeps on the left side, or when the body is full of thick blood or other thick humours, especially after eating, it feels like there is a great weight on him, so much so that he does not feel like he can move or flip over; or it seems like he is going to drown and wants to help himself but cannot, and he wants to cry for help but does not seem to have a voice. Sometimes the person cries out and cries during such a dream, expressing regret. Some call this a demon dream or incubus, saying that it is an animal like a satyr, or a hobgoblin, that goes around at night and bothers people this way; and some call it the bogeyman. Despite what people will tell you, this dream has a natural cause. When someone lies on his left side, where the heart is, thick blood and certain other humours flow there and surround the heart, and, being full and not able to move freely or draw in the spirits or expel them, of which it is the source and main seat, causes anguish and anxiety in the person, as if he were drowning, blocked from his natural movement, which never rests. Therefore, the whole body is disposed, and the imagination informed, according to that feeling in the heart, which sometimes is so great that a person drowns and dies. The heart has this feeling when one is sleeping, but also when a person is awake and alert. Some call it a heart deficit, others fainting, and others call it syncope or ecstasy. In the case of those who sleep on their right side, the liver might get heated up and obstructed, and then a person dreams of being hot with fever, or of being heated up out of wrath or too much fatigue, so that he cannot catch his breath or breathe, or he dreams of seeing fire, or that he is burning or struck by lightning. Sometimes, if the bed linens or an arm or a hand get too close to the throat, a person will dream that hands have been put around his neck to strangle him. When his head and neck or some other member hurts because it was in the wrong position, the person will dream that it should be cut off. When a person is lying on his back, evil and bothersome dreams occur. First, there are dishonourable and evil dreams, such as when the kidneys and the back get heated up, with the inner organs that lie atop them pressing on them, and the seminal humour moves and descends towards the generative members, and that movement moves the fantasy and the imagination to dream of things for which that humour runs its full course. Therefore, a man who wants to live chastely should be careful not to lie that way. Also, when lying this way we dream of heavy and bothersome things, because the memory part, which is on the side of the back of the head, is squeezed beneath and weighed down by the other parts of the brain, which are on top of it; and the fantastic part, being useless, because it is turned backward, the former part being blurred and almost drowned, the latter worthless and faint, receives heavy and bothersome fantasies because the memory is exhausted, and it makes dreams according to that disposition. The best and healthiest way to lie is with your mouth open, or almost, so that all the interior parts can stay put, unless you have a cough, or asthma, or some other infirmity, which would make it a problem or bothersome to keep your mouth open.

We are allowed to observe all the ways and means of dreams, with their causes, which are written, because they are natural, not because they signify what might happen, but as effects that follow from their causes.

There are certain other external causes for dreams, which the philosophers write about in their books, and in which I have little faith. Nevertheless, we want to write a bit about them here, so that our treatise will not be lacking.

Some sages say that if you put a laurel branch under a sleeping person's head he will have true dreams, and they say that the seed of wild lettuce will not allow someone to dream worthless dreams. The philosophers Antiphon and Artemon write this in their books.[303] And Hevax says[304] that if you keep a diamond on your person when you sleep, you will not be allowed to dream fearful and worthless things, as he says:

---

303 Passavanti appears to be following the tradition according to which the
fifth-century BCE orator Antiphon was also the author of *An Interpretation of
Dreams*. Little is known about Artemon, who also may have written a treatise on
dreams. See Passavanti, ed. Auzzas, 537.

304 On Hevax, an Arab king, see Passavanti, ed. Auzzas, 537.

Et noctis lemures, et somnia vana repellit. He says that the sapphire causes revelations in dreams, as he says: *Et qui portat eum, nequit ulla fraude noceri, / ut divina queat per eum responsa mereri.* They say that the emerald makes one a diviner, who knows what will happen in the future: *Commodus iste lapis scruptantibus abita fertur, cum prescire volunt aut divinare futura.* Of coral they say that it is good against illusions and fears that the devil makes; so they write: *Umbras daemoniacas ac thessala cuncta repellit.* They say similar things about certain other precious stones, like chrysolite and zirconium, of which they write: *Et dulces sompnos, et dulcia somnia prestat,* and *Contra nocturnos fortis tutela timores.* They write the opposite about another stone called onyx, of which they say: *In sompno lemures et tristia cuncta figurat, multiplicat lites ad commovet undique rixas,* that it makes one dream of shadows and sad and fearful things, and it causes arguments and quarrels. With regard to many other stones, they write about how chalcedony and heliotrope and chelonite and graphite have the power to make one have true and good dreams. They write of the magnet that, among its other virtues, if a man wants to know whether his wife is faithful to him he should put a piece of magnet under her head when she sleeps. If she is chaste and faithful, she will turn over and embrace her husband; if she is an adulteress and unfaithful, she will not be able to tolerate the power of the stone, but, as if repulsed, she will tumble from the bed to the ground. If that is true, then jealous husbands should safeguard it carefully. It is well known and proved that one part of a magnet attracts iron and the other repels it, but I do not know if it can draw a chaste woman towards her husband, or chase away the unchaste woman, and I do not believe it is true, unless the wife were already made of iron. The philosophers write that in a certain part of the world, i.e., towards the meridian, near the torrid zone, there are mountains of magnet, which draws human flesh to it, and therefore people cannot live there or travel there. Indeed, there was a case in which a person, heading there, had his flesh drawn in opposite directions as he passed through those mountains of magnet, and was lifted into the air and died there, appearing to laugh. Perhaps because the magnet has the above-mentioned power, jealous husbands look for it, in order to test their suspect wives and be freed of their jealousy, and for the wives to be freed of their bother.

We are not fully allowed to heed these dreams, because although herbs and stones have certain heavenly virtues, and according to their qualities and species can repair and remove certain impediments in human bodies, still I do not believe that they have as much efficacy as the philosophers give them.

The other external reason for dreams is spiritual. This comes at times from God, who through the ministry of the holy angels reveals certain hidden mysteries and high things, beyond human senses, to people whom He chooses, according to the order of His providence. He did this with the prophets, to some of whom he revealed prophecies in a dream, which they then preached to the people and wrote in books. As God said in the book of Numbers: *Si quis fuerit inter vos propheta Domini, in visione apparebo ei, vel per sompnium loquar ad illum* [Nb 12:6]: If there shall be any prophet of God among you, I will appear to him in a vision, and I will speak to him through a dream. In the Holy Gospel we read that the angel of God appeared to the Magi and often to Joseph in a dream, as is written above.[305]

I will not explain here why such visions and revelations come in dreams rather than when we are awake, and the difference between those dreams and others, because it would not be very useful and it would take too long, although the doctors do discuss it. There is just one thing to clarify, and that is how we can know whether such visions come from God and not from other sources. Although some try to talk about signs, I myself believe that every other sign can be erroneous unless that same spirit that makes the revelation reassures the person to whom he shows the vision by means of a special cognitive and spiritual light, causing a spark in his mind that such a revelation is from God and that he should have faith in it.

Visions that happen this way can, indeed must, be heeded. Some saints, through prayer and fasting, have asked God to reveal certain necessary things to them, like some strong passage in Scripture, or some other uncertain thing, or to show God's glory either by proof of faith or by something else that is in God's honour or for the good of one's neighbour. I believe this can be done without sin, with humility and without presumption.

The other external spiritual source of dreaming can be the devil, who, as said above,[306] can make someone dream by impressing imaginary apparitions and fantastic visions in sleepers' heads, revealing certain hidden things or things that are going to happen, as far as he knows; we have written about this earlier. The devil is motivated to put someone to sleep, either on his own, through his malice, in order to disturb or scandalize people, so that typically he bothers good people in dreams (who, by trying to stay awake, resist defeat), or to distance them from the good by frightening and alarming them with fearsome and terrible visions, or to incline them to evil by drawing them in with pleasant and delightful images of fleshly lust and dishonourable corruption.

---

305 See p. 238.
306 See p. 226.

Sometimes, the devil is motivated to cause someone to sleep, because these magi and evil men use their magical art to induce him to do so. They have certain seven-word incantations and a few rituals, with which they invoke the demons when people go to sleep. They make a sacrifice to them of their own blood, or of the hair on their heads or other body hair, and they ask them specifically to appear before them or others, in whose name they perform their art, through dreams, and to reveal whatever it is they want to know or hear or let someone else know. Sometimes, without making an explicit invocation or sacrifice, they carry, or have others hold, little cases or other writings, with certain names and figures and signs in which are contained certain hidden and tacit pacts with the demons, which we spoke of above.[307]

To seek to have such dreams and visions, or to have faith in them or heed them, is a most grave evildoing. Because, as St. Paul says [2 Cr 11:14], the devil is often transfigured into an angel of light, one should not follow or heed dreams or visions unless he is certain they are revelations from God. Nor should one easily trust his own judgment, because we are often deceived in our opinions, just as in our desire. Therefore, although the dream appears to be a revelation from God, a person should not believe it if he does not have some certain experience, because while that person believes it comes from God, it could be from the devil. There are many who are so deceived. St. John puts it well: *Nolite omni spiritui credere, sed probate spiritus si ex Deo sunt* [1 Jn 4:1]: Do not believe every spirit, but test the spirits, to inspirations and desires of others, and of the doctrine and advice that is often given to others, because one should be very careful about whom to trust, since the deceits are many.

Many have already taken up the interpretation of dreams, and they have written books about them, where they teach how to skilfully interpret, i.e., to know and show others what the dream signifies, and what should come from such a dream. They so trust in their own vanity that they set about to interpret every dream, saying that all dreams have some meaning. If they were to say that every dream has a source, they would be telling the truth; but it is wrong to say that all dreams have a meaning that can be interpreted, especially about what is going to happen, almost as if dreams and the reason for dreams are why they occur. Although some can interpret them, understanding interpretation broadly to be any knowledge, such as dreams that have natural internal or external causes, as we said above, which the doctor and the

---

307 See p. 234.

astrologer and a good natural philosopher can know by his science, still many other dreams cannot be interpreted or known in any way, either by science or by human art. These include those that do not come about from natural causes, or for which the reasons are very hidden and uncertain, or when many reasons, similar and contrary, come together in a single dream. This happens often, because there are many reasons for a dream, both internal and external, and each will have some effect on the head of the dreamer, who will dream scrambled, confused things without any order, either several together or one after another, with so much confusion that the dreamer himself will not be able to recount it. So go ahead and say that such dreams can be interpreted, and that it's possible to know what they mean.

In the case of dreams that do not proceed from natural causes but are revelations from God, which He makes according to His hidden will, to signify some hidden things or what is going to happen, sometimes through dreams about dissimilar and contrary things, sometimes through similar, obvious things, and sometimes by hidden things: how can such a dream be interpreted by a living man? God's will, which is the source of the dream, is hidden, and the rule of the art of like and unlike things in such a dream does not apply, nor can it be used.

To better understand what I am saying, let's take a case and an example. Let's assume that there is a great drought, as there is now, and the moon and the stars and the elements are not naturally aligned in such a way that it might rain in the next month, but that God, who can do whatever He wants, by His grace and through the prayers of some holy persons, wants to make it rain for the next three days. He reveals that in a dream to a good person, not through a vision of rain or water, but through something contrary: for example, if that person were to dream that he was picking up three handfuls of dry dirt and tossing them in the air, and God were to reveal to him sooner or later that these three handfuls meant three days, and the dirt the rain, and tossing it in the air meant the water descending upon the earth. What astrologer or philosopher or interpreter, hearing such a dream, could or would understand it or interpret it? Not a one, unless he had already received from God by His grace and gift the supernatural ability to interpret, as God gives the gift of prophecy and of tongues to some of us. That is shown clearly in Scripture concerning the dream of the Pharaoh, king of Egypt, and of that of Nebuchadnezzar, king of Babylon, that there was no one in those realms, where astronomers and philosophers and magi, diviners, and evil enchanters and interpreters especially abound, who knew how to understand or interpret those dreams. Only those two young saints,

Joseph and Daniel, who were abstinent and chaste and had the spirit of God in themselves, knew how to interpret them.

No one should presume therefore to say or believe that a mortal man can understand or interpret, through any field of knowledge, dreams that come from God, unless he has already received from God that which not just mortal men, but demons as well, cannot by their own knowledge know. Even the holy angels, through whose ministry God makes visions and revelations, at times do not know God's mysteries and secret sacraments except as God chooses to reveal them. It is not just God's secrets but also certain secret and hidden things of nature that men do not know, no matter how wise, gifted, and expert they may be, because if they knew them, they would suffer many evils of death, infirmity, and other dangers, which others would eschew. It also happens, in this regard, that we do not know how to judge or interpret some dreams, even those having natural causes, either because they are hidden or for many other reasons. Let's assume that someone dreams about laughing very hard, feeling like he is being tickled. There can be many reasons for this dream, so it is difficult to know them all or to hit upon the correct one. One reason could come from within, either a great happiness that one might have or expect to have, or a superabundance of blood, or if the person is very afraid of being tickled. An external reason could be that the person had seen someone laugh a lot who was tickled, or if he had been tickled and laughed a great deal, or if someone else had wanted to tickle him and he had fled. A doctor or natural sage could easily say that these could be the reasons for such a dream, but he would not be able to decide which of them it was, unless he had already heard about it from the dreamer.

There could be another hidden reason for such a dream, which would be difficult, or perhaps impossible, for any physician to know. This would happen if some vermin, like those that develop in corruptible and bothersome human bodies, in approaching and touching the heart or the spleen, the liver or the lung, should tickle him before sticking his head in. This would cause harm to the person, and the abovementioned dream would ensue, since such a thing has already occurred when the person was awake, for the reason given. What doctor or astrologer could understand or interpret said dream? Many others arise from such hidden reasons, although properly speaking we should not call the understanding of the reasons for dreams interpretation, but rather call interpretation the understanding and knowledge and ability to set forth the meaning the dream might have with regard to what might happen, whose cause is the dream or the reason for the dream. Therefore, as already suggested, most dreams cannot be interpreted, because they are not the reason why something should happen, but the final and ultimate effect of reasons that came before, either internal or external, which do not reach beyond the dream that they cause, as is shown in the example given of the dream about laughter when a man feels like he is being tickled. Whatever the reasons, either vermin or fear of tickling or something else, it ends in that dream, and it does not extend farther to signify something else, nor likewise does the dream.

So it is with all dreams having specific and determinate causes. But dreams that have common and general causes mean something else, as far as the efficacy and power of those causes goes. For example, if the moon were in such a sign and in such an arrangement as to make it rain, and it made an impression in this regard on the brain of some person who was disposed to receiving that impression, and he dreamed that it was raining or something else cold and wet, then the natural sage could interpret that dream and say: "This dream means it will rain," not that the dream is the cause of it, but attributing such an effect to the disposition of the moon, which is the reason for both the dream and the rain.

It is indeed true that, when there can be several specific causes for the same dream, setting aside the general common one, we can easily err in interpreting it, because, with the interpreter believing that the common reason is why the dream happens, he will say that another effect should follow besides the dream. If the specific cause is the cause for the dream, which will have no other effect than the dream itself, the interpreter would be wrong to claim that that dream signifies something else. To clarify, and for brevity's sake, let's return to the example of the rain. There is no doubt that outside of the moon, which is the common cause, there can be several other specific reasons why someone might dream that it will rain. This does not mean it will rain, because the power of those reasons does not extend to making it rain the way the moon does, although they can make someone dream, as the moon also does. When cold and wet humours abound in the body, and especially in the head, either when a person thinks very hard about water, or when someone desires or very much wants the water to come or might be worried that it is not going to rain, these would be specific reasons for someone to dream about rain, and their power would not extend beyond the man, or the dream, to make it rain. So the interpreter would go too far and would be wrong if he interpreted the dream of rain as coming from a specific cause, which does not have the power to make it rain, like that which comes from the common reason, whose power extends to making it rain. This is the error and deceit of these worthless dreamers and presumptuous interpreters who set about to interpret in this way, according to their knowledge and art, indeed, according to their own fantasies, both dreams that cannot be interpreted and those that can. They would daringly presume to interpret the above-mentioned dream about laughing because of tickling, even though it cannot have an interpretation. They would follow two general rules of their art. The first is to interpret according to the contrary, such as when they say that when someone dreams of his own death or someone else's, it means a longer life; or by similitude, such as when they say that when he dreams of black clothes, it means sadness and tribulation. So, interpreting by the contrary, they would say that dreaming about laughter means pain and crying, whose cause would be someone else's cruelty as signified by the tickling; or else, interpreting by way of similitude, they would say that laughter means happiness and joy, whose cause would be someone else's praise and flattery, as signified by the tickling. Anyone who has any understanding and remembers what was said above about the difference between dreams that can and cannot be interpreted is easily aware of how much emptiness and falsehood there is in this.

In like manner they dare to interpret dreams, or visions, which come from God through the ministry of the holy angels, which although they have an interpretation, it is not by either human art or knowledge but by divine revelation, as was shown above.[308]

Of dreams that come from heaven, i.e., from the influence of the stars and planets, and from the disposition and influence of the elements, good natural philosophers and good astrologers can make a true interpretation. But there are precious few of them, and those few who do know would be more wary to judge, fearing that they might err, than those who know little. Sir Martin-of-the-threshing-floor and Lady Bertha-of-the-mill would more daringly set about to interpret dreams than would Socrates and Aristotle, sovereign masters of natural philosophy. Indeed, we read that Socrates, discussing dreams in his school, and having said what can be said and known about them through natural science, as he had certain doubts about the causes, effects, and meanings of dreams, which he did not know how to explain and solve, said what St. Jerome adds in the prologue of the Bible, written above for another purpose: *Hoc unum scio, quod nescio*. The noble master was not ashamed of confessing the truth of his ignorance about those things that human ingenuity cannot know, even though Lady Bertha says that she knows well. Instead he said: I know one thing, which is that I don't know. This means: what you, my audience and disciples, would like to know from me on the question of dreams, which I am speaking to you

---

308 See p. 238.

about, I do not know, and I know perfectly well that I do not know; as if to say: I well recognize my ignorance in this case.

One thing is certain about dreams that come from the devil: they can be interpreted not by natural science or human art, but by diabolical science and magical art, of which one sure part is making someone dream, as is said above.

Interpreting those same dreams is equivalent to spreading the devil's knowledge, which he has shown and taught to men in order to deceive them about those things that they want to know and to promote reverence to him, removing them from obedience to God and from the purity of the Christian faith. Our faith teaches us to flee and disdain the devil's vanities and falsehoods, which are contained in the books of magical art from which the diviners, necromancers, and all the other evildoers draw all of their evil deeds and lying vanities with their false opinions. This art, with its artifices, abounds among the pagans, such as the Egyptians, Chaldeans, Persians, and Indians, and other oriental nations where the devil first taught it. We read that the magus Zoroaster, king of the Bactrians, having learned the magical art from demons, taught and left it in writing, following his teachers' advice, on a sculpted marble column, so that floodwater would not extinguish it, and on a terracotta column, so that fire could not obscure it. We read of this Zoroaster, the demons' first disciple and the first writer and master of the diabolical art, that the demons, indignant towards him, killed him as he deserved, burning his body, depriving it of material life, and leading his wretched soul to the eternal fire. Some say that he was that third son of Noah, Cam, cursed by his father. Others say that they were not the same person, but that Zoroaster came from that line.

In those places and among those peoples, where it had its beginning, the devil's knowledge has endured up till now, because they are all idolaters and do not have faith in Jesus Christ, who condemns that iniquity. Instead, the devil rules over them, leading them with those illusions all the way to hell. He did this in the west, where we live, throughout the Roman Empire, while paganism held sway. But since St. Peter and St. Paul first disseminated the true faith, finding approval through great miracles and through the blood of their martyrdom, with Simon Magus, master of that confused and dead art, and after that St. Laurence, St. Sylvester, and the other martyrs and doctors and confessors of the Catholic faith, idolatry ceased, and with it the magic art. Some relics in which the devil is hidden have remained, however, and he effectively makes use of those who have faith in him, as he does in his main art. Although in these lands there are not many books, nor many masters of that art (and perhaps there are more whom we don't know about; because they are hidden, because civil and ecclesiastical law condemns them), nevertheless, many people have been corrupted by it, and if not everywhere, at least in certain parts. Although the devil cannot fully drown the Christian people in the sea of infidelity, he can at least toss us about and send up many splashes of that sludgy iniquity in which he is sealed up and hidden, either by not showing himself or making it seem to be a good and licit thing, or through the desire for what he does and teaches. And even though we believe that it is bad, he draws many people to a tacit idolatry and to a believable paganism. This is as serious for the Christian as it is for the apostate, baptized in the faith and a transgressor of the vow he made, and others for him, to renounce the devil and all of his vain and false shows, the sum of which are all the enchantments, evil deeds, and superstitious rituals of which we have spoken extensively above. Also, the heeding and interpreting of dreams, which is still among us, where many vanities and falsehoods are committed by people, and especially in interpreting them, of which these stupid dreamers and shameless coiners, and perhaps blind deceivers, believing that they have seen the light, make a great effort to prove it true. They write and argue not only with general reasons, which can be adapted to dreams both generally and specifically, but by positing singular and specific dreams, which any person of any condition has without distinction, and for whatever reasons. Because it is granted to them that some dreams can be interpreted, they presumptuously and sophistically argue that that can be done for all dreams.

In order to cut down their presumptuous vanity, or expose their ignorance, and wanting by now to conclude the matter of dreams, which we have spoken about for a long time, I want to attack their statements by using them against them, using one proof alone, which every young girl and boy will understand.

Among the other things that they say, interpreting dreams without distinction, is that whenever someone dreams that all or some of his teeth are falling out, this means that some relative or friend of the dreaming person is going to die. They also say that whenever somebody dreams about flying, this means that that dreamer is going to go on a pilgrimage, and that he will have authority and command over many people. And he who might dream of being called, if he answers, should soon die. They also say that whenever someone dreams of being struck by lightning, it means that he will be assaulted by his enemies, or that he will suffer great damage to his property, by arson set by his enemies. Anyone who dreams of seeing dead people, or of speaking with them, and hears from them and they appear to be alive, will soon die. They interpret many other dreams as well, which I won't mention for brevity's sake. I have recounted a few of the most common ones, which people commonly dream, so that, having shown how these lying interpreters tell lies when interpreting these common dreams, we can show that they do not tell the truth when interpreting the ones that are harder to understand. Whoever reads or hears this treatise should recall whether he ever dreamed any of the aforesaid dreams, and whether what these blowhards stubbornly affirm ever happened. If not, as I believe, he should hold them to be liars. And if even one those things were to happen, it would not be because of the dream, but for some other reason, because things happen every day, and if they accord with a dream, that would be a coincidence. I myself have dreamed the above-mentioned dreams many times in my life, and so I offered them, rather than others, as examples. As I recall – indeed, I am sure of it – none of the things predicted by those who say what those dreams mean ever happened to me. Ever since I was very young, and often after that, and even recently, I dreamed that I was called upon and saw dead people, with whom I appeared to speak as if they were alive, which they say means that the dreamer is going to die. God willing, I am still alive, and I am more than fifty years old. I have often dreamed of flying, and I never had authority or command over anyone at all, nor do I want to. Nor did I ever go on a pilgrimage except to Rome for absolution, and I do not have any intention to. I have sometimes dreamed that I was struck by lightning, and I have never been attacked by my enemies, and I don't have any enemies that I know of, and I never suffered damage or loss of things in a fire, as they say that dream signifies. I have dreamed many times about my teeth falling out, and not a one of them has ever fallen out, except for my baby teeth, nor did I ever become aware, after having such a dream, that a relative or friend of mine had died, although sooner or later many of my relatives and friends did die. So experience, which teaches certain things, shows that the so-called interpreters are wrong; because that judgment could be about dreams other than those we have offered as an example. The only thing they have going for them is that for somebody who had one or another of those dreams or had them interpreted by others, what they were said to mean had in fact happened. But the dreaming could be for some special reason, because one person dreams in a way that another does not, and one person has truer dreams than somebody else. There is no doubt a great difference in how people dream, according to their constitutions and thoughts, feelings, and the variety of their jobs, studies, and activities, which are the reason for dreams. There are people who never dream, others who always dream while they are sleeping, still others who dream right when they fall asleep and then no more, many others who dream in the middle of their sleep and not at the end, and some dream closer to the end. Also, there are people who remember all their dreams and can recount them later, and many who do not remember them and cannot recount them. There is thus a great variety of dreams for various reasons, both internal and external, and because of the varied disposition of the visualizing organ, where the imaginary appearance and vision of the dream is received. Therefore, the so-called interpreters should not give a general rule for them, saying that when someone dreams such a thing, it means that it will happen thusly. Rather, they could say, if they knew that it was true: if somebody dreamed such a thing, it happened to him in this way, or thus should happen to him, for such-and-such a reason. By not giving a reason for their interpretation, and generalizing from what perhaps happened at one time to one person, or for some special reason, it so happens that they do not prove that what they say is true, but their statement should be criticized as insufficiently proven. And when they see by reason and experience that they are wrong, they dig in and, stubbornly defending their error, they insist that what they say about the meaning of all dreams is true, but that it can take time before that which is signified by the dream occurs. So they say that for a dream that happens between the first and third hour of the night some time may pass before whatever should happen, twenty years or twenty months or twenty weeks or twenty days or twenty hours. For a dream that happens between the third hour and the sixth, its interpretation will be affirmed within fifteen years, or at most seventeen years. For a dream that occurs between the sixth hour of the night and the ninth, its interpretation will be fulfilled in four or five years. Of the dream that is dreamed between the ninth hour of the night and dawn, they say it should be fulfilled within a year, or six months or three, or within ten days. And those dreams that happen around dawn, they say, are the truest dreams there are, and their meanings can be interpreted best.

They say many other things in their blowhard way, as they are used to doing, and which I won't record here, so that it doesn't seem like I myself am dreaming, as those lying dreamers are who think that can make others believe, according to their own fantastic imaginings, that we should wait twenty years for the meaning of a dream to come to pass. If they had talked about those dreams whose cause are the stars and the planets, which complete their course in a certain and determinate time, what they say would have some appearance of possibly being true, that as the star is the cause of the dream with its influence and its movement, so too would it be, with the completion of its course, the reason for fulfilling the meaning and effect of the dream. But saying that indiscriminately about any dream, even though they make a distinction according to the time of the dream, is to be ridiculed.

I do not want to appear to reject the science of dreams and their interpretation completely, for, if the reader has kept in mind what is written above, I don't fully deny it; indeed, I approve it in part, as far as those dreams that have natural or supernatural signification are concerned. Therefore, as we end this treatise, it is appropriate, almost as an epilogue, to summarize briefly what was written at length above, setting forth what one should hold to be true about dreams and exposing all the other prevarications and mental gyrations. One may heed dreams and their interpretations, and trust in them as coming as revelations by God or the holy angels. Also, one can, without sin, heed those dreams and their meanings that come from natural internal or external causes, not going beyond where the power of those natural causes extends. To heed dreams that do not have natural causes, or whose causes are not known, but which by certain rules of magical art are given certain meanings they do not have, is a grave sin and diabolical vanity. Likewise, it is a grave sin and idolatrous sacrilege to seek out dreams and their meanings from the devil, through either invocations or sacrifices or through other agreements, tacit or explicit, or to trust or pursue, even though they have not been procured, dreams or revelations that others know, believe, or suspect come from the devil.

There is but one thing left to clarify, which, according to what was said above, is already very clear. Nevertheless, because it is commonly held by almost everyone and could create a common doubt, it is useful to restate it here. This is that every person commonly experiences that what he dreams comes to pass the same day as the night he dreamed it. As a result, when the person sees before him what he has dreamed, he remembers the dream and says: "This is what I dreamed last night." So it appears that some dreams are true and sometimes come true. Our interpreters would say that that happens with dreams that happen at daybreak, which a man always remembers, and that they come true no later than that very day. This, like their other statements, is worth little or nothing, because neither the time of the dream, nor the dream itself, nor remembering the dream can be the reason why it comes true. By remembering the dream one could easily be motivated to do or not do something, as was shown above, but it cannot be that something else happens beyond the person, or that he is motivated to do or not do something because of the dream. It also cannot be that whatever happens to make someone remember having dreamed it is the reason why the dream happened, because that thing had not yet happened when the dream took place: and that which is not cannot be a reason for something that is. It is necessary therefore that the dream, and what happens that causes someone to remember the dream, which is not the cause of the dream, nor the dream the cause of it, be reduced to some common cause, such as something natural or supernatural, as in the example offered above of the moon,[309] which is the natural and common reason for making someone dream that it is raining, and for it to rain, and not that dreaming that it is raining is the reason why it rains. Nor was the rain, when it was not yet raining, the reason for someone to dream that it would rain. This goes for all similar natural things and their effects. Of supernatural causes, which are God and the devil, it is also necessary to say that such effects can be traced back to them. God sometimes makes a person dream and has the dream come true, for example, making someone dream that he was giving alms to a poor man and inspiring that poor man to go to church or to the piazza where that dreamer could find him, whereupon, finding him there and giving him alms, he would remember that he had dreamed it. The dream and the giving of alms would not however be the cause of one another. Likewise, the devil will make someone dream that he came to words and fisticuffs with some friend and neighbour. He will then create a reason for that person to go to where he will find the person he dreamed about, and first off something will appear to them both that will lead them to squabble and fight. Then the person, remembering that he dreamed the dream, will be able to say: "Here is the dream I had last night, it all came true." But the dream will not be the cause of the argument, nor the argument for the dream: the devil will be the reason for both.

Of dreams that we find written about by authors worthy of trust, that have been verified and came true, like Valerius Maximus who writes of the death of Julius Caesar, and of those two companions of Arcadia, and many others, and as we read in the legend of St. Ambrose, archbishop of Milan, that, having fallen asleep on the altar in Milan as he was about to perform the mass for the burial of St. Martin of France, it should be said that there were no natural causes for that, that the power of nature does not extend that far, but that there were supernatural reasons. These could be either God, through the ministry of the holy angels, in the dream, or truly a vision or rapture of St. Ambrose, or the devil in the dreams that Valerius writes about, which were about idolatrous pagans and that the devil has great power and command through them in such things.

Enough said about dreams, which have been written about extensively in the present treatise.

---

309 See p. 249.

Index